Brian Friel's Models of Influence

Zosia Kuczyńska

Brian Friel's Models of Influence

Zosia Kuczyńska
Nottingham, England

ISBN 978-3-031-17904-4   ISBN 978-3-031-17905-1   (eBook)
https://doi.org/10.1007/978-3-031-17905-1

© The Editor(s) (if applicable) and The Author(s), under exclusive license to Springer Nature Switzerland AG 2023

This work is subject to copyright. All rights are solely and exclusively licensed by the Publisher, whether the whole or part of the material is concerned, specifically the rights of translation, reprinting, reuse of illustrations, recitation, broadcasting, reproduction on microfilms or in any other physical way, and transmission or information storage and retrieval, electronic adaptation, computer software, or by similar or dissimilar methodology now known or hereafter developed.
The use of general descriptive names, registered names, trademarks, service marks, etc. in this publication does not imply, even in the absence of a specific statement, that such names are exempt from the relevant protective laws and regulations and therefore free for general use.
The publisher, the authors, and the editors are safe to assume that the advice and information in this book are believed to be true and accurate at the date of publication. Neither the publisher nor the authors or the editors give a warranty, expressed or implied, with respect to the material contained herein or for any errors or omissions that may have been made. The publisher remains neutral with regard to jurisdictional claims in published maps and institutional affiliations.

Cover image: © Zosia Kuczyńska

This Palgrave Macmillan imprint is published by the registered company Springer Nature Switzerland AG
The registered company address is: Gewerbestrasse 11, 6330 Cham, Switzerland

Paper in this product is recyclable.

Acknowledgments

The doctoral and postdoctoral research on which this book is founded was made possible by funding from the Irish Research Council. Additional funding for 'Don't Anticipate the Ending' came from the Arts Council of Ireland, Cavan Arts, and Dublin City Council. 'Don't Anticipate the Ending' was co-produced by the Museum of Literature Ireland (MoLI), Smock Alley Theatre, and Tonnta, with further research support from Dance Ireland, the UCD Humanities Institute, the National Library of Ireland, and the Brian Friel Estate.

Archive materials are reproduced courtesy of the National Library of Ireland and by kind permission of the Brian Friel Estate and the Edwards-Mac Liammóir Estate. The chapter 'Creative Encounters: *Faith Healer* and Artistic Practice' is adapted from the article '"A Disoriented Vision of ... Fact": Brian Friel, Francis Bacon, and *Faith Healer*', first published in *Irish University Review* 50.2 (November 2020).

Thanks to Emilie Pine for her exemplary mentorship and relentless encouragement; for asking me 'but what do you actually *want* to do?'; and for generally being the kind and supportive academic role model I never knew I needed.

Effusive thanks to Robbie Blake and Jessie Keenan for making my first experience of collaborative practice-based research (in the middle of a pandemic, no less) a joy. Thanks to Bláthnaid Conroy Murphy, Marion Cronin, Lucia Kickham, Michelle O'Rourke, and Sarah Ryan for their creative contributions and artistic generosity throughout the project. Thanks to our production team: Steve O'Connor, Matt Burke, Seán Mac Erlaine, Benedict Schlepper-Connolly, Eoin Kilkenny, Sophie Coote, Natalie Hands, Michelle Cahill, and LaurA Fajardo Castro.

Thanks to Manuela Moser and the Belfast Book Festival for giving us a place to share our work in progress, and to Dance House and Smock Alley for the rehearsal space.

Particular thanks to MoLI for their generosity in giving 'Don't Anticipate the Ending' a permanent digital home, as well as providing filming locations and extensive in-kind and technical support. Thanks to Simon O'Connor for being on board with my proposal in the first place. Special thanks to Benedict Schlepper-Connolly for giving me a free curatorial rein whilst working to make the resultant exhibition a digital reality in a way that reflected the intricately interconnected chaos in my head (whilst doing what seemed to be five jobs at once at any given time). Thanks to digital producer Ian Dunphy and developer Stuart Cusack.

Thanks to Palgrave Macmillan for giving my research a home and for being accommodating when I had to keep extending my deadline due to COVID-19. Thanks to Aishwarya Balachandar for being my ever-patient point of contact throughout the publication process. Thanks to the NHS and the HSE for vaccinating and boosting me, and to the Irish Research Council and University College Dublin for extending my postdoc in extraordinary circumstances.

Thanks to my benevolent wizard PhD supervisors Nicholas Grene and Chris Morash for guiding me through the early research on which this monograph is built, and for their rigorous feedback this time around. Thanks to my erstwhile external examiner Shaun Richards for valuable feedback on multiple chapters. Thanks to Gerald Dawe, my internal examiner, for some early advice on how to develop my doctoral thesis. Thanks to Fran Brearton for her MA supervision, Bernard O'Donoghue for his formative seminars on Friel, and to my A Level Drama teacher, the much-missed Dave Lumb, who once compared Sir from *Living Quarters* to Inspector Goole from *An Inspector Calls* and set the wheels in motion for my thinking around Friel and time.

Special thanks to Alfie Coates and Simon Blakey at The Agency for being accommodating and quick to respond on the issue of permissions. Thanks to James Harte and the staff at the National Library of Ireland for being helpful and accommodating at all times. Thanks to Michael Travers of the Edwards-Mac Liammóir Estate.

Thanks to the UCD Humanities Institute for giving me a research community. Thanks to Anne Fuchs for running the ship; Valerie and Ricki for being the most helpful administrators on the planet (as well as all-round good eggs); my fellow postdocs for being the best work colleagues and office pals I could've asked for; and the PhD crowd for sharing their research, company, and cake. Special thanks to Dr Stephan Ehrig for the 3pm office dance breaks which saved my sanity on more than one occasion.

Thanks to the Information Systems Research Group at the University of Oslo for giving me temporary office space when I had none. Thanks to the HumSam Library at UiO for being a great place to work, even though I 'don't even go here'.

Thanks to friends old and new, especially Joe Lines, with whom I have commiserated at length on the thanklessness of monograph writing. Thanks to housemates past and present, especially Ben Power and Lara Comis. Thanks to Laurence Price and Enrico Emanuele Prodi for their help on Theology and Ancient Greek, respectively.

Last but in no way least, thanks to Katherine Wyers, without whose love, support, and instinctive knowledge of when to put the kettle on I would never have got this book over the line, and whose being in my life makes it more. Thanks to my Mum for her support and for keeping a roof over my head whilst I was between funding awards; thanks to my Dad and my Babcia, neither of whom will get to see this book published but whose love and support have been instrumental. Thanks to my sister Halina, brother-in-law Joe, and baby Oskar for your general existence. (I hope you like books, but if you don't, that's ok too.)

Contents

1 **Introduction: 'Don't embalm me in pieties'** 1
  Overview 4
  On what has been done; on what has been left undone 6
  A note on theory 9
  A note on the archive 11
  A note on Friel's composition process 11
  A final note 14

2 **Creative Encounters: *Faith Healer* and Artistic Practice** 17
  Early plays: 'the changing landscape of fact' 18
  ***Crystal and Fox** and **The Freedom of the City**: 'that reality far from which we live'* 21
  ***Faith Healer**: 'a disoriented vision of a fact'* 30
    The character of chance 33
    The language of distortion 39
    Triptych 42
  Making History: *'an "art" of the facts'* 46
  ***Give Me Your Answer, Do!**: orthopraxis* 53

3 **A Story Told Through People: Friel's Embodied Intertexts** 67
  Embodiments 68
  Friel's sources 69
  The enterprise of consciousness 85

4	**Form and Core: Brian Friel and Denis Donoghue**	107
	Where is the crisis?	108
	The Communication Cord	111
	Wonderful Tennessee	123
5	**Influence as Model: Friel's Performing Muse**	145
	'How dare you, Mr Janáček?'	147
	'Play—play—play', O Muse…	159
	'Excellent testimony!'	164
	'Stupid, useless, quirky mind…'	170
6	**'Don't Anticipate the Ending': Towards a Legacy of Artistic Practice**	191
	Project background	196
	Into the archive	197
	Robbie Blake: 'Running the Ending'	203
	Jessie Keenan: 'So What Is Surfacing'	215
	Don't anticipate the ending	229
7	**Conclusion: So What Is Surfacing (?)**	245
	(A)	246
	(B)	247
Appendix: Friel's Sources		253
Bibliography		261
Index		271

List of Figures

Fig. 6.1	Robbie Blake's transcription of Friel's markings on a draft from MS 37,104/1 dated 19 May 1989	206
Fig. 6.2	Robbie Blake's first attempt at producing a graphic score inspired by Friel's creative process	207
Fig. 6.3	Performers Michelle O'Rourke, Marion Cronin, Sarah Ryan, Lucia Kickham, and Bláthnaid Conroy Murphy workshop 'Running the Ending' by Robbie Blake, using copies of their final five-page score taped to the studio walls (Dance House, 14 August 2020)	207
Fig. 6.4	Screenshots from 'Running the Ending' by Robbie Blake (Performers left to right: Bláthnaid Conroy Murphy, Lucia Kickham, Marion Cronin, Michelle O'Rourke, and Sarah Ryan)	214
Fig. 6.5	Double-exposure of Marion Cronin, Sarah Ryan, and Lucia Kickham performing live improvisations to a recording of Michael's opening monologue from *Dancing at Lughnasa* (Dance House, 3 September 2020)	222
Fig. 6.6	Marion Cronin and Sarah Ryan performing in a live improvisation to a recording of Michael's opening monologue from *Dancing at Lughnasa* (Dance House, 3 September 2020)	223
Fig. 6.7	Screenshot from 'So What Is Surfacing (Trio)' with Marion Cronin	228

CHAPTER 1

Introduction: 'Don't embalm me in pieties'

A life's work is never done; nor is a literary archive ever complete. There are only the remains of what was once being made—the material traces of a live process that can only be encountered in the 'now'. The Brian Friel Papers and Brian Friel Papers (Additional) at the National Library of Ireland (NLI) are a record of a life's work in progress. They represent a way of working and of making art over a period spanning more than fifty years. This book is the first of its kind in its attempt to interrogate the role of the Brian Friel Papers in Friel's legacy as a working artist with a richly developed creative practice. By means of an unprecedented focus on Friel's copious notes towards his plays, I ask not only how and *by whom* Friel was being influenced and inspired, but also how and *for whom* Friel's artistic process might come to be an inspiration. In so doing, I suggest that an expansion of archival access and engagement that is grounded in artistic practice might provide the tools for setting a major creative legacy not in stone but rather in motion.

By 'artistic practice', I mean nothing more or less than the process through which artists make art—a process in which 'the artist' is a state of doing rather than a privileged state of being. In this, the question of influence is key. No artist creates in an intellectual vacuum, and the way

---

Brian Friel, *Plays Two* (London: Faber, 1999), p. 330.

© The Author(s), under exclusive license to Springer Nature Switzerland AG 2023
Z. Kuczyńska, *Brian Friel's Models of Influence*,
https://doi.org/10.1007/978-3-031-17905-1_1

a given artist engages with their many sources of inspiration—whether painstakingly researched, haphazardly chanced-upon, or almost subconsciously absorbed as part of a cultural milieu—is an essential part of any creative process. For Brian Friel, inspiration came in many forms and was more likely in the first instance to have come less from his sense of his own place in a given literary canon than from the review pages of the *Times Literary Supplement* or the *New Yorker*. As the archive will attest, Friel's plays are saturated with an eclectic array of contemporary thinking on subjects that range from linguistics to historiography, from dissident Russian writers to neglected muses, and from the praxis of living painters to the history of timekeeping.

Though fascinating in and of themselves, these sources are only part of what makes Friel's archive invaluable. Uncovering the 'what' of literary influence is, technically speaking, relatively simple these days if you happen to have access to a good quality archive, a reliable internet connection, and an uncensored search engine that includes at least some of the contents of digitised books. None of these things are a given, but they are certainly more available than they were when Friel donated his archive to the NLI in the year 2000. Take the time to familiarise yourself with an author's way of working and develop a knack for guessing when they're quoting rather than inventing, and a basic Boolean search will most likely yield revelatory results.

Here, the elephant in the ivory tower rears its ugly head. Time, of course, is more difficult to come by than all the above, insofar as time can only be bought with research funding, access to financial support, or independent wealth. I have been working intermittently with Friel's archives for nearly ten years, first as a funded doctoral researcher and then as a funded postdoctoral researcher in the city in which Friel's archives are housed, and have been able to rely on my family and my partner for support in the interim. I have had the resources and the breathing space to get to know the Brian Friel Papers well enough to trust my instincts.

It is in the knowledge that time is a privilege, then, that I make no apology for the fact that technology has made the 'what' of influence easier to ascertain. Whilst I do not doubt for a moment that Friel would on some level have disapproved of this unceremonious clearing of the mist, I would argue that being able to answer the question of 'what' more quickly has merely freed up researchers to focus on something far richer: the '*how*' of influence. To this end, the focus of this book is Friel's engagement with source materials that he came upon largely in the course of his day-to-day reading, and which he subsequently incorporated not only into his work but also into his way of working.

In recovering these sources, my aim is not to establish a new genealogy of Irish theatre per se, but rather, in some respects, to destabilise an overtly genealogical model of influence, within which male authors wrestle anxiously with their literary forefathers in the manner of Harold Bloom. This is because such a model is largely inattentive to the temporality of the creative process itself, considering the artist in the context of generational time rather than the time of generation itself. Certainly, insofar as Friel's archive reveals the operation of influence, it shows the extent to which Friel was engaging with material in a present moment—citing it, questioning it, reworking it as part of a live creative process. This remains true even when acknowledging that Friel was an artist who always seemed to have one eye on posterity. Though supremely self-conscious in his writing, highly ambitious, and remarkably jealous of his own written word, Friel still encountered his source materials in a 'now' conditioned by both personal and professional considerations. Indeed, there were times where he was demonstrably aware of having been inspired by a chance meeting of minds on paper. It is creative encounters such as these that are documented by Friel's archive as part of a wider record of his artistic practice.

Crucially for this book, encounter is also a means of understanding the relationship between archive and archive user—whether scholarly, artistic, or otherwise. My understanding of encounter in this setting is informed, in the first instance, by one of two seminal works underpinning this monograph that consider the archive in a performance studies context: Rebecca Schneider's *Performing Remains* (2011), in which she conceptualises the physical archive as both 'a house [...] built for live encounter with privileged remains' and a site for 'live practices of access'.[1] This is a foundational understanding that has been enriched and enhanced through the development of my own archival praxis as both a scholarly researcher and a facilitator of artistic research—a development that has coincided with a growing personal and professional interest in what it means to research queerly. Of particular relevance in this respect is what Ann Cvetkovich terms 'the convergence of the archival turn with the affective turn'[2] in the context of queer archival methodologies. Introducing the edited volume *Out of the Closet, Into the Archives* (2015), Cvetkovich not only emphasises the extent to which its contributors 'practice forms of the archival turn that put relentless curiosity and unapologetic passion to use as methods for intellectual invention' but also 'affirm[s] the importance of the archive as a site of practice': 'archives are [...] places where we do things with objects'.[3]

When I say 'encounter', then, I mean a foregrounding of the materiality, temporality, and subjectivity of being brought face to face with the written word as a record of a way of thinking and/or working. What happens when, on a day unlike any other, and with our receptivities dulled or heightened by factors of which we are both aware and unaware, we as archive users participate in a real-time encounter with a mind at work? It is in this spirit that the book includes an analysis of my own original collaborative practice-based research project, during which I worked with dancer-choreographer Jessie Keenan and performance-maker Robbie Blake to produce creative responses to Friel's archive. In this way, I hope to extend Friel's legacy of artistic practice to new ways of working that might emerge from a practical engagement with his archive.

Overview

The book begins and ends with the question of influence at the level of artistic practice, and is structured in a way that facilitates an exploration of its different facets rather than adhering to a strictly chronological approach. Following this introductory chapter, I use a case study of the play *Faith Healer* (1979) in Chapter 2 to showcase a period in Friel's creative life when he was demonstrably open to the influence not only of other artists but also of other artists' ways of working. I suggest that his chance encounter with a series of interviews with painter Francis Bacon may have influenced the play's development on a structural level. I also use case studies of the plays *Crystal and Fox* (1968), *The Freedom of the City* (1973), *Making History* (1988), and *Give Me Your Answer, Do!* (1997) to situate Friel's encounter with Bacon's interviews in the context of the development of Friel's thinking in two key areas: the relationship between 'art' and 'fact', and the role of the artist in navigating that relationship.

Having made a case for the importance of creative encounter to Friel's praxis, I devote the majority of Chapter 3 to a case study of *Translations* (1980). It asks how Friel's sources function as embodied intertexts in the context of theatre as the art of the transformation of space. Specifically, I examine *how* Friel combined his sources to create a piece of writing that is not only greater than the sum of its parts but also functions as live theatre—as 'a story [...] told *through* people'[4] (my italics). I give particular attention to a long neglected work by George Steiner, *In Bluebeard's Castle* (1971), which I suggest may be of as much significance to the play as its best-known source, Steiner's *After Babel* (1975).

Chapter 4 examines the genesis of two Friel plays: *The Communication Cord* (1982) and *Wonderful Tennessee* (1993). Both are linked by Friel's engagement with the writings of Denis Donoghue, whom I suggest ought to be considered as one of Friel's major influences. The chapter also focuses on a way of conceptualising Friel's composition process in terms borrowed from his own notes. I propose that a key component of the 'how' of Friel's process involved selecting or inventing a dramatic form that best expressed what he often called the 'core' of a given play. I go on to suggest that this framework might be a useful means of assessing the successes and failures Friel experienced when attempting to incorporate secondary material into his work. In this way, the chapter provides a window into a vital part of Friel's praxis whilst recovering a significant source for his work.

Chapter 5 moves towards a consideration of archival encounter from the researcher's point of view, as a means of generating new critical perspectives. By way of a case study, I privilege my own response to Friel's source materials for *Performances* (2003) over the imperative to verify the extent to which Friel engaged with them. Combining Friel's known engagement with works by George Steiner with his more uncertain engagement with Francine Prose's *The Lives of the Muses* (2002), I suggest that what I call Friel's 'performing muse' may be a productive lens for engaging with Friel's gender politics elsewhere in his oeuvre. To this end, I make a case study of *Molly Sweeney* (1994) in an attempt to address some of the more problematically apologist critiques of the way Friel wrote female characters for the stage.

The final Chapter 6 prior to the conlcusion extends the notion of archival encounter to artistic engagements with Friel's archive. Here, I reflect on the process and outcomes of a collaborative practice-based research project I conducted with Jessie Keenan and Robbie Blake, titled 'Don't Anticipate the Ending'. As part of the project, Blake and Keenan engaged directly with archive material in the NLI pertaining to Friel's *Dancing at Lughnasa* (1990). In a process supplemented by my research, they responded to Friel's creative process as revealed through their own archival encounters, incorporating elements of Friel's way of working into their own practices. As part of the project, they produced two short films:

'So What Is Surfacing (Trio)' by Keenan and 'Running the Ending' by Blake. These are now a central part of a digital exhibition I curated for the Museum of Literature Ireland (MoLI). Looking back on the project, I posit these artworks and the process by which they came about as an extension of the significance of Friel's archive as a piece of cultural heritage, acknowledging the centrality of Friel's artistic practice to his ongoing legacy.

On what has been done; on what has been left undone

This book is largely a record of archival encounters: Friel's; my creative collaborators'; my own. Though I engage with other voices in the field where I feel it would enrich the discussion or where my work has already been done by others before me, my dialogue is mostly with the archive itself. This is not to dismiss those voices, nor to leave their scholarship unacknowledged. I am well aware that I am hardly the first researcher to make extensive use of the Brian Friel Papers since they were made available to the public in the early 2000s. Anthony Roche, Christopher Murray, Marilynn Richtarik, and Jessica Adolf have all produced book-length studies that draw heavily on the available archive material. Moreover, running in parallel to my own experiments in expanding archival outreach via partial digitisation, artistic interventions, and public outreach has been the National Lottery funded 'Friel Reimagined' project at Queen's University Belfast.[5] At the time of writing, it too has now launched its own, much larger-scale partial digitisations and outreach programmes.[6] It is also increasingly common for Friel scholars able to travel to what is, at the time of writing, and despite such efforts as these, still a significantly undigitised Dublin archive, in order to make use of its contents in journal articles and conference papers. I have even seen archive material in the occasional newspaper article on Friel. Put simply, the archive is very big and very rich, and there is enough painstakingly and expertly catalogued material in there to keep generations of Friel scholars busy excavating the parts they find most compelling. No one researcher could cover it all in one book. (I know for a fact that I share with Anthony Roche the wish that I could have gone into detail about that time Friel was considering putting talking animals in *The Home Place* (2005).).

It is with this in mind that I see fit to call my engagement with the Brian Friel Papers 'unprecedented', not because I believe I can have been the only one ever to have found the material that has been showcased in this book but because of my sustained focus on the archive itself as a record of Friel's artistic process. It is true that the book contains a detailed analysis of several sources for Friel's work that have never been discussed in print and which have never before been associated with Friel's work in a scholarly context. It is also true that I have been able to spend many years almost exclusively on archival detective work and have therefore had the time to chase down a fair number of the unacknowledged sources buried in Friel's notes. Nevertheless, I maintain that the book's true value as an intervention in Friel studies is in its use of the archive to make a case for Friel's legacy as work in progress, both in the sense of its being a representation of a live creative practice and in the sense of its facilitating the creation of new work.

Though I have consulted nearly every box in the archive at one time or another, there are many stones that have been left unturned here: I have barely touched upon the archive as a record of production history, for instance. There was also a great deal of material I wanted to include but which would not have furthered a discussion of Friel's models of influence in a productive way. As a queer researcher, I had hoped in particular to be able to include a chapter that focused on Friel's dealings with homophobic censorship whilst attempting to have *Philadelphia, Here I Come!* (1964) staged in London in the mid-1960s. However, by the time the British Library had opened its doors again in the aftermath of successive lockdowns due to the ongoing pandemic, I was no longer in a position where a research trip would have been financially viable, and so there are crucial pieces of archival material I am unable to access at the time of writing. I had also hoped in the same chapter to get to grips with *The Gentle Island* (1969), which ends with one of its two openly gay characters being shot and maimed by the island's self-styled King and resident dinosaur Manus. MS 37,064/1 contains some particularly revealing feedback from actor Micheál Mac Liammóir, whose partner Hilton Edwards had directed some of Friel's earlier plays. Writing on 1 December 1971, Mac Liammóir was about as frank as he could be given the ongoing criminalisation of homosexuality in Ireland, and told Friel that he had found the play 'repellent [...] not merely [in] its pointless brutality [...] but also [in] its (forgive me) strange naïveté on one of the leading themes of the play': 'Honestly, Brian, your view of homosexuality is not very well-informed'. Mac Liammóir was particularly vocal about the way in which Friel had 'put into the mouth of your leading man a great coda

[...] entirely composed of the most vicious ignorance the Western world has suffered from':

> Now really, Brian! Give such lines to the silly ass, or the Knave of Clubs or whom you will, but not to a grand, central figure [. . .] Such rhetoric, with such a content, comes from an abyss of [. . .] ignorance [. . .] and I cannot see that it is in its place in the summing-up of what could be a fine melodrama about human beings.

It would certainly have been gratifying to have been able to delve into Mac Liammóir's criticisms of the play (with which I whole-heartedly agree). However, I ultimately felt that there was not enough archive material available to write an entire chapter on homophobia as a model of (social) influence in Friel's work *at the level of* artistic practice, which has been the main focus of the book. I include it here because it is valuable for queer scholars to have an outspoken critique of ill-informed LGBTQ+ representation from Mac Liammóir—a self-styled 'member of the tribe'[7]—in print. I hope to be able to do justice to these archival findings in the near future.

Two other entirely regrettable omissions are *Living Quarters* (1977) and *Aristocrats* (1979). I am fond of both, and though they are mentioned several times in passing, there simply wasn't space to include them as major case studies. Moreover, most of what is interesting to me about *Aristocrats* has little to do with the way Friel engaged with his source materials, which—given that the play has long been acknowledged as an extension of his short story 'Foundry House'—are not particularly revealing. There is, perhaps, a case to be made for the play as a partial dramatisation of a poem by Alastair Reid printed in the *New Yorker*, which appears in Friel's notes. Titled 'My Father, Dying',[8] there are certain moments where the staging appears to seek to embody elements of the poem. This, however, is hardly enough for a substantial portion of a chapter. In short, the composition process is rich, but not hugely relevant to this book.

Also notable by their absence are Friel's many versions, translations, and 'plays after'. My rationale for their exclusion is that the archive does not shed a great deal of light on Friel's process beyond the inclusion of some of the literal translations from which Friel worked. Given the comparative lack of the usual 'notes to self' you would expect to find at the inception of an original Friel play, this is not particularly fertile ground for an archive-based exploration of the operation of influence. In short, these plays are a little beyond the scope of the book, though I do hope that future scholars find a way of tackling them usefully.

After ten years of working with the same archive, I am, understandably, keen to move on to pastures new. I may or may not develop the material that didn't make it to the book, but it would be a real shame if all my research on Friel's influences stayed buried. In the spirit of sharing, I have therefore included a non-exhaustive appendix of Friel's source materials, where scholars who have neither the time nor the resources to go digging around in the archive for several years can find a list of secondary works I have found so far that have influenced Friel's plays to some degree. It is my hope and expectation that future scholars will be able to make use of and indeed add to it. Until such time as the archive has been mined for every last bit of evidence of Friel's influences, however, I refer you to a post-it note that lived above my desk for the duration of my postdoctoral research: 'IF IN DOUBT, TRY THE *TLS*!'.

A note on theory

The bulk of the theoretical and/or philosophical content of the book is derived from Friel's engagement with his source materials. I have taken care to provide detailed summaries of this material where needed in the main bodies of the relevant chapters, with the exception of some cases where existing Friel scholarship has already covered the ground in question. In addition to Friel's source materials, there are two main theoretical strands that underpin this book, which overlap significantly on the theme of embodiment. One concerns theatrical space; the other concerns performance-based approaches to archives/archival access. Given that this book is focused on the 'how' of influence—including not only the embodiment of Friel's source materials in bodied speakers onstage, but also the relationship between body and archive in the practice-based elements of my research—it is important that the thinking that informs its engagement with ideas of embodiment is acknowledged at the outset.

Due in part to its being adopted by multiple disciplines, 'embodiment' as a term can be flexible at best, nebulous at worst. For this reason, I will be drawing largely on three specific engagements with embodiment from two different disciplines. Some are based primarily on its being a literal bodily housing of ideas and/or information; others also incorporate a more abstract sense of embodiment as the actualisation or physical manifestation of those ideas. These approaches can usefully be summarised as follows:

1. IN RELATION TO THEATRICAL SPACE
    Vimala Herman (1997)
    In the context of theatre as 'the art of the transformation of space',[9] the speaking body is the primary reference point not only for calculations of time and distance, but also for their manipulation. Words as they are spoken when corporeally situated (as opposed to words as they are written) have the power to transform theatrical space.

2. IN RELATION TO ARCHIVES/ARCHIVAL ACCESS
    Diana Taylor (2003)
    Practices that are normally considered to be ephemeral *and which require bodily presence/participation* (e.g. dance, song, storytelling) are both ways of knowing and ways of transmitting knowledge. In other words, performance can be understood as an embodied archive, where the body is both a site and a means of transfer, particularly with regard to cultural memory and identity.[10]
    Rebecca Schneider (2011)
    The practice of archival access itself is to be included in the category above. In other words, as a live encounter with 'privileged remains',[11] archival access is also to be understood as a process in which the body is both a way of knowing and of transmitting knowledge.

As has already been noted, Taylor and Schneider's performance-based approaches to archival access and engagement have been instrumental to my thinking around the idea of 'encounter'. They have also provided a solid and well-established foundation for developing my own archival praxis in a direction inspired by queer archival methodologies that privilege affective encounters with material objects in time.

A NOTE ON THE ARCHIVE

This book draws on two collections currently housed at the National Library of Ireland (NLI): the Brian Friel Papers (MSS 37,041–37,806) and the Brian Friel Papers (Additional) (MSS 42,091–42,093; 49,209–49,350). The Brian Friel Papers (BFP), compiled by Helen Hewson in 2003, comprise 116 boxes given by Friel and his children to the NLI in the year 2000, with an additional 14 boxes presented by Curtis Brown of London (Friel's agent). These papers comprise 'material relating to his early days as a short story writer, and the subsequent writing and production of 30 radio and stage plays' and include 'documents concerning the establishment and administration of the Field Day Theatre Company, correspondence with actors, directors, producers, writers and academics and articles and theses on Friel and his work',[12] spanning the years 1957–2001. The Brian Friel Papers (Additional) (BFPA) is a collection of '48 small archival boxes' presented to the NLI in 2007, 2009, and 2011 by Friel's children and 'consists mostly of material dating from 2000 to 2010, with a few items dating from before 2000 relating to productions of plays, Brian Friel's membership of the Seanad (1987–1991), and the acquisition of Brian Friel's papers by the National Library of Ireland (1993–2009)'.[13] This later collection was compiled by Fergus Brady with assistance from Karen de Lacey, Avice-Claire McGovern, and Nora Thornton in September 2011. In both collections, the material is organised by work, and those works are placed in chronological order. For each work, there are multiple boxes of folders containing manuscripts (including early notes) and typescripts, translations, and productions in chronological order. This book focuses largely on Friel's manuscripts—specifically on his early handwritten notes and ideas.

A NOTE ON FRIEL'S COMPOSITION PROCESS

Friel's composition process seems, with minimal variation, to have been one he followed throughout his career as a dramatist, although admittedly there are no records of the composition process of his earliest three stage plays. We also don't know from this archive what relationship this bears to the composition process for his short stories. What we do know is that, very early on, Friel would begin by making a series of notes which, helpfully for Friel scholars, he very quickly learned to date. This was, presumably, so that he could refer back to his earlier notes with ease.

These notes would usually be in black ink—occasionally biro—with additions made in pencil and sometimes in coloured felt-tip pens. Many of these were written on cream A5 paper, hole-punched on the top left-hand side, and then collated into booklets kept together with treasury tags. These booklets would then be labelled 'A', 'B', 'C', and so on. Many of these pages are crossed through diagonally in pencil, not to the extent that the words are obscured but apparently to indicate that these are ideas that have either been discarded, or from which Friel has moved on, or which Friel has in some way addressed, developing them further in subsequent notes. I have indicated these crossings-through where appropriate, along with scored-through words. Where the word that has been erased is legible, I have indicated this with a strikethrough; where the word that has been erased is illegible, I have indicated this with a square-bracketed, struck-through '[illegible]'. Where words have been added, I have taken the liberty of inserting them in their proper place as indicated by Friel rather than imitating his own formatting. However, where words have been inserted clearly above the line, I have indicated this by enclosing them in a pair of slashes '\gesturing upwards/'; where words have been inserted below the line, I have indicated this by enclosing them in a pair of slashes '/gesturing downwards\'. It is not uncommon for only one or two ideas to be written on a given page, and Friel usually restricted himself to writing on the one side of the page when forming his early thoughts on a given play.

The contents of these early holographic writings vary from notes on specific characters to the development of thematic ideas to fragments of dialogue to quotations from his various source materials. These quotations are not immediately apparent, but there are usually tell-tale signs when Friel isn't using his own words. If the title of the book does not appear, then perhaps a page number or the author's initials will be present. Sometimes it is simply the case that it doesn't *sound* like Friel or is written too fluently to have been written off-the-cuff at that level of complexity. Other times, Friel's sources are more obvious, as in *The Communication Cord* or *Making History*, where the relevant articles from the *Times Literary Supplement* are included in the archive alongside his notes. Similarly, the textbooks and articles on sight loss/gain that Friel used for *Molly Sweeney* are likewise included in the archive. These notes also contain the many questions that Friel asked himself (and occasionally answered), as well as the odd stern note to self or wry moment of particularly heightened self-awareness.

Once Friel felt that enough preliminary work had been done to establish what I have come to think of as both the form and core of the play, he would begin writing in a series of hardbacked notebooks (usually A4) and draft the play scene by scene in pencil, writing first on the right-hand page and then making emendations on the left-hand page. These would again be struck through in pencil once Friel had moved on from the draft version in question. In the front would be potential titles and a series of numbered questions or notes, which again would be struck through—presumably once they had been addressed. At the same time, he would work from the back on anything that was out of sequence, often leaving a section of blank pages where the two halves of the notebook failed to meet. There would be several of these notebooks, usually one per act or couple of acts, followed by a typed-up version of the manuscript pasted or taped into a notebook on the right-hand page, again with emendations on the left-hand page. Several typed drafts would follow. Friel did not, generally speaking, date these pencilled or typed drafts, but it is logical to assume that he continued to make at least some loose/treasury-tagged notes at the same time. Given that Friel's handwritten drafts were made in pencil, we can reasonably conjecture that the pencil markings on the ink notes were made during this part of the process, suggesting that he was engaging with them whilst drafting dialogue.

Once a play was written, Friel would send copies for feedback. Earlier in his career, he was more likely to receive constructive criticism that he would either heed or ignore; later, or so assorted archived letters from literary critics of the 1990s will avow, he was more likely to receive blanket adulation. So too was Friel more likely to respond to directorial input at the beginning of his career than towards the end. Anthony Roche has already written extensively of Friel's early, often collaborative relationship with director Hilton Edwards, who first staged *Philadelphia* at the Gaiety and went on to direct its Broadway run.[14] So too is the mentorship of Tyrone Guthrie well documented by Roche and others. Kelly Matthews, meanwhile, has shed valuable light on the influence of Belfast radio drama producer Ronald Mason on Friel's early, pre-Guthrie career.[15] Still others have written of what became Friel's notorious aversion to directors, to the extent that he preferred to direct plays like *Molly Sweeney* himself rather than allowing for alternative interpretations of his work.

A FINAL NOTE

The aim of this book is not, as Denis Donoghue would have it, 'to explain everything and preferably to explain it away'[16] with regard to Friel's creative practice; nor is it to make definitive claims as to the 'true' origins of the ideas that underpin his work. Rather by bringing to light certain elements of Friel's composition process, revealing new source materials for his plays, and setting a precedent for engaging with Friel's archive at the level of artistic practice, I hope to open up an increasingly canonical body of work not only to new readings but also to new approaches to their production. It is my hope that the material presented in this book will be of interest not only to Friel scholars (or theatre scholars more generally), but also to artistic practitioners across a variety of disciplines, from directors and dramaturgs to theatre makers and performers in a more experimental vein. Indeed, in Friel's willingness to experiment in order to find forms for his plays that would do justice to what he would often refer to as their 'core', other practitioners might find ways of thinking and working that will resonate with, challenge, or enhance their own practice. I am particularly keen that an approach to literary archives that foregrounds the liveness of encounter might inspire further critical and/or practice-based engagements in which the relationship between the body and the archive is taken into consideration.

What the Brian Friel Papers give us is an invaluable insight into a mind at work that, once glimpsed, enriches immeasurably. Through his creative practice, Brian Friel consistently shows his commitment to a subtle experimentation that belies his plays' accessibility. Friel may be famous for his use of George Steiner's signature work *After Babel* in *Translations*, but this is just one example among many largely unsung instances of Friel's intellectual preoccupations informing not only the thematic content but also the form and staging of his work. What is surfacing, then, is a picture of Friel's composition process that shows him to be as much a Frank Sweeney as a Frank Hardy—as much a keen autodidact with what might be termed a 'quirky mind'[17] as he was an artist in search of a faith. The Brian Friel Papers have the potential to transform the way we think about Friel's legacy without seeking to impose a dominant critical narrative upon a body of work strong enough and flexible enough to withstand fresh interpretation and increasingly inventive staging. Effectively, they ensure against his being embalmed in pieties.

Notes

1. Rebecca Schneider, *Performing Remains: Art and War in Times of Theatrical Reenactment* (Abingdon: Routledge, 2011), p. 108.
2. Ann Cvetkovich, 'Foreword', in *Out of the Closet, Into the Archives*, ed. by Amy L. Stone and Jaime Cantrell (Albany: SUNY Press, 2015), pp. xv–xviii (p. xvii).
3. Cvetkovich, pp. xvii–xviii.
4. Dublin, National Library of Ireland (NLI), Brian Friel Papers (BFP), MS 37,085/1.
5. 'Friel Reimagined', Queen's University Belfast <https://www.qub.ac.uk/sites/friel-reimagined/> [Accessed 25 July 2023].
6. 'Brian Friel Digital Archive', Queen's University Belfast <https://www.jstor.org/site/qub/brian-friel-digital-archive/?searchkey=1690297998020> [Accessed 25 July 2023].
7. Letter from Micheál Mac Liammóir to Brian Friel, 1 December 1971 (3 pages), in NLI, BFP, MS 37,064/1.
8. Alastair Reid, 'My Father, Dying', *The New Yorker*, 15 November 1976, p. 50.
9. Vimala Herman, 'Deixis and Space in Drama', *Social Semiotics 7*, No. 3 (1997), pp. 269–283 (p. 269).
10. See Diana Taylor, *The Archive and the Repertoire: Performing Cultural Memory in the Americas* (Durham and London: Duke University Press, 2003).
11. Schneider, p. 108.
12. Helen Hewson, 'Collection List No. 73: BRIAN FRIEL PAPERS' (Dublin: National Library of Ireland, 2003), p. 1. <https://www.nli.ie/sites/default/files/2022-12/frielb.pdf> [Accessed 25 July 2023].
13. Fergus Brady, with Karen de Lacey, Avice-Claire McGovern, and Nora Thornton, 'Collection List No. 180: Brian Friel Papers (Additional) (Dublin, National Library of Ireland, 2011), pp. 6–7 <https://www.nli.ie/sites/default/files/2022-12/180_brianfrielpapers_additional.pdf> [Accessed 25 July 2023].
14. See Anthony Roche, *Brian Friel: Theatre and Politics* (Basingstoke: Palgrave Macmillan, 2011).
15. Kelly Matthews, 'Brian Friel, the BBC, and Ronald Mason', *Irish University Review* 47 (2017), 470–485.

16. Denis Donoghue, *The Arts Without Mystery* (London: The British Broadcasting Corporation, 1983), p. 12.
17. Friel, *Plays Two*, p. 488.

CHAPTER 2

Creative Encounters: *Faith Healer* and Artistic Practice

The Brian Friel Papers at the National Library of Ireland are, fundamentally, a record of a life's work in progress. To read Friel's notes is not only to encounter a mind at work but also to witness Friel's own encounters with other minds on paper. Friel's early notes in particular give archive users a crucial insight into how this playwright's influences operated at the level of artistic practice. What I have found especially noteworthy is the extent to which Friel's work was frequently the product of his encounters not only with the work of other artists but also with their different ways of working. There is one period in Friel's creative life that stands out as something of a turning point in this respect: the composition process for his play *Faith Healer* (1979). It is my view that it was Friel's chance encounter with David Sylvester's *Interviews with Francis Bacon* (1975), at around the same time that he was becoming receptive to the writings of George Steiner, that was a significant catalyst for a creative leap in Friel's thinking around two of his enduring intellectual concerns. The first is the relationship between art and 'fact'; the second is the role of art and the artist in navigating that relationship.

This is perhaps best illustrated chronologically, though a little temporal back-and-forth is unavoidable. I will begin with a series of short case studies that elucidate the way these concerns manifested themselves in the writing of Friel's earlier plays. Moving on, I will take a slightly more detailed look at Friel's engagement with Proust's thinking around '[t]he

© The Author(s), under exclusive license to Springer Nature Switzerland AG 2023
Z. Kuczyńska, *Brian Friel's Models of Influence*, https://doi.org/10.1007/978-3-031-17905-1_2

great quality of true art'[1] in *Crystal and Fox* (1968) and *The Freedom of the City* (1973). I will then offer a detailed study of the 'how' of influence in *Faith Healer* at the level of artistic practice as the chapter's main case study. Following on from this will be another pair of shorter case studies, exploring how Friel's chance encounter with painter Francis Bacon's ways of working might usefully be posited as a significant recalibration in Friel's intellectual trajectory, focusing on *Making History* (1988) and *Give Me Your Answer, Do!* (1997). 'Okay? Okay',[2] as Teddy might say. 'Why don't I do that? Why not?' (Friel, *Pl*, 366).

Early Plays: 'The Changing Landscape of Fact'[3]

The relationship between art and 'fact' is one that is characterised almost from the outset of Friel's playwrighting career as one in which the definition of a fact is mutable. Material relating to the composition process of Friel's short stories and earliest forays into theatre is either non-existent or in short supply in the Brian Friel Papers. Even the manuscripts for *Philadelphia, Here I Come!* (1964) are relatively light on early notes, despite being rich in drafts and production history. Nevertheless, archive-based examples from his extant early notes provide a sense of Friel's intricate and constantly evolving explorations of the nature of fact, even though he was still essentially honing his craft on the job. There is certainly evidence of a sustained engagement with the distinction between fact and fiction. For instance, although it would not be articulated in print until Friel's 'Self-Portrait' of 1972, *Philadelphia* famously blurs this distinction in a pivotal scene in which Gar Public attempts to share a treasured memory of a fishing trip with his father. Seeking corroboration, Gar is instead faced with the possibility that what he remembers 'never happened' (Friel, *Pl*, 95) because his father contests certain details. The definition of autobiographical fact that informs this scene was later clarified by Friel as both 'something that happened to me or something I experienced' *and* 'something I thought happened to me, something I thought I experienced'. In other words, it is a subjective truth that does not necessarily acknowledge the difference between a verifiable 'fact' and an unverifiable 'fiction':

> My father and I [. . .] are walking home from a lake with our fishing rods across our shoulders. [. . .] That's the memory. That's what happened. [. . .] But [. . .] there is no lake along that muddy road. And since there

is no lake my father and I never walked back from it in the rain with our rods across our shoulders. The fact is a fiction. [. . .] For some reason the mind has shuffled the pieces of verifiable truth and composed a truth of its own. For to me it is a truth.[4]

Friel complicated the *Philadelphia* model still further during the composition process of *Lovers: Winners* (1967):

> There is a world, a cerebral world, in which people do + say things (kind, cruel, absurd, outlandish) which is in keeping with our concept of them. And there is a world, not cerebral and yet not fully "external", in which people behave unintelligibly from our point of view. And finally there is a world—"external reality"—in which we live; where action + human behaviour is made up partly of both wor[l]ds above.[5]

Unlike the muddled fact/fiction binary, this tripartite model is one that hinges on the idea of intelligibility: there is an internal world of ideas in which people behave in ways that we understand; there is an in-between world in which people behave in ways we do not understand; and there is external reality, in which people act in ways we both do and do not understand. Tantalisingly, this is not something upon which Friel expands directly. Nor is this exact framework of three different realities directly traceable to his secondary reading. Though Friel often omitted his sources, there are usually clues—quotation marks, page numbers, an author's initials, and a recurring phrase—to suggest that Friel is transcribing secondary material. None of these apply to this particular note. Though there is an unnamed philosopher figure who expounds on the nature of external reality elsewhere in the MS, this character was left undeveloped.

The closest philosophical affinity I am able to suggest without supporting archival evidence is with Gottlob Frege (1846–1925), who proposed a Third Realm of timelessly true 'thoughts [that] are neither things of the outer world nor [internal] ideas'.[6] Though Frege may be a useful precedent for Friel's 'not cerebral and yet not fully "external"'[7] world, however, this resonance should not be overstressed. Frege's Third Realm of thought is one that accommodates such truths as Pythagorean theorems, which exist and are true even if not known, understood, or believed. As Frege puts it, a thought (as opposed to an idea) is like 'a planet which, already before anyone else has seen it, has been in interaction with other planets'.[8] Moreover, where Friel writes of the intelligibility of human behaviour, Frege writes of sensibility or perceptibility: 'The thought belongs neither to my inner world as an idea nor yet to the outer world of material, perceptible things'.[9] In other words, Frege's Third Realm is not a space in which truths cannot be fully understood, but rather a space in which truths cannot be perceived purely by sensory means, existing independently of their bearers. I would, therefore, suggest that this is a framework of Friel's own devising, in which the subjectivity of the distinction between a fact and a fiction is heightened by the question of intelligibility.[10] Expanding on the *Philadelphia* model, in which the truth of something that never happened can be part of the 'subsoil'[11] of the self, the *Lovers* model suggests that a truth can only be understood if it can be reconciled with the individual's internal sense of reality. Hence the lingering senselessness of the tragedy of the two drowned children Mag and Joe, despite our being privy both to the official version of events and their rich inner lives: their deaths do not make sense given what we know of them and of the events of the day.

Friel's demonstrable preoccupation with the nature of fact remained with him for the duration of his career. The Brian Friel Papers show us that he revisited the question time and time again, both directly and indirectly, incorporating different source materials as he encountered and absorbed new perspectives over the years. It is there in every conflict between the official record and individual testimony in Friel's oeuvre—in *The Freedom of the City* (1973), in *Living Quarters* (1977), and in the much later *Making History* (1988). And what we see by the time of this more mature play is something altogether different to the usual juxtaposition of clearly demarcated official and unofficial truths. Moreover, due partly to Friel's sources for the play and partly to what I suggest is the catalysis of Friel's engagement with the *practice* of art during the writing of *Faith Healer*, a more practice-based definition of fact emerges. Indeed, by the time of *Making History*, Friel had clarified something latent in his thinking around fact, conceptualising it as something that has been *produced* through discursive, cognitive, or artistic practices of engaging with reality as we experience it.

Crystal and Fox AND *The Freedom of the City:*
'THAT REALITY FAR FROM WHICH WE LIVE'[12]

But how did this clarification take place? Before answering that question, it is necessary to focus for a time on the evolution of Friel's thinking around art and the role of the artist. Prior to *Faith Healer*, Friel's plays had taken a largely abstract view of art rather than focusing on art as a practice or set of practices. These were works that had arguably been written with a view to making the unsayable or unknowable tangible through stagecraft in a fundamentally positive way, unhappy endings notwithstanding. This is an impulse that governs many of Friel's early experiments with non-naturalistic techniques. See, for instance, the relatively straightforward device of the soliloquy as used in the Wagnerian rhapsodies of *The Loves of Cass McGuire* (1966), whose Pirandellian overtones were acknowledged by Friel in a letter to Hilton Edwards.[13] So too does this attempted restorative objectification of the subjective occur in Friel's serial reinventions of the idea of a chorus, of which Sir in *Living Quarters* is one. Certainly, the archive suggests that Friel had been combing the *Reader's Encyclopedia of World Drama* for a working definition of a chorus, landing on Northrop Frye's *Anatomy of Criticism* as a guiding focus.[14] It is examples like these that suggest a view of art and the artist that is best summarised by one of the so-called *Maxims of Marcel Proust* (1948), in a passage from *Le Temps Retrouvé* quoted by Friel during the composition process of not one but two pre-*Faith Healer* plays:

> The great quality of true art is that it rediscovers, grasps, and reveals to us that reality far from which we live, from which we get farther and farther away as the conventional knowledge we substitute for it becomes thicker and more impermeable, the reality that we might die without having known and which is simply our life, real life, life finally discovered and clarified, consequently the only life that has been really lived—that life which in once sense is to be found at any time in all men as well as in artists.

The maxim continues:

> But they do not try to analyze it. Thus their past is cluttered with innumerable snapshots that are useless because the intelligence has not "developed" them.[15]

In other words, for Proust, art is a means of reconnecting both artists and ordinary people with the reality of their own lives, having grown away from that reality through an unwillingness or an inability to analyse it.

Friel first engaged with this Proustian maxim during the composition process of *Crystal and Fox* (1969), a play that in the history of Friel criticism is usually seen as a thematic forerunner of *Faith Healer*. There are certainly similarities: both plays contain a rag-tag performance troupe poised between 'transcendence and squalor',[16] astonishing acts of viciousness by self-destructive men who have grown 'exhausted with the effort of believing [their] own creation',[17] and wives reduced to 'object[s] within the private world of the thinking male'.[18] Over a series of episodes, the troupe's leader, Fox Melarkey, 'dismantles the hierarchy and affiliations of his family, his livelihood and his own identity in order to regain his dream of childhood innocence',[19] mostly by alienating and abusing his loved ones. This he does in a series of increasingly shocking acts that include poisoning a dog and telling his own wife Crystal (untruthfully) that it was he who informed on their murderous son Gabriel to the English police, causing her to abandon him in disgust. The play ends with Fox, alone at a crossroads, spinning a battered wheel of fortune, not renouncing chance but rather embracing it.

Friel's engagement with Proust occurred some months into the fairly short composition process for *Crystal and Fox*. The earliest dated notes for the play are from November 1967; Friel sent a copy of the finished play to Hilton Edwards on 27 March 1968. The Proust appears in Friel's notes on 4 January 1968, along with a further note from the same day that makes its significance explicit: 'It now seems best to start directly as scripted—straight into the roadshow [...] And at the end of that first episode, Fox explains to Crystal his search, his vague necessity, his groping for *the reality far from which we live*'.[20] [My italics.] As Friel's note implies, he had again deliberated at length over an appropriate form for the piece. For instance, one undated note floats the possibility of a form that Friel would ultimately be put to use in *The Freedom of the City*:

The circus action is interpolated by very high sounding speeches by

(a) Clergyman,
(b) Politician,
(c) trades-unionist
(d) anthropologist

all done by the same actor.[21]

A further undated note, meanwhile, makes Friel's motivation for entertaining such a form apparent:

> How to represent officialdom—the social welfare woman [. . .]; the guard who mentions road tax, insurance, parking lights, TV licence, radio licence; the priest.
> It seems they must be done realistically. But there is an inclination to put them as a face and voice in isolation.[22]

It is worth noting here that some of these forms of officialdom are also thorns in the sides of Teddy, Grace, and Frank, but that Friel's eventual chosen form for *Faith Healer* does not give them any physical representation.

As with several of his pre-*Faith Healer* plays, Friel was asking himself how best to use dramatic form to distinguish between binaries—official and unofficial, public and private—in order to explore, once again, the relationship between fact and fiction. For instance, on 10 November 1967, Friel wrote: 'I now think the story must lean towards a revelation of the impossibility of a coexistence between fact + fiction. The show world cannot exist in a real world determined to impose reality (in the form of law, religion, sociology, trades unionism) on it'.[23] As in *Lovers: Winners*, Friel seems to suggest that it is largely the public world (best represented by varying forms of officialdom) that stands in the way of the possibility of 'fusing fact + fancy into a liveable whole' in private.[24] Consequently, the show world is insufficient for Fox, who looks for alternative means of recovering the life he thinks he remembers with Crystal at a time when they were young and full of 'warm hopes'.[25]

Although *Crystal and Fox* is similar to *Faith Healer* in many respects, it is notes like these that show that Friel had not yet found a way of engaging productively with art as a practice rather than in the abstract or as an aspect of the fictional in the context of a fact/fiction binary. Indeed, it is arguably as a man and not as an artist that Fox (whose role in the show world bears more of a resemblance to that of Teddy the showman-manager than that of Frank the artist) makes his disastrous attempt to rediscover 'that reality far from which we live'. Although there is certainly a case to be made that Fox's artistry is in his creation of a fictional show world rather than the 'rotten dramatic material'[26] he churns out, there is little archival evidence that Friel was thinking of Fox as anything other than an ordinary man, albeit with a talent for showbiz. There is no troubling implication here that, like the Frank of Teddy's monologue in *Faith Healer*, a man behaving badly might be excused if he can be understood as an artist. This does not diminish or invalidate readings of the play in which Fox is a proto-Frank figure who shapes and destroys the show world as 'one of his fictions' (Friel, *P1*, 353), albeit in search of lost time (as it were) rather than in an attempt to understand his craft. However, it does illustrate that, at this point in his writing life, Friel was not equipped to tackle an important question raised by Proust's maxim: how, and by what processes, might art achieve this discovery and clarification of 'the only life that has been really lived'? This is not a question that is ever addressed in the play. Fox does not achieve his epiphanic vision of a temporally distant reality through the process of carving out a make-believe world that he and his loved ones can inhabit as knock-off versions of characters from popular films. Instead, he experiences, in the midst of his disillusionment, a moment when 'the fog lifts, and you get a glimpse, an intuition; and suddenly you know that [...] there has to be something better than this'.[27] Essentially, he has a mid-life crisis.

Certainly, it seems that, in this play, Friel was drawing on Proust primarily as one of two precedents for the otherwise incomprehensible behaviour of a man who attempts to destroy the present as a means of recovering the past. As Friel recognised when interrogating himself in note form on 2 December 1967, Fox's motivation was a question in dire need of an answer, part of which he felt ready to provide at the time:

> Basic importance
> Why does Fox destroy his own show?
> Because he loves it; because it is his life.[28]

Friel's justification for Fox's motivation? One of the more famous (and problematic) parts of Oscar Wilde's *The Ballad of Reading Gaol*:

> This is a perfectly compatible contradiction: loving + killing simultaneously.
> Yet each man kills the thing he loves
> By each let this be heard;
> Some do it with a bitter look,
> Some with a flattering word.
> The coward does it with a kiss
> The brave man with a sword.[29]

With the addition of the passage from *Le Temps Retrouvé* (Time Regained) a month later, a picture of what Friel may have been trying to achieve emerges: Fox's wrecking of his own show is an attempt to regain the past (Proust); the destructiveness of his actions is not an act of hate but an act of love (Wilde).

That these attempts to make Fox's behaviour intelligible are neither especially apparent nor sufficiently convincing in the finished play is undoubtedly a factor in *Crystal and Fox*'s absence from the roster of frequently revived Friel plays. It has not aged particularly well. Pioneers of Friel scholarship may well have been willing to see Fox as an example of the recurring Frielian trope of 'the inner man in conflict with the public world [...] trying to make himself whole and to complete his vision of the world by satisfying the world's demands'.[30] By the mid-2000s, however, critical attitudes towards Fox had become less sympathetic, as Frank McGuinness's pithy appraisal of Fox's final moments will avow: 'His yelps of pain do not go unnoticed. They do go unpitied'.[31] Though McGuinness ultimately believes that Friel's 'rough, rabid, devious texts' of the late 1960s were a necessary unleashing of 'monsters' by a playwright still honing his craft, there remains evidence to suggest that Fox's unsympathetic nature was a stumbling block for the play's readers even before the text was staged. Moreover, though I would tend to agree with McGuinness that the 'creative challenge[s]'[32] of some of these earlier plays were necessary experiments, Friel would most certainly have disagreed with McGuinness as far as Fox's monstrosity is concerned. Indeed, Friel was demonstrably horrified by the some of the early feedback he received on Fox's character from his U.S. publisher, Robert Giroux, and wrote to the play's director Hilton Edwards to tell him so:

> Evil—nonsense! Destructive—perhaps, but [. . .] I would accept the term only when it is completely divorced from the idea of gratuitous malice. [. . .] For example, when Fox insists that "She's to know nothing" [. . .] his <u>only</u> thought is to protect the woman he loves passionately from any tiny hurt. [. . .] The lines of an evil, destructive man?

Indeed, Friel went so far as to say that if, as Giroux claimed, Fox 'hurts for the sake of hurting [...] then he's a stranger to me and I've created something I don't recognise'. In short, for Friel, Fox 'may not be admirable or lovable or even pitiable but I think that he is within our understanding'.[33]

Though Friel may have been right to object to the simplistic dismissal of Fox's actions as those of a malign madman, his apologist view of Fox's actions remains naïve if not problematic. The trouble with Fox is, in many ways, the trouble with *The Ballad of Reading Gaol*: the philosophically motivated aesthetic erasure of victims of physical and psychological violence, othered and abstracted as 'the thing he loves'.[34] In this respect, it is worryingly close to the latent gender politics of *Faith Healer*. However, where Frank Hardy's behaviour is inextricably and therefore problematically linked with his being an artist, Fox Melarkey's acts of increasingly shocking cruelty are not a deliberate weaponisation of his artistic practice but the means of pursuing a personal obsession. Indeed, whether we pity the Fox or not, whether we see him as man or artist, he is not a character who displays any kind of conscious relationship with an artistic practice. It would, therefore, be a misdirection to see *Crystal and Fox* as a precedent for *Faith Healer* in terms of the latter's engagement with the practice of art, despite being 'its obvious analogue'[35] in other respects.

The second play in which Friel engages with Proust's maxim taken from *Le Temps Retrouvé* is arguably a more successful engagement with the practice of art in terms of his own craft as a playwright. However, it is an engagement that reinforces the idea that art is a fundamentally restorative practice capable of articulating the impossible rather than acknowledging its potential for violence—something that Friel would go on to explore in *Faith Healer*. The play in question, *The Freedom of the City*, is superficially a very different piece to *Crystal and Fox*. One is the relatively naturalistic unfolding of the slow destruction of a band of itinerant performers by its inscrutable leader. The other is a more obviously temporally fragmented and overtly political portrayal of the events surrounding the murder of three unarmed civilians by British troops after the violent dispersal of a civil rights march in Derry, as a kind of fictional equivalent to Bloody Sunday.[36] The origins of the two plays, however, are less disparate than their subject matter would suggest. The genesis of this later play was certainly earlier than is generally imagined. Indeed, the real-world event from which Friel would draw some early inspiration occurred a mere two months after the premiere of *Crystal and Fox* in November 1968.

The Freedom of the City was originally conceived as a play on the general theme of the burgeoning civil rights movement in the North of Ireland, potentially in the light of the Burntollet Bridge attack of 4 January 1969.[37] Friel was making a few preliminary notes on his civil rights play by the end of April 1970:

> The P[eople's].D[emocracy].take over the Mayor's parlour; drink cabinet, cigars, ceremonial clothes [Do Straus [*sic.*] waltz to transistor].
> McCann, the leader, preaching revolution to his supporters who are ultimately too flippant, too joyous, to go to his logical extremes.
> They receive various deputations (and TV? press?).[38]

By 'McCann', Friel means Eamonn McCann, the civil rights activist, journalist, and erstwhile People Before Profit MLA on whom the character of Skinner is partially based. Later, in September 1970, Friel specifically mentioned Burntollet:

> Still on the Civil Rights theme:
> Set in route during the Burntollet march.
> In a byre after the attack OR
> In a large hall, full of rugs + sleeping bags, before Burntollet.[39]

Following the events of Bloody Sunday, however, the play altered its trajectory. This is evident from the contents of MS 37,066/3 and MS 37,067/1, which contain a copy of the Derry Supplement of the *Irish*

Independent devoted to 'Derry's Bloody Sunday' and a copy of the now discredited Widgery Report of April 1972, respectively.[40] The play's many juxtapositions of differing socio-political viewpoints, meanwhile, can be traced to Friel's wider reading. For instance, the interpolations of the sociologist, Dr. Dodds, are heavily based on Oscar Lewis's *La Vida: A Puerto Rican Family in the Culture of Poverty—San Juan and New York* (1965).[41]

As has been noted, the interpolative form of *The Freedom of the City* is essentially a development of an unused idea for *Crystal and Fox*. This recycling of discarded forms was not uncommon for Friel. *Living Quarters*, for instance, makes use of a version of a Pirandello-style conceit that Friel was considering for *Lovers: Winners*: 'The whole play a dress rehearsal/run through with interruption by the director: and every time he [...] interrupts the boy or girl tells the audience what they really saw + remember'.[42] Whereas *Crystal and Fox* would most likely have used interpolators to represent the imposition of officialdom on private lives, however, in *The Freedom of the City* they also function as an extension of the three citizens' inability to articulate their experiences and political views in a language of their own. Hence Michael's tirade against 'bastards like [Skinner], bloody vandals that's keeping us all on our bloody knees' (Friel, *Pl*, 147) is an echo of the Priest's sermon, which portrays the 'initially peaceful and dignified' Civil Rights movement as one that has been 'contaminated [...] and ultimately poisoned' by 'certain evil elements' intent on 'deliver[ing] this Christian country into the dark dungeons of Godless communism' (Friel, *Pl*, 156). Similarly, Skinner's attempt to explain Lily to herself finds its more long-winded counterpart in sociologist Dr. Dodds's condescension. Dodds suggests that 'once [the poor] become aware that their condition has counterparts elsewhere [...] they have broken out of their subculture' (Friel, *Pl*, 111); Skinner tells Lily that she marches '[b]ecause for the first time in your life you grumbled and someone else grumbled [...] and you heard each other, and became aware that there were [...] millions of us all over the world', and that the movement is 'about us—the poor—the majority—stirring in our sleep' (Friel, *Pl*, 154). In a letter to Friel, literary agent Warren Brown observes that Dodd's speech 'amounts to a considerable chunk of Mr. Lewis's own nonsensical twaddle' and advises Friel to alter the lifted material or else seek permission to include it 'since this character of Dodds is going to play satirically'.[43] Though the 'sometimes stilted and often hypocritical officialese'[44] of the authority figures represented by the interpolations is also a feature of Dodds's speech, there is nevertheless a suggestion in Friel's notes that Dodds's views, if not his condescending middle-class manner, were not intended to play entirely satirically. Indeed, Friel stipulates that '[t]here must be "character development" along the lines of Dr. Dodds's opening speech—the psychological and social core must be broken by Skinner'.[45] Here Friel is referencing Lewis rather than the fictional Dodds, whose opening speech borrows heavily from *La Vida*. Where Lewis observes that '[a]ny movement [...] which organizes and gives hope to the poor and effectively promotes solidarity [...] destroys the psychological and social core of the culture of poverty', Dodds opines that 'any movement which [...] organizes them gives them real hope, promotes solidarity [...] inevitably smashes the rigid caste that encases their minds and bodies' (Friel, *Pl*, 111). In short, Friel borrows from Lewis not simply to create an unfeeling official discourse but rather to suggest a roadmap for some of the ways in which each character is 'adjusted'[46] over the course of the play.

Nevertheless, the interpolators' speeches stand in stark contrast to those expanded, abstracted moments before the deaths of the three citizens when they attempt to articulate their experiences independently of judicial, sociological, religious, or political frameworks. One of these mini monologues in particular is directly attributable to the same passage of Proust Friel used for *Crystal and Fox*, and is cited in the MSs for *The Freedom of the City* on 3 June 1972.[47] Ironically, given that Lily's reasons for marching find no analogue in any of the interpolations, her moment of self-realisation is largely a Proustian echo. Her feeling 'that life had eluded me because never [...] had an experience [...] been isolated, and assessed, and articulated' (Friel, *Pl*, 150) is one that is borrowed from the tail end of the maxim (not cited in Friel's notes): 'their past is cluttered with innumerable snapshots that are useless because the intelligence has not "developed" them'.[48] The realisation that she has therefore 'never experienced' her own life is its defining and most tragic experience. The reason she feels she 'died of grief' (Friel, *Pl*, 150) is that her life turns out truly to have been a reality she 'die[s] without having known'.[49]

This is a far more successful integration of Proust than in *Crystal and Fox* insofar as the finished play's juxtaposition of discourses gives formal expression to the ideas contained in the maxim. The last hours in the lives of Skinner, Michael, and Lily—two of whom articulate themselves using the language of pre-existing socio-political frameworks, one for whom none of the official discourses represented is equipped to speak—are presented in fragmented, frequently interrupted snapshots when alive; their dead bodies are represented in camera snaps, scatter patterns, and bullet wounds. Admittedly, there is little in Friel's notes that suggests a sustained engagement with Proust: if Friel was thinking about how best to find a form that would enable an exploration of the ideas contained within the maxim, he wasn't thinking on paper. Nevertheless, earlier drafts of the characters' dying monologues were much more an attempt at an articulation of their political views: Michael affirms his '[belief] in progress'; Skinner, pessimistically, suggests that we are ultimately '[neither] our own architects nor our own executioners'; Lily 'cant now begin to think in terms of what [her] regrets are' because her life's anxieties were the 'necessary worries' of poverty and she can't imagine what it would have been like 'if [she] had had money'.[50] The versions of their revenant epiphanies that appear in the play, by contrast, are an impossible space carved out of time in which the three struggle to articulate the things for which they didn't have the time to find the words at the moments of their deaths. Michael addresses his 'disbelief, [...] astonishment, [...] shock' at the 'mistake' that has been made; Lily is 'overwhelmed by a tidal wave of regret'; Skinner dies 'in defensive flippancy' (Friel, *Pl*, 149–150). These are not statements of belief but 'time regained' in practice—the claiming of a moment that exists only as fiction, to say things for which there is no official forum, and to assess the reality of their lives that has been hidden, until now, even from themselves. Here, the art of Proust's maxim is Friel's art as a dramatist, by which the dead are made to live again and experience, however heartbreakingly, 'that reality far from which we live'.

Faith Healer: 'A DISORIENTED VISION OF A FACT'[51]

Friel's plays of the 1960s up until the mid-1970s represent an active engagement with the relationship between a largely abstract idea of art and a slowly evolving definition of 'fact'. Over the course of multiple plays, the latter emerges as a necessarily unstable construction; as one of a number of ways of giving form to aspects of reality, and to the differing subjectivities of public and private or official and unofficial truths. There is a burgeoning sense of art as that which is likewise capable of giving form (i.e. a kind of fictional factuality) to 'that reality far from which we live', in a way that official discourses are unlikely to be able to accommodate. However, there is little consideration either to the *practice* of art or to the role of the artist up to this point. This was all about to change, thanks to the composition process of a play that is in many ways a vital example of the intersection between different artistic practices: Friel's subtly ground-breaking play of 1979, *Faith Healer*.

A memory play of aching complexity, *Faith Healer* comprises four contradictory monologues for three actors. Though it has no plot to speak of, the events it recounts concern the life, marriage, bereavements, and untimely deaths of Frank and Grace Hardy, aided, abetted, and witnessed by Frank's manager Teddy. Frank is an itinerant faith healer, pathological liar, narcissistic charmer, and emotionally abusive alcoholic. Grace worked in the legal profession before eloping with Frank, and endures a life of psychological torture and material squalor, during which time she suffers several traumatic miscarriages. Teddy, the affable cockney showman, drives the three of them around the dying villages of Scotland and Wales where Frank 'performs' (or more usually fails to perform) miracle cures. Upon their return to Ireland, Frank is murdered by the friends of a man he failed to heal that night in a bar; Grace tries to process her trauma with the help of a largely inadequate therapist in England, but later commits suicide; Teddy is left with the poster for Frank's act, his reminiscences, and his unrequited feelings for at least one of the pair. The play ends with Frank recounting his own death as a renouncing of chance, relinquishing what he sees as his lifelong struggle with the crippling uncertainty of his healing gift.

The intellectual development of the play was marked by a series of what Friel would later think of as chance encounters with secondary material. For instance, the composition process was partially underpinned by a cautionary mantra derived from an interview with playwright Howard Brenton in an issue of *Theatre Quarterly* published in February 1975, shortly before the earliest dated note in the *Faith Healer* MSs (15 April 1975): 'Beware of the huge, jokeless, joyless allegory'.[52] Elsewhere, on 24 May 1975, Friel cites an interview with Russian writer and dissident Andrei Sinyavsky (better known as Abram Tertz) that had appeared in the previous day's *Times Literary Supplement*, in which the latter posits the artist as 'a failed miracle-worker, or, in simpler language, a magician who casts a spell on reality through his images':

> The magical transformation of the world by means of art is unattainable, but art lives and breathes by such stimuli. Hence the tragedy of the artist, who is incapable of carrying out the primordial injunction that has been

laid upon him. And therein lies the great strength and joy of art: to create images by transforming life and thus on a sheet of paper or on the page of a book to play the artist's immemorial role—that of sorcerer and mythmaker.'[53]

This evocation of the doomed male artist unable to fulfil his miraculous calling is certainly sympathetic to a reading of the play that posits its titular faith healer as a tragic figure destined to fail in his vocation. Such a reading is, however, only one of three versions of events portrayed by Friel's multifaceted play, and the one closest to that espoused by its deeply problematic and unreliable lead at that. As the archive suggests, the idea of the miracle man as artist so neatly supplemented by Sinyavsky's idea of the artist as miracle man was already being shaped by another, knottier source that would influence the play on a deeper, more structural level: David Sylvester's *Interviews with Francis Bacon* (1975).

Whilst Sinyavsky and others remain important touchstones for the play, it is Friel's encounter with Bacon's interviews that has possibly the most significance for *Faith Healer* and the plays that followed it. As the archives indicate, this encounter occurred around the same time that Friel was beginning to digest George Steiner's ideas on language—some three years prior to the first dated archive material pertaining to *Translations*. In a note dated 25 June 1975, Friel saw the definite 'possibility of a creative confluence in the distinctive elements of [George] Steiner + F. Bacon + the faith-healer': 'Steiner—language; Bacon—chance; faith-healer the vehicle of the indecision of now'.[54] Here, the combination of Steiner and Bacon is illustrative of a point in Friel's creative development when he was demonstrably receptive to new ideas about the possibilities and limitations of linguistic representation. Significantly for *Faith Healer*, for instance, Steiner's *After Babel* (1975) is notable for its argument on 'the creativity of falsehood'. In a passage quoted in Donald Davie's review in the *TLS* (which Friel is likely to have read), Steiner goes so far as to say that '[t]he very concept of integral truth ... is a fictive ideal':

> We speak less than the truth, we fragment in order to reconstruct shared alternatives, we select and elide. It is not 'the things which are' that we say, but those which might be, which we would bring about, which the eye and remembrance compose.[55]

There is certainly a case to be made for Steiner's influence on the elided truths of *Faith Healer* in a theoretical sense. However, to my mind, it is Friel's concurrent reading of Bacon's interviews that provided him with the strongest *practical* example of the creativity of falsehood, not as linguistic theory but as artistic practice. Indeed, Bacon's ideas on the role of the artist, the workings of chance, and the extent to which the practice of art is a form of violence may have been a significant influence on not only the character of Frank Hardy but also the thematic core and form of a monologue play that redefined its genre.

The character of chance

On 18 May 1975, Brian Friel was in need of a breakthrough. The play he had been working on for the past month or so about an as-yet unnamed 'S.S.' or Seventh Son—a faith healer—was still in its early stages. Already it was struggling under its own symbolism whilst resisting Friel's efforts to find a suitable form ('[b]eware of the huge, jokeless, joyless allegory' indeed). In the days and weeks that followed, there would be no definitive lightbulb moment. As the archive reveals, it would take a series of encounters over several months with various artists and thinkers across different media and disciplines before a play recognisable as *Faith Healer* would emerge. Nevertheless, 18 May 1975 remains a significant date for *Faith Healer*. Among Friel's notes on this day are the first pieces of concrete evidence that one of the most important of these creative encounters was already taking place: Friel was reading David Sylvester's *Interviews with Francis Bacon*.[56]

At the surface level of influence, Bacon's interviews can be seen to have had an important role in shaping not only the character of Francis 'Frank' Hardy but also the character of his gift of faith healing. Both had been giving Friel trouble. Although he had hit upon an analogy that would provide him with the bare bones of a plot by 17 May 1975, it was one with which he almost immediately found fault:

17 May '75.

The Salmon

The salmon is born in a certain river.
He crosses thousands of miles.

> He returns to the same river, to the place of his birth; and to get there he has to circumvent seine nets, drift nets, fishermen, poachers.
>
> 18 May.
> And then, when he returns ....
> [One of the weaknesses of the analogy is that the nets, rods, etc. aren't manned by salmon!][57]

It was on the same day that he was taking his extended salmon metaphor to task that Friel chose to express his frustration in terms of Bacon's interviews, referencing French poet and philosopher Paul Valéry. Indeed, Bacon's wish 'to do the thing that Valéry said—to give the sensation without the boredom of its conveyance' (Sylvester, 65)—was paraphrased by Friel in a square bracketed addendum to a separate note from 18 May:

> More real progress would be made if the concentration were on the truth + validity of S.S. and his situation and if the image were allowed to speak for itself through them.
>
> [Valery: I want to go direct to the sensation + avoid the boredom of the conveyance].[58]

That Friel spoke in terms of 'the image' is telling. As Sylvester notes, Bacon used the word 'image' to mean a number of different things:

> Sometimes [. . .] a picture he is making or has made, or one by someone else, or a photograph; sometimes [. . .] a subject he has in mind or in front of him; sometimes [. . .] a complex of forms which has an especially powerful and suggestive resonance (Sylvester, 7).

Although it is unclear which of these was meant by Friel, what is clear from his notes is that he was thinking of the play in terms of Bacon's artistic practice. As Friel's paraphrasing of Bacon and Valéry will attest, he was eager 'not to avoid storytelling' altogether but rather to avoid 'the boredom [that] comes upon you' at 'the moment the story enters' (Sylvester, 65). In other words, Friel was keen that the play and its form should emerge through the character and situation of the faith healer rather than relying on 'symbolism in isolation', which he felt had 'taken possession and killed the environment necessary for its survival'.[59]

Of particular interest to Friel in terms of developing the character of the faith healer was the role of chance in Bacon's work. In a note dated 19 May, Friel wrote:

> Since the kernel is healing ... and presumably healing by belief, then we are concerned at least as much with the possibility of faith in certain situations as we are with the empirical fact of a cure.
> So that in some respects S.S. works as blindly as Francis Bacon, believing in chance, in accident.[60]

By this, Friel meant Bacon's consistent practice of emphasising the workings of chance and accident in his creative process. For Bacon, 'if anything works for me, I feel it is nothing I have made myself, but something which chance has been able to give me'. This chance must subsequently be manipulated, though there remains the additional uncertainty of 'never know[ing] how much it is pure chance and how much it is manipulation of it' (Sylvester, 52). On 21 May, Friel condensed a slightly longer exchange between Sylvester and Bacon and added his own commentary:

> Francis Bacon.
> Q: Can you say why you feel that an image will tend to look more inevitable the more it comes about by accident?
> F.B. It hasn't been interfered with. The hinges of form, come about by chance, seem to be more organic + to work more inevitably. The will has been subdued by the instinct.
>
> The above
>
> Signposts for the formal direction of the whole play.
> And, as important, a peep-hole into the handling of S.S., the artist, the medium, chance's handmaiden.
> Also the 'chance' of reading Bacon at this time.[61]

This last note gives us a particular insight into how Friel saw both his character and himself in relation to the role ascribed to luck and accident in Bacon's work. The thematic thread of chance that runs through *Faith Healer*, itself directly related to Friel's reading of Bacon, is altogether more positively expressed in Friel's own sense of having had a fatefully significant encounter with the right book at the right time.

For all that Friel's notes attest to his having found definite potential in Bacon's musings on the role of chance, both the play and its titular character are nevertheless greater than the sum of their parts. Friel's consideration of the relationship between his creative practice and that of an artist working in a different medium ultimately produced a character that was neither fish nor flesh. Neither the hardy homecoming salmon nor quite the confidently self-mythologising artist Francis Bacon, the resultant Francis Hardy is an artist whose journey home is beset by psychological snares of his own making that come from his inability to reconcile himself with the workings of chance. Much like his partial namesake, Frank is an artist who is 'possessed' (Friel, *Pl*, 333) by a gift he does not understand. However, where Bacon accommodated his relationship with 'accident' into 'the vocabulary of an obsession'[62] that was arguably part of a 'strategic' construction of 'the interpretative framework of his *oeuvre*',[63] Frank is plagued by 'nagging, tormenting, maddening questions' (Friel, *Pl*, 334). In this, Frank is perhaps more like his creator than the artist on whom he appears to be partially modelled. Friel's own composition process was one that was likewise driven by questions that ranged from detailed interrogations of character to ruminations on broader thematic concerns and how they might be manifested formally. Indeed, the earliest dated note in the *Faith Healer* MS (15 April 1975) comprises a list of questions:

The Seventh Son.

Is a faith-healer a poet, a saint, a charlatan?
Offering tangible images that evoke a response.
At what cost to himself?
Is faith-healing an art? A craft? A technique? A con?
When the play opens at what stage of his career is he? At his peak? Declining? Only discovering himself?
Is there any question of—or any need of—healing himself?
[. . .]
Has he faith? In what? And how + what does he heal?[64]

Although this is hardly unusual for Friel, who routinely used questions as a means of ensuring that even his most theoretically dense plays were a 'story [...] told through people',[65] what is notable here is the fact that it is not the answers to these questions but rather the questions themselves that went on to determine the character of Frank. This is particularly evident from the beginning of Frank's first monologue, in which Friel's earliest questions to himself about Frank are remarkably similar to Frank's own relentless self-questionings:

Am I endowed with a unique and awesome gift? ... *Am I a con man?* ... Was it all chance?—or skill?—or illusion?—or delusion? Precisely what power did I possess? Could I summon it? When and how? Was I its servant? Did it reside in my ability to invest someone with faith in me or did I evoke from him a healing faith in himself? Could my healing be effective without faith? But faith in what?—in me?—in the possibility?—faith in faith? And is the power diminishing? (Friel, *Pl*, 333-4) [Italics in original]

Where Friel's sense of Bacon as an artist was gained through the medium of the question and answer (the interview), Frank exists as a series of questions, many of which are sufficient in and of themselves to form his character.

Despite the fact that Frank appears to identify less with Bacon's more positive creative relationship with chance than Friel—who saw his encounter with the Sylvester interviews as essentially serendipitous—there is evidence nevertheless to suggest that Friel was keen to construct a character for Frank that hinted at a fundamental receptiveness to the accidental. On 21 May 1975, Friel wrote:

[With reference to Francis Bacon:-]
 There must be some practical example in his non-professional life of S.S.'s openness to chance—e.g. gambling, ... drink. Just as in his work he is always positioning himself in exposure to chance.[66]

These practical examples likewise appear to have their origins in Bacon's interviews. For instance, Teddy's account of Frank's cure of ten people in Glamorganshire after which Frank and Grace absconded to 'a posh hotel in Cardiff' with the contents of a grateful farmer's wallet and 'lived it up until the wallet was empty' (Friel, *Pl*, 360) bears a strong resemblance to Bacon's account of how he would behave after a big gambling win (Sylvester, 51). That Frank 'always knew, drunk or sober ... when nothing was going to happen' (Friel, *Pl*, 334) also has its roots in Bacon's gambling, when he thought he 'heard the croupier calling out the winning number at roulette before the ball had fallen into the socket' (Sylvester, 51).

Of still greater significance is the role of alcohol in *Faith Healer* as an aspect of what Bacon referred to as a kind of will to despair. Asked by Sylvester about the process of painting his *Three Studies for a Crucifixion* (1962), Bacon said he had completed the triptych 'under tremendous hangovers and drink; I sometimes hardly knew what I was doing':

> DS Have you been able to do the same in any picture that you've done since?
> FB I haven't. But I think with great effort I'm making myself freer. I mean, you either have to do it through drugs or drink.... Or will.
> DS The will to lose one's will?
> FB Absolutely. The will to make oneself completely free. Will is the wrong word, because in the end you could call it despair. Because it really comes out of an absolute feeling of it's impossible to do these things, so I might as well just do anything. And out of this anything, one sees what happens.

This struggle to maintain '[t]he will to lose one's will' (Sylvester, 13) is something that is at the very heart of *Faith Healer* and indeed the key to the ending of the play, as a note dated 21 May 1975 attests:

> What about the ending, then? Does his going to meet the lads represent an ultimate chance OR does he accept its finality? OR Is the apparent certainty enhanced by the remote possibility of the chance ingredient? OR Are the two concepts—chance + inevitability—mutually exclusive? OR Is his final going out his renunciation of chance—and therefore his artistic death?[67]

On 15 July 1975, Friel added: 'Not exclusively artistic—the renunciation of chance is everyone's death'.[68]

For Bacon, chance and inevitability are interconnected: when '[t]he will has been subdued by the instinct', images will 'come over without the brain interfering with the[ir] inevitability' (Sylvester, 120). Friel, however, wonders whether there is an element of mutual exclusivity at play insofar as inevitability might also be taken as a kind of 'finality' or 'certainty'. Ultimately, he appears to have decided that Frank cannot go out to meet 'the lads'[69] believing in both. Frank's artistic and actual death is a triumph of will over instinct: he is no longer in that despairing state of freedom where the impossibility of what he is trying to achieve allows him to 'just do anything' and '[see] what happens' (Sylvester, 13). Frank's renouncing of chance, then, is at once a self-liberating and a self-imprisoning act: just as the will is freed from its subjugation to instinct, so the artistic freedom that comes of this self-imposed, despairing openness is lost to a suicidal certainty. '[R]enouncing chance' (Friel, *Pl*, 376) is, in many ways, Frank's final act of narcissism—a self-destructive reassertion of self-will.

The language of distortion

Friel's encounters with Bacon's interviews, then, facilitated an exploration of artistic practice on an unprecedented scale. Both Frank's character and the *process* of creating Frank's character are built on what Bacon would have seen as the artist's manipulative relationship with chance. These manipulations have further implications for *Faith Healer* on a linguistic level. Key in this respect is Bacon's belief that chance was essentially a means of formal innovation:

> [Accident] has given me a disorientated vision of a fact I was attempting to trap. And I could then begin to elaborate and try and make something out of a thing which was non-illustrational. (Sylvester, 53)

By 'non-illustrational', Bacon meant a form that, instead of telling you 'through the intelligence immediately' what it is about, 'works first upon sensation and then slowly leaks back into the fact' (Sylvester, 56), in a manner not unlike Frank's litany of dying villages. Moreover, accident was a necessary component in recording an image in a post-technological world. The advent of photography had 'altered completely this whole thing of figurative painting' and had turned it into 'a kind of game' (Sylvester, 28):

> I think that [. . .] there is the possibility of an extraordinary irrational remaking of this positive image that you long to make. And this is the obsession: how like can I make this thing in the most irrational way? So that you're not only remaking the look of the image, you're remaking all the areas of feeling which you have apprehensions of. (Sylvester, 27–28)

That Bacon saw his creative practice in part as an obsessive game of remaking through factual disorientation is potentially vital to a critical understanding of the way in which language functions in *Faith Healer*.

Here is a play in which the use of the counterfactual is informed, I would argue, less by Steiner's theoretical sense of its creative potential than by Bacon's practical awareness of the same—an awareness that, as we shall see, acknowledged the threat of violence implicit within such creative acts. Though Steiner certainly acknowledges the rather more serious moral implications of 'philosophic, political non-truth' on a global scale such as 'the un-saying of history',[70] he appears to see much more destructive potential in a deliberate silence than in lying more generally. Indeed, while he insists on referring to Lear's youngest, frankest daughter as 'murderous Cordelia',[71] 'the unboundedness of falsehood' is something he deems 'crucial both to human liberty and to the genius of language'.[72] For Bacon, however, the distortive process of painting a portrait is one that is explicitly fraught with the risk of injury:

> FB What I want to do is to distort the thing far beyond the appearance, but in the distortion to bring it back to a recording of the appearance. [. . .]
> DS In what sense do you conceive it as an injury?
> FB Because people believe—simple people at least—that the distortions of them are an injury to them—no matter how much they feel for or how much they like you.
> DS Don't you think their instinct is probably right?
> FB Possibly. [. . .] But tell me, who today has been able to record anything that comes across to us as a fact without causing deep injury to the image? (Sylvester, 39–41)

That Friel drew on Bacon's artistic practice to form the basis of a poetics of violence in *Faith Healer*—particularly in the context of marital relations—is strongly suggested by an earlier version of the play. Titled *Bannermen*,[73] it comprised two monologues—*The Faith Healer* (Frank) and *The Faith Healer's Wife* (Grace)—bookending a subsequently abandoned mini-play called *The Game*. A duologue between married couple Agnes and Noel Devine (a dissatisfied commercial artist), it is less 'a vicious portrait of private, intimate bewilderment'[74] like *Faith Healer* than 'a bitter, bitchy battle'.[75] In fact, the Devines are in many ways the forerunners of another unhappy pair, Gráinne and Garret Fitzmaurice of *Give Me Your Answer, Do!*. However, where the Fitzmaurices' public bickering depends on 'audiences … that impose limits' and prevent either from 'deliver[ing] the final thrust, that mortal wound',[76] the Devines use the titular Game as a framework within which such wounds can be delivered. Superficially a staring contest, the Game is effectively won by whoever is able, through a narrative act, to so disorient, distract, or disgust the other as to render them unable to keep looking.

Bacon's influence on *The Game*, I suggest, extends well beyond Noel Devine's occupation as a commercial artist, insofar as his thinking is discernible in the mechanics of the Game itself. At one point, Noel nearly wins the Game by verbally reducing Agnes to a distorted image of herself with an unmistakably misogynistic vehemence:

> [I]n the beginning I saw you with what seemed to me then to be absolute, objective clarity. [. . .] And when I focussed on you again you had dissolved into a body of mist without colour or shape or definition [. . .]. And now I have a new epiphany—a sudden and intuitive perception into the core of your reality: You are a *distortion*. Mrs. Devine is [. . .] one enormous hostile watching equine eye [. . .]. Correction. Mrs. Devine is a cavern that could be mistaken for a mouth. Hades [. . .]. Correction. Mrs. Devine is a totem-pole that's shaped like a nose. That's it. No doubt about it. The final judgement [. . .]. That's what you are, my darling—A Nose—good for nothing but smelling out public causes—good for sweet goddam nothing else.[77] [My italics.]

As Noel speaks, Agnes is essentially transformed into a Francis Bacon triptych—a tripartite study for a head with distorted and grotesquely emphasised features 'returning fact onto the nervous system in a more violent way' (Sylvester, 59). In other words, Noel deliberately weaponises the injurious potential of non-illustrational painting as part of the Game.

The possibility of calculated violence in the artistic distortion of 'anything that comes across to us as fact' (Sylvester, 41) is crucial to understanding the multitude of discrepancies within the story that unfolds across the four *Faith Healer* monologues. As with *The Game*, Friel translates this distortion into a series of narrative acts. In Grace's monologue, for instance, we see that the basis of her 'groping' (Friel, *Pl*, 346) towards a verdict on Frank's pathological lying has its origins in Bacon's artistic process:

> It wasn't that he was simply a liar—I never understood it—yes, I knew he wanted to hurt me, but it was much more complex than that; it was some compulsion he had to adjust, to refashion, to re-create everything around him. (Friel, *Pl*, 345)

There are irresistible linguistic resonances here: where Bacon speaks of his 'obsession' with 'the possibility of an extraordinary irrational remaking' (Sylvester, 28) of an image, Grace speaks of Frank's 'compulsion [...] to refashion' (Friel, *Pl*, 345); where Bacon speaks of 'causing deep injury to the image' (Sylvester, 41), Grace speaks of 'hurt'.

Problematically for a play that is notable for its convincing portrayal of a woman married to an emotionally abusive narcissist, Friel effectively posits Frank's behaviour as part of his artistic practice. Although Grace's assessment of Frank's 'talent for hurting' usually comes across in performance as an astute if hesitant indictment of 'a twisted man' (Friel, *Pl*, 345), Frank's own attitude to Grace channels Bacon by implying that her reaction to her artistic distortion is that of a 'simple' person (Sylvester, 41). Though Friel's portrayal of a deliberate weaponisation of the process of artistic distortion in *The Game* gives us an additional pinch of salt with which to take Frank's monologue, there is an irrefutable double standard at play. When Agnes wins the Game, it is an emasculating act wherein Noel falls victim to 'her castrating ploys'.[78] Frank's victimisation of Grace, however, is an extension of his own emasculation as a man whose 'bloody brains has him bloody castrated' (Friel, *Pl*, 357), rendered impotent by his role as 'chance's handmaiden'.[79] Moreover, Frank's inexcusable gaslighting of Grace when he returns to the scene of her miscarriage is floated by Teddy as a coping mechanism exacerbated by an artistic temperament that simultaneously excuses it. Indeed, there is a nagging and unpleasant possibility that we may in fact be expected to take Teddy's word for it that Frank's 'strange gift' means he 'had to have his own way of facing things' (Friel, *Pl*, 365), even when taking into account Teddy's unresolved feelings for Frank. Certainly, Bacon's interviews add a new dimension to the gender politics of a play in which, like Bacon, a superficially unrepentant Frank retreats guiltily to the isolation of the monologue in order to be 'totally alone' (Sylvester 40) with the memory of those upon whom he 'would rather practise the injury in private' (Sylvester, 41).

Triptych

For Bacon, then, the remaking of an image in an irrational way is a personal obsession that entails a process of potentially injurious distortion that nevertheless allows for more affective ways of meaning. The possibility of such distortions being weaponised is one that Friel actively explored in both *The Game* and *Faith Healer*, making the connection between Frank's artistry and Frank's emotional violence explicit. This is a marked contrast to Friel's engagements with Proust's idea of art as something close to restorative justice (which is effectively how Lily's monologue in particular functions in *The Freedom of the City*). So too does *Faith Healer* present a far more troubling apologism for emotional abuse than the marital cruelties of *Crystal and Fox* insofar as Frank's obliterations are apparently committed in the name of his craft. Fox is no longer capable of evoking a sympathetic response from an audience (if he ever was in the first place); Frank's excuse for his bad behaviour is one that is still very much in evidence when it comes to abusers who happen to be artists.

Paradoxically, it is Friel's engagement with Bacon's obsession with non-illustrational forms on a *formal* level that goes some way towards destabilising the play's hierarchy of sympathies. Indeed, Bacon's artistic practice may be a significant factor in understanding how *Faith Healer's* final four-monologue structure empowers its audience. The play's eventual format is, after all, one that permits each speaker to do violence to fact on an individual level whilst locating the play's factuality squarely in the eye of the beholder. This in turn allows for a great deal of flexibility in performance: there is no guarantee whatsoever that Frank Hardy will get a free pass in the name of great art.

That *Faith Healer* was a monologue play in the first place owes a great deal to Friel's sense of Bacon's desire to remake the longed-for image in a non-illustrational, 'irrational' (Sylvester, 27) way. Indeed, Friel's goal in finding a form for the play was one he chose to articulate in Bacon's own terms, again referencing Valéry: 'TO GIVE THE SENSATION WITHOUT THE BOREDOM OF ITS CONVEYANCE'.[80] Certainly, the question of the play's form was at the forefront of Friel's mind almost too early in the composition process and ran the gamut of experimental possibilities. For instance, on 1 May 1975, Friel wrote:

> The major portion of the [. . .] set would be the hall—the people arriving—The Trusting + The Maimed—and waiting. Perhaps their individual stories. Soliloquies.
> [. . .]
> Possibility: The sick, who are both themselves + chorus, could sing their commentaries to the air of hymns. (?)[81]

On 5 May, Friel was considering '[t]wo vague possibilities' which raised a question that prefigured the technique he would use for *Dancing at Lughnasa* (1990):

1. That the play will not find itself in any kind of naturalism or realism [...].
2. It is even possible that the action will progress from a kind of tableau-to-tableau.

   Question: Could there be a marriage of two forms—a formal, almost recitative style, and occasional 'lapses' into a naturalism?[82]

Although, as he wrote on 7 May, Friel was dogged by '[a] persistent conviction that the play must be unrealistic',[83] he also considered (on 18 May) a more naturalistic setting in a hall that would then function in a similar way to *The Freedom of the City* (1973): 'this reality is suddenly silenced—frozen—and in these "interruptions", a past is formally created by brief unrealistic scenes'.[84] In an attempt to marry the two forms, he even considered a technique reminiscent of the as-yet unwritten *Living Quarters*, in which characters encased in a seanchaí-style narrative frame would then '[move] out of the "realistic" action [...] explaining his/her version or attitude to the narrator'.[85]

Though Friel had, '[b]y November of 1975 [...] drafted [...] a single monologue, spoken by Frank Hardy, scarcely long enough (at 14 pages) to make a one-act play', the journey to the 'final, formal perfection' of *Faith Healer* was, as Anthony Roche puts it, 'arbitrary [...] contingent and [...] downright messy'.[86] As Nicholas Grene points out, '[i]t took him a long time, one substantial wrong turning and two crucial practical prompts from theatrical colleagues [actor Niall Tóibín and producer Oscar Lewenstein], to yield the four-part play'.[87] In other words, there is a well-documented production history of the play that runs alongside the intellectual history I am suggesting here. To suggest that *Faith Healer's* eventual format was either Friel's original intention or a direct and deliberate transposition of Bacon's ideas onto the form and structure of the play would, therefore, be something of an overstatement. Nevertheless, there are some tantalising possibilities that are worth teasing out. For instance, it may well be significant that, when Friel had completed a typed script of a three-part version of the monologue play, it was called 'TRIPTYCH'.[88] As Friel noted in a letter to D.E.S. Maxwell on 16 February 1977, the word was already an 'emotive' one for reasons relating to the documentation required for border crossings.[89] So, too, is there a more immediately obvious association with the art of Christian altarpieces. There remains, however, the additional suggestion of an affinity between Friel's chosen structure and Bacon's work that is undiminished by the fact that 'Triptych' turned out to be an unsuitable title for what would ultimately become a four-part play. Indeed, Bacon's triptychs are significant not because of their tripartite structure but because they are an iteration of his preferred method of displaying his canvases:

> DS And do the vertical breaks between the canvases of a triptych have the same sort of purpose as those frames within a canvas?
> FB Yes they do. They isolate one from the other. And they cut off the story between one and the other. It helps to avoid story-telling if the figures are painted on three different canvases. [. . .] [T]he story that is already being told between one figure and another begins to cancel out the possibilities of what can be done with the paint on its own. (Sylvester, 23).

Like Bacon's studies, Friel's monologues exist on separate canvases, which—in a departure from Bacon's medium—has implications for his characters not only as subjects but also as artists. Each monologist is able to practise the injury of distortion upon the facts they are attempting to trap uninhibited by additional presences onstage. The cumulative effect is a non-illustrational dramatic form—not three stories but three acts of remembrance in four parts that, for Bacon, are closely tied to the process of creating an image:

> DS Are you saying that painting is almost a way of bringing somebody back, that the process of painting is almost like the process of recalling?
> FB I am saying it. And I think that the methods by which this is done are so artificial that the model before you, in my case, inhibits the artificiality by which this thing can be brought back (Sylvester, 39).

As a 'revenant drama'[90] peopled by the dead, *Faith Healer* uses the monologue format to heighten the artificiality needed in order to create an image that 'works first upon sensation and then slowly leaks back into the fact' (Sylvester, 56). It negates the possibility of scenes in which multiple characters interact to 'cancel out the possibilities of what can be done with the paint'—or, in Friel's case, language—'on its own' (Sylvester, 23).

In deliberately altering certain facts as the play grew from a single monologue to a multi-canvas affair, moreover, Friel was consciously using form in order to explore new ways of navigating what he would later, in an echo of George Steiner, call 'the landscape of ... fact' (Friel, *Pl*, 419). In an earlier, pre-Teddy version of Grace's monologue, for instance, Grace's account of the burial of her stillborn child specifies that 'Teddy made a wooden cross' and that 'Teddy just said a few prayers'.[91] With the addition of Teddy's monologue early in 1977, in which Teddy's account would seem to corroborate this, Grace's monologue was changed to the effect that 'Frank made a wooden cross' and 'Frank just said a few prayers' (Friel, *Pl*, 344–5). To highlight these discrepancies, Friel added certain anchoring phrases and locations, most notably 'Kinlochbervie, in Sutherland, about as far north as you can go in Scotland' (Friel, *Pl*, 337) and altered Frank's monologue accordingly. Indeed, in an earlier version of Frank's monologue, Frank was not in Kinlochbervie at all when he claims to have heard of the death of his mother (or, as Grace would have it, his father) but 'in the Rhondda Valley in South Wales'.[92] By experimenting with a Bacon-like triptych form and by privileging acts of remembrance over plot, Friel implicated his audience in a new development in his career-long exploration of the nature of fact. This was no longer the juxtaposition of a subjective truth against an official truth that laid an erroneous claim to objectivity as in *Lovers: Winners* or *The Freedom of the City*. Rather Friel was juxtaposing three distorted images and relying on words, in the same way that Bacon relied on paint, to allow the audience to access a fact through feeling rather than thought.

Making History: 'an "art" of the facts'[93]

Friel's notes on the composition process of *Faith Healer* testify both directly and indirectly to the influence of Francis Bacon's artistic practice on that play's linguistic distortions, dramatic form, and character development. Frank's creative process is inextricably linked with his openness to chance; the play's twisted truths are forms of non-illustrational artistic distortion that are fraught with the potential for violence; the play's form makes use of the dramatic monologue in the same way Bacon uses arrangements of separate canvases 'to give the sensation without the boredom of its conveyance' (Sylvester, 65). There is more to this 'chance' encounter, however, than its role in the creation of a landmark play. *Faith Healer*'s formal innovation in particular gestures towards a far wider significance in terms of Friel's evolving preoccupation with the relationship between the world as we experience it and forms of representation. Indeed, Friel's formal innovations in that play set a precedent for making space for *multiple* truths rather than a relatively straightforward divide between unfeeling officialdom and the realm of personal truths.

Friel's early plays establish both 'fact' and 'fiction' as credible ways of processing what we experience as reality. Staging a series of conflicts between official (public) and unofficial (private) discourses, they make a case for the validity of the latter as a more subjective form of truthfulness. Where Friel engages with art in these earlier works, it is largely in the abstract rather than as a form of creative practice. Moreover, where he begins to engage with his *own* practice as a Proustian means of rediscovering 'that reality far from which we live [...] which is simply our life [...] finally discovered and clarified', it is as a kind of restorative justice for the characters of *The Freedom of the City*, whose monologues are a means of regaining lost time. This was clearly a necessary intervention: the officialdom of that play is in part a dramatisation of a real-world example of official discourse as a tool of state violence (the Widgery report); the other interpolations of the play are likewise indicative of real lives being overwritten by a deafening chorus of socio-political discourse from the academy to the pulpit, and from state media to the soap box. In dealing explicitly with the aftermath of Bloody Sunday, Friel was attempting to use his craft to carve out a space for 'real life'[94] in amongst all that dehumanising noise. In *Faith Healer* and the plays that followed, however, Friel was demonstrably alert to the potential for violence within the practice of art as a conscious distortion. In other words, there is an extent to which Friel's post-*Faith Healer* plays consider 'fiction' and 'fact' as being equally capable of doing harm, not because he changed his views on the validity of 'fiction' but because both involve a *process* of 'remaking' (Sylvester, 26). It is in this sense that Friel's encounter with Bacon's interviews functions as a catalyst in the clarification of Friel's prior thinking, in which the constructedness of different truths had always been implied if not articulated. Now Friel was turning his attention to the question of constructedness itself.

A particularly rich illustration from later in Friel's oeuvre is *Making History* (1988), which stages 'the life + The Life'[95] of Hugh O'Neill, Earl of Tyrone (c.1550–1616). Central to the play are scenes from O'Neill's domestic life immediately following his marriage to Mabel Bagenal. One of the New English 'Upstarts', her family is closely associated with the enforcement of English rule in Ireland: her brother, Sir Henry 'the Butcher'[96] Bagenal, is the current Queen's Marshal, like his father before him. As 'two deeply opposed civilizations' (Friel, *P2*, 283) make their claims upon O'Neill's loyalty in a time of rapid political change, O'Neill finds himself reluctant to 'interfere with that slow sure tide of history' (Friel, *P2*, 284) by choosing a side. Ultimately, O'Neill joins an open revolt against the English, culminating in an Irish/Spanish defeat at Kinsale. In the timeline of the play, Mabel dies in childbirth while O'Neill is 'skulking about' (Friel *P2*, 304) in the Sperrins after Kinsale; the real Mabel Bagenal had already died some years previously.[97] O'Neill leaves Ireland as part of the so-called Flight of the Earls, and ends his days as a 'bitter émigré' (Friel, *P2*, 330) in Rome. Meanwhile, Archbishop Peter Lombard is writing '*The History of Hugh O'Neill*' (Friel, *P2*, 338). Lombard, who believes that 'art has precedence over accuracy' in matters historical (Friel, *P2*, 283), aims to transform the defeat at Kinsale into a 'triumph' in 'the telling of it' (Friel, *P2*, 332), hoping to unite a relatively disunited Irish people behind a heroic narrative. O'Neill, meanwhile, who believes not in multiple truths but in a single version of the truth, sees the book as his 'last battle' against being 'embalm[ed] […] in a florid lie' (Friel, *P2*, 329). The play ends with Lombard reciting the introduction to the book as O'Neill recites his surrender to Queen Elizabeth I in counterpoint. O'Neill breaks down as he begs forgiveness of Mabel, having failed to secure her a 'central' (Friel, *P2*, 330) role in Lombard's history.

Whilst researching *Making History*, Friel came to consider historical fact in the light of historiography, as extrapolated from a review of four different works on the subject by historian Hayden White for the *TLS* in January 1986.[98] (White had already written extensively and influentially on the relationship between history and literature.[99]) This was an encounter that, as with *Faith Healer*, occurred at a time when Friel felt that his play had 'lost its centre, if it ever had one'.[100] In a serendipitous echo of Bacon's language, White describes the search to define historical knowledge in terms not only of 'a "science" of the past' but also an '"art" of facts'—in other words, as a practice. It is easy to see why White's synthesis of historiographical thought may have caught Friel's imagination in the first instance. In a gloss of Paul Veyne's *Writing History* (1986) highlighted by Friel, White is speaking the playwright's language in a very real sense:

[I]n so far as historians provide understanding of the worlds about which they speak, they do so by telling interesting, complex and *intelligible* stories about them. This means fitting the "facts" they have made out of the events they have studied to the forms of plots met with in imaginative literature or fiction.[101] [My italics.]

Crucially, White goes on to emphasise the close relationship between 'fact' and 'fiction', not in terms of assessing their inherent validity but in terms of their both being *constructed*. Indeed, in White's conclusion—bracketed by Friel in red pen—there is a renewed emphasis on the relationship between the making of history and the practice of art:

In short, it is events that belong to objective reality; facts are constructions created by the subjection of events to the protocols of different discursive characterizations. This means that there can be as many [. . .] "true" interpretations as there are different discursive protocols recognized in any given culture as permissible ways of making sense of the world. In this respect, even fiction can be said to deal in "facts" even when the "events" of which it speaks are openly admitted to be "imaginary".[102]

Once more, it is easy to see how this idea of there being as many truths as there are 'permissible ways of making sense of the world' might have appealed to Friel. Not only is it compatible with his view of the subjective truths of which he wrote in 'Self-Portrait', but it is also in keeping with his view of what he termed 'the authority of fiction'[103] when justifying the historical inaccuracies of *Translations* (see the following chapter).

There is, however, a significant extent to which Friel differs from the ideas summarised in White's review—the question of violence. As part of his gloss of Veyne, White writes:

Historical events, it appears, can be plotted in a number of ways and with equal plausibility and *without in any way doing violence to the factual truths* derived from study of the documentary record.[104] [My italics.]

This is demonstrably at odds with Friel's understanding of the practice of art, which was influenced at least in part by the thinking of an artist for whom to engage in the construction of truths was to risk doing violence: 'who today has been able to record anything that comes across to us as a fact without causing deep injury to the image?' (Sylvester, 41) Certainly, Friel was aware of his own complicity in a process of deliberate distortion, albeit possibly in a tongue-in-cheek sort of way: 'Lombard writing about O[']N[eill] is like Friel writing about Lombard + O['']N[eill]—fashioning event-facts into an acceptable fiction—inventing a plot that will endow the events with intelligibility'.[105] Less ambiguous is a note dated 29 March 1984, in which Friel explicitly acknowledges that '[v]iolence would have to be done to certain historical facts'[106] in order to make Mabel a key figure in the play. Indeed, perhaps the biggest irony of the play is that the hill O'Neill chooses to die on—the centrality of Mabel's role in his life—is based on Friel's own very conscious act of creative violence. Despite identifying himself with the closest thing the play has to an antagonist, then, it would appear that Friel, much like Bacon, considered what he had once called the infliction of 'tiny bruises'[107] on history to be a necessary evil of his craft—a kind of occupational hazard that, whilst uncomfortable to confront in one's own practice, can be excused by it. Consequently, Friel came to see the essence of *Making History* not as a conflict between the lived life and the constructed Life but rather as what he described as a 'dual' conflict: 'the drama of the "events" and the structuring of those events into "facts", and then the interpretation of those "facts" into a comprehensive "exploration" that claims to correspond with some objective truth'.[108] Thus Lombard and O'Neill are at loggerheads not so much over the course of events themselves but rather over how those events ought to be reshaped and structured into facts and, subsequently, how these facts ought to be interpreted and explored.

In a significant development for a play in which officialdom is contested both in theory and in practice, the Life and the life of Hugh O'Neill do not necessarily map neatly onto public and private, respectively. Nor does Friel use dramatic form as a means of distinguishing between the two. This is in contrast to much of Friel's earlier work which, although undoubtedly complex in its exploration of the nature of fact, has an observable tendency to juxtapose a subjective truth against an official or externally validated truth that lays an erroneous claim to objectivity. These juxtapositions are made possible, moreover, by means of certain 'techniques' (as Friel often called them) in order to differentiate between public and private truths. In *Making History*, however, Friel resists giving the play a form where, as in *The Freedom of the City*, having multiple interpolators is another means of creating a clearly defined boundary between official, public discourse in all its forms on the one hand and unknowable privacies on the other. Even at a point where Friel was considering presenting the story of Hugh O'Neill 'in a very formalized, non-naturalistic way',[109] it was clearly with a view to establishing different viewpoints rather than staging official intrusions:

> Could the story be mediated through several narrators—each of whom has a different viewpoint + style—and in this way overcome most of the standard objections to the historical play?[110]

Indeed, archival evidence suggests that what Friel had in mind here was a similar technique to that employed by Welsh poet Dylan Thomas in his radio play *Under Milk Wood* (1953)—a work that appears in Friel's notes for more than one play: '4–5 narrations: Milk Wood: on chairs?'[111] As has been established, the form of *Making History* would ultimately be shaped by Friel's encounter with White's *TLS* article in 1986: 'The play itself is a form of fictional historiography'.[112] However, prior to this change of direction, it is evident that Friel was at least considering a formal conceit similar to that of *Faith Healer*—a multi-canvas play comprising multiple attempts to fashion events into facts.

Making History was finally staged in 1988 as a play whose formal experimentation was remarkably subtle. Nevertheless, the legacy of *Faith Healer* is still apparent in its plurivocity. This comes across in the closing moments of the play, where Lombard and O'Neill recite opposing histories in counterpoint, gesturing towards the kind of dialogic history advocated for by Dominick LaCapra (as glossed by White):

> For LaCapra, when historians speak about the past (without having first sought to listen to the many messages it emits by way of the historical record) or when they subject its objects to the rigours of some monolithic explanatory method, so as to "reduce" its plurivocity to the dead hum of the machinery used to interpret it, they offend against the morality of their vocation even while remaining true to the ethics of their profession.[113]

In the play's final moments, O'Neill does not offer a private testimony but rather an extract from an historical record that complicates the monolithic, pious, embalming history being composed by Lombard—the text of his submission to the Crown. It is only at the very last moment that he cries out in apology to the dead.

There is also something of *Faith Healer's* intellectual foundations that is evident in the way Lombard's stance on historiography plays out on stage, insofar as there is an element of moral ambiguity at work that is not admitted by White's metahistorical framework. It is, however, most certainly present in Friel's engagement with the possibility of violence in Bacon's artistic distortions. Indeed, there is a sense from Friel's notes that Lombard's actions are antagonistic not because they lack validity but because Lombard, like Bacon, understands his power and yet, unlike Bacon, abuses it with wanton sophistry. He does so, moreover, without any of the implied guilt that made Bacon want to 'practise the injury in private' (Sylvester, 41). In an abandoned snippet of dialogue intended for the Historian of the piece, for instance, Friel suggests that Lombard believes his role as a cleric eradicates the potential for tension between vocational morality and professional ethics:

> There is no conflict between the imperatives of my vocation/priesthood and the ethics of my profession. They share the same morality.
> There is only one way, one truth, one life.[114]

In other words, by identifying as a cleric rather than an historian whilst continuing to practise an historian's craft, Lombard cynically exempts himself from the moral imperative to listen to the many voices of history. He sees his reduction of history's plurivocity to 'the dead hum of the machinery used to interpret it' not as a perversion but rather as an extension of the morality of his priestly vocation. Indeed, he sees the 'complementary' nature of the 'four [...] stories' the Four Evangelists made of 'the haphazard events in Christ's life' (Friel, *P2*, 334) rather than the richness of their discrepancies as the true value of the Gospel's methodology as an explanatory method. In this way, Lombard gives himself licence to do violence to the past by weaponising his craft, in much the same way as Noel Devine abuses his own powers of distortion in *The Game*. Indeed, Lombard insists that what others perceive as violence is, in reality, a necessary function of his practice as an '"art[ist]" of [the] facts'.[115] After all, what is '[i]mposing a pattern on events that were mostly casual and haphazard' if not the appropriation and wilful misuse of the artistic manipulation of chance?

Though I would not go so far as to claim Bacon as a direct inspiration for Lombard, the influence of Bacon's interviews on *Faith Healer* remains pertinent to *Making History*, and to other plays that take a multi-canvas approach to meaning without overtly privileging a single viewpoint. Indeed, the '"chance" of [Friel] reading Bacon at this time'[116] may have been a game-changer for *Faith Healer*, but it also served as a catalyst for a major development in Friel's experiments with form. Specifically, I would suggest that *Faith Healer* marks a point in Friel's career when he was beginning to look for ways of staging the juxtaposition of different truths, not in order to say which was the more valid, but rather to create a space within which an audience exposed to multiple truths might construct their own reality. Examples that spring to mind are the multiple monologues and divided stage of *Molly Sweeney* (1994) and the subtle experimentation of *Dancing at Lughnasa* (1990), where an absent boy is the medium through which life as it is and life as it is remembered exist side by side. Like *Making History*, these are plays in which Friel was using dramatic form to explore a more morally ambiguous many-voicedness than in his earlier plays. It is a plurivocity that is enriched by its inconsistencies and which acknowledges the violence of the potential for artistic distortion as a weaponisable function of those 'different discursive protocols recognized in any given culture as permissible ways of making sense of the world'. Though plays like *Making History* were shaped by their own creative encounters, *Faith Healer* marks the beginning of a phase in which such acts of distortion are not exclusively a function of a disconnected officialdom inflicting its discourse on the private sphere. Indeed, I would contest that, beginning with *Faith Healer*, such distortions become an acknowledged feature of the power dynamics of making art, occurring not only between public and private but also 'between privacies' (Friel, *Pl*, 446).

Give Me Your Answer, Do!: ORTHOPRAXIS

The composition process for *Faith Healer* signals a significant adjustment in Friel's sense of the role of the artist and of artistic intervention. In the plays that followed, Bacon's interviews are a discernible factor in Friel's altered thinking, despite the fact that Bacon's sense of art as a manipulative practice would soon be absorbed by the more linguistic focus afforded by Friel's engagement with Steiner. The creative encounters of *Faith Healer* also marked a major development in Friel's thinking around art itself. Indeed, with the possible exception of his brief engagement with Proust, it was not until *Faith Healer* that Friel began to think in terms of the *practice* of art in a sustained manner. In the plays that followed, Friel would even go so far as to treat it as subject matter.

Although there are multiple artist figures that appear in the plays after *Faith Healer* (Lombard being a controversial example), Friel would not engage explicitly with the role of the artist again until *Give Me Your Answer, Do!* (1997). In this play, novelist Tom Connolly (who has been suffering from writer's block for years) is having his archive assessed for possible purchase by a Texan university. He and his wife Daisy have a daughter, Bridget, who has been institutionalised and whom Tom visits regularly, telling her the family news in a series of fantastical invented stories that bear a tangential relationship with reality. Over the course of the afternoon and evening on which the play is set, the Connollys await the assessor's verdict. The play is characterised by the uncertainty with which the Connollys live (creative, financial) and by the question of the value of certainty. In this sense, it is testament to a change of trajectory in which Bacon's interviews were a catalyst. As in *Faith Healer*, the certainty provided by the 'tangible evidence' that 'the work has value' (Friel, *GMYAD*, 79) is judged to be antithetical to the life of the artist: 'being alive is the postponement of verdicts' (Friel, *GMYAD*, 79–80). In this respect, *Give Me Your Answer, Do!* harks back to a note from the composition process of *Faith Healer*: 'Not exclusively artistic—the renunciation of chance is everyone's death'.[117]

Though the play itself is something of a disappointment, Friel's engagement with his immediate inspirational touchstones for *Give Me Your Answer, Do!* is indicative of his practical and intellectual trajectory in the years since *Faith Healer*. In an undated note, Friel lists them as follows:

> Pascal: He carried out the gestures and by doing this he found faith
> Wittgenstein: Whereof . . . .
> Dante: . . . . . Rushes of Repentance[118]

This is a Dante who comes via Eamon Duffy's *The Stripping of the Altars* (1992), in which Purgatory is painted in a positive light consistent with the play's embrace of uncertainty. The Wittgenstein is cited in full in the finished play: 'Whereof one cannot speak, thereof one must be silent'.[119] This line, quoted by Garrett, was at one point suggested as a possible interjection by a recurring figure that is never alluded to in the finished play, known only as 'the Presence'. Though never fully developed, this figure appeared frequently in Friel's notes: 'even though It is the heart of the work itself, It cannot be fully known, comprehended, even described. Hence the Writer's turmoil'.[120] Some days later, he went on:

> Perhaps the Presence is in fact <u>HIS OWN</u> core, centre, authenticity, integrity, \HIS SOUL?/ That is what he has lost touch with. That is what he needs to be put in touch with again.[121]

That the Presence does not appear as a dedicated theatrical Other in *Give Me Your Answer, Do!* may have been due in part to Friel's unease at revisiting *Philadelphia* so blatantly: '[u]nhappy echoes of Philadelphia's Public + Private'.[122] It is also testament to Friel's development as a playwright. Indeed, a characteristic of many of Friel's mature plays is that, while he may have flirted with the idea of introducing more obviously experimental figures in the manner of Gar Private, the Commentators, or Sir during their composition processes, these plays generally resist representing such theatrical Others as an external presence.

The third of Friel's touchstones for the play was something Friel had found in the ever-fruitful pages of the *Times Literary Supplement*: seventh-century French thinker Blaise Pascal's practical approach to the divine. Although the *TLS* had run articles on Pascal (including one by George Steiner, no less) in previous years, this particular snippet of his theology was to be found embedded in a review of Alain Peyrefitte's *C'était de Gaulle* (1994): 'As to the General's attitude to Europe, [Peyrefitte] writes that he followed the advice of Pascal: he carried out the gestures, and by doing this he found faith'.[123] For Friel, this idea of fidelity to the gestures of one's craft was the key to a question that, like Frank's questions to himself in *Faith Healer*, '<u>CANNOT</u> be answered'[124]—that of whether or not Tom Connolly is a good writer:

> That question will be put, maybe by others, maybe by himself.
> "I wish I knew. No, I don't wish I knew. All I can say is that <u>I was faithful to it—kept</u> with <u>faith with it and in it. And I listened, with attention. And the love was never silenced by despair. And over maybe 40 continuous years it certainly gave me moments of delight.</u>["][125]

As with Friel's response to Bacon decades earlier, there is a sense of a found affinity here. Friel's own creative practice certainly had its ritualistic elements. In his so-called sporadic diary for *Give Me Your Answer,*

Do!, for instance, Friel recorded the commencement of a writing process that had altered little in its material idiosyncrasies since the early 1960s: 'Began. The A4 pages cut in half. The treasury tag. The capital A in red ink on the front page'.[126] At other times in the writing of this play, moreover, there is evidence of Friel's own adherence to these gestures as a point of principle rather than out of inspiration. On one occasion when Friel sat down to write *Give Me Your Answer, Do!*, for instance, he simply wrote in brackets: '[Off colour y'day + today. Sitting here as duty.]'. Striking a line through this, he then wrote: 'The writer drifts around. Doesn't engage'.[127] In the play, as we have seen, the influence of Pascal survives as a rare exchange between Garrett and Tom about the practice of their shared craft. In many ways, then, despite its shortcomings as theatre, *Give Me Your Answer, Do!* answers some of the questions posed by *Faith Healer* regarding the nature of faith: this is a play in which, artistically speaking, orthopraxis is a means of achieving orthodoxy.[128]

Friel's creative engagement with Bacon's interviews may have been one among many such chance encounters, but it was, I would suggest, one of the more significant and far-reaching ones in terms of its legacy. Serving as a catalyst for Friel's evolving preoccupation with the relationship between art and any number of mutable realities, it arguably equipped him with a conceptual framework for engaging with the practice of art. It is a framework that he would, as he matured as a playwright and encountered other sources of inspiration, learn to reconcile with the more abstract, theoretical, quasi-spiritual ideas about the role of art and the artist with which he had grappled earlier in his career. Indeed, *Faith Healer* can be seen to mark the beginning of a stage in Friel's life as an artist where he was beginning to think differently about the possibilities and limitations of art when it came to articulating those subjective, autobiographical facts that 'can be pure fiction'.[129] Moreover, Bacon's ideas laid some of the groundwork for a poetics of violence that would potentially inform his relationship with Steiner's approach to creative untruths. It also set in motion a phase of more subtle formal experimentation that allowed him to stage multiple realities without resorting to making binary distinctions between public and private, official and unofficial, or fact and fiction, embracing dramatic uncertainty and moral ambiguity on a structural level.

Perhaps the most important legacy of this creative encounter, however, is that it allows us to think of influence at the level of artistic practice. *Faith Healer* is, at its core, the product of an intersection of different creative processes by artists working with very different media. It was, above all, Bacon's *way* of working rather than his work that came to permeate *Faith Healer*, providing Friel with an opportunity to experiment with his own form of extended verbal triptych—three attempts to trap an elusive fact across four canvases. In this sense, the creative encounter as a model of influence ought to be considered as integral to Friel's praxis rather than as a curiosity of textual genetics. As Friel's archive becomes more available through scholarship, it is the potential of this model of influence to which we should be alive. If a painter's way of making could produce a new approach to the monologue play, what new ways of working might contemporary artists in their various disciplines find through their encounters with Friel's creative practice? And what practical questions of access need to be answered in order to facilitate those encounters? 'But', as Frank's first monologue concludes, 'we'll come to that presently. Or as Teddy would have put it: Why don't we leave that until later, dear 'eart? Why don't we do that? Why not? Indeed'. (Friel *P1*, 341)

Notes

1. Marcel Proust, '361', in *The Maxims of Marcel Proust*, ed. and trans. by Justin O'Brian (New York: Columbia University Press, 1948), p. 191. This maxim is taken from p.48 of *Le Temps retrouvé* (Vol. II) in the standard French edition (Paris, Gallimard, Editions de la Nouvelle Revue Française, 1923–27).
2. Brian Friel, *Plays One* (London: Faber and Faber, 1996), p. 365. Further references in parentheses in the text as 'Friel, *P1*'.
3. George Steiner, *After Babel: Aspects of Language and Translation* (Oxford: Oxford University Press, 1976), p. 21.
4. Brian Friel, 'Self-Portrait (1972)', in *Brian Friel: Essays, Diaries, Interviews: 1964–1999*, ed. by Christopher Murray (London: Faber and Faber, 1999), pp. 37–46 (p. 39).
5. Dublin, National Library of Ireland (NLI), Brian Friel Papers (BFP), MS 37,054/1. Note towards *Lovers: Winners*. Double underlining in original.
6. Gottlob Frege, 'The Thought: A Logical Inquiry', *Mind* 65.259 (1956): 289–311 (p. 302).
7. NLI, BFP, MS 37,054/1. Note towards *Lovers: Winners*.
8. Frege, p. 302.
9. Frege, p. 308.

10. If a future Friel scholar were to prove me wrong, I would of course be delighted to learn the source of Friel's thinking; at present, I remain stumped.
11. Friel, 'Self-Portrait', p. 39.
12. Proust, p.191. See also NLI, BFP, MS 37,060/2, note towards *Crystal and Fox* dated 4 January 1968 and NLI, BFP, MS 37,066/1, note towards *The Freedom of the City*, dated 3 June [1972].
13. See NLI, BFP, MS 37,052/1, which contains a draft of a letter to director Hilton Edwards dated 7 April 1965 in which Friel describes himself has having been 'praying to Pirandello' at the play's inception.
14. See NLI, BFP, MS 37,072/1, note towards *Livjng Quarters* dated 9 January 1976. See also 'chorus', in *The Reader's Encyclopedia of World Drama*, ed. by John Gassner and Edward Quinn (New York: Dover Publications, 2002), p. 131. Friel had consulted this text during the composition process of *The Communication Cord* (1983). For further reference, see Northrop Frye, 'Third Essay: Archetypal Criticism: Theory of Myths', in *Anatomy of Criticism: Four Essays* (Princeton: Princeton University Press, 1957), pp. 131–223.
15. Proust, p. 191.
16. Anthony Roche, *Brian Friel: Theatre and Politics* (Basingstoke: Palgrave Macmillan, 2011), p. 88.
17. Frank McGuinness, 'Surviving the 1960s: three plays by Brian Friel 1968–1971', in *The Cambridge Companion to Brian Friel*, ed. Anthony Roche (Cambridge: Cambridge University Press, 2006), pp. 18–29 (p. 21).
18. Christopher Murray, *The Theatre of Brian Friel: Tradition and Modernity* (London: Bloomsbury Methuen Drama, 2014), pp. 43–44.
19. Richard Pine, *Brian Friel and Ireland's Drama* (London: Routledge, 1990), p. 81.
20. NLI, BFP, MS 37,060/2. Note towards *Crystal and Fox* dated 4 January 1968.
21. NLI, BFP, MS 37,060/1. Undated note towards *Crystal and Fox*.
22. NLI, BFP, MS 37,060/1. Undated note towards *Crystal and Fox*.
23. NLI, BFP, MS 37,060/1. Note towards *Crystal and Fox* dated 10 November 1967.

24. NLI, BFP, MS 37,054/1. Undated note towards *Lovers: Winners*. 'READ THIS (9 NOV. 1966)' added in green ink.
25. Brian Friel, *Collected Plays: Volume One* (London: Faber and Faber, 2016), p. 385.
26. McGuinness, p. 20.
27. Brian Friel, *Collected Plays*, p. 366.
28. NLI, BFP, MS 37,060/1. Note towards *Crystal and Fox* dated 2 December 1967.
29. NLI, BFP, MS 37,60/1. Note towards *Crystal and Fox* dated 2 December 1967. It is uncertain whether Friel was writing from memory or whether he was quoting from a specific edition, as his punctuation does not match the original. See, for instance, the version printed in Oscar Wilde, 'The Ballad of Reading Gaol', in *Oscar Wilde: The Major Works*, ed. by Isobel Murray (Oxford: Oxford World Classics, 1989), p. 549.
30. Pine, *Brian Friel and Ireland's Drama*, p. 17.
31. McGuinness, p. 22.
32. McGuinness, p. 28.
33. NLI, BFP, MS 37,061/1. Letter from Brian Friel to Hilton Edwards dated 30 September [1968].
34. See Karen Alkalay-Gut, 'The Thing He Loves: Murder as Aesthetic Experience in "The Ballad of Reading Gaol"', *Victorian Poetry* 35, No. 3 (1997), pp. 349–366.
35. Scott Boltwood, *Brian Friel, Ireland, and The North* (Cambridge: Cambridge University Press, 2009), p. 73.
36. As has been well documented, this is a potent echo of the events and aftermath of Derry's Bloody Sunday when, during a peaceful protest against internment on 30 January 1972, '[t]he firing by soldiers of 1 PARA caused the deaths of 13 people and injury to a similar number, none of whom was posing a threat of causing death or serious injury'. See Report of the Bloody Sunday Inquiry Volume 1 Chapter 5, https://webarchive.nationalarchives.gov.uk/20101017064040/http://report.bloody-sunday-inquiry.org/volume01/chapter005/.
37. This pivotal event of the Troubles occurred when a People's Democracy march from Belfast to Derry was ambushed by Loyalists, aided and abetted by off-duty members of the B Specials.
38. NLI, BFP, MS 37,066/1. Note dated 29 April 1970.
39. NLI, BFP, MS 37,066.1. Note dated 15 September 1970.

40. The findings of the controversial Widgery Tribunal of 1972 into the events of Bloody Sunday. The tribunal is now widely regarded as a rushed job and its findings have been labelled a whitewash insofar as it largely absolved British soldiers of any wrongdoing. In 1998, the Bloody Sunday Inquiry (or Saville Inquiry) was set up; the results, published in 2010, instead exonerated the victims and held the actions of British soldiers to be unjustified.
41. See NLI, Brian Friel Papers, MS 37,067/1. Letter to Friel dated 20 December 1972 from Warren Brown of Curtis Brown literary agency.
42. NLI, BFP, MS 37,054/1. Undated note towards *Lovers: Winners*.
43. NLI, BFP, MS 37,066/1. Letter from Warren Brown to Brian Friel dated 20 December 1972.
44. Elizabeth Hale Winkler, 'Brian Friel's *The Freedom of the City*: Historical Actuality and Dramatic Imagination', *The Canadian Journal of Irish Studies* 7, No. 1 (1981), pp. 12–31 (p. 27).
45. NLI, BFP, MS 37,066/1. Undated note towards *The Freedom of the City*.
46. NLI, BFP, MS 37,066/1. Note towards *The Freedom of the City* dated 16 March 1972.
47. See NLI, BFP, MS 37,066/1.
48. Proust, p. 191.
49. Ibid.
50. NLI, NFP, MS 37,066/1. Note towards *The Freedom of the City* dated 20 May 1972.
51. David Sylvester, *Interviews with Francis Bacon* (London: Thames and Hudson, 1975), p. 53. Further references in parentheses in the text.
52. See NLI, BFP, MS 37,075/1. Notes dated 11, 12, and 25 June [1975]. See also Howard Brenton, 'Petrol Bombs Through the Proscenium Arch', *Theatre Quarterly* 5, No. 17 (1975), pp. 4–20 (p. 6).
53. Michael Glenny, trans., 'Sinyavsky: Fiction and Reality', *Times Literary Supplement*, 23 May 1975, p. 560. See also Abram Tertz (Andrey Sinyavsky), *A Voice from the Chorus*, trans. by Kyril Fitzlyon and Max Hayward (London: Collins and Harvill Press, 1976), p. 200. See also NLI, BFP, MS 37,075/1. Note dated 24 May [1975].

54. NLI, BFP, MS 37,075/1. Note dated 25 June [1975]. In an interview with Paddy Agnew (1980), Friel claims to have come to Steiner's *After Babel* when he was translating *Three Sisters* (1981), and that '[t]he work ... somehow overlapped into the working of the text of *Translations*' (Murray, ed., *Brian Friel: Essays, Diaries, Interviews*, p. 84). However, it remains highly probable that Friel was at least aware of Steiner's latest ideas from Donald Davie's review of *After Babel* in the 31 January 1975 edition of the *TLS*, which he is likely to have read. It is also possible that he is referring to an earlier work by Steiner; Friel does not elaborate in these notes.
55. Steiner, p. 220. Cited in Donald Davie, 'The clans and their world-pictures', *TLS*, 31 January 1975, 98–100, (p. 98).
56. Subsequent editions were expanded and revised to incorporate later interviews with Bacon.
57. NLI, BFP, MS 37,075/1. Notes dated 17 May [1975] and 18 May [1975]. Square brackets in original.
58. NLI, BFP, MS 37,075/1. Note dated 18 May [1975]. Square brackets in original.
59. NLI, BFP, MS 37,075/1. Note dated 23 May [1975].
60. NLI, BFP, MS 37,075/1. Note dated 19 May [1975]. Double underlining in original.
61. NLI, BFP, MS 37,075/1. Note dated 21 May [1975]. See also Sylvester, p.120. For Sylvester and Bacon's discussion of the artist as medium in relation to Duchamp, see Sylvester, pp. 104–105.
62. John Berger, *Portraits: John Berger on Artists*, ed. by Tom Overton (London: Verso, 2017), p. 345.
63. Victoria Walsh, '"... to give the sensation without the boredom of conveyance": Francis Bacon and the Aesthetic of Ambiguity', *Visual Culture in Britain 10*, No. 3 (2009), pp. 235–252, (p. 249).
64. NLI, BFP, MS 37,075/1. Note dated 15 April [1975]. Friel's use of the term 'images' may indicate that he had already encountered Bacon's interviews at this point.
65. NLI, BFP, MS 37,085/1. Undated note towards *Translations*.
66. NLI, BFP, MS 37,075/1. Note dated 21 May [1975]. Square brackets in original. Double underlining added in magenta ink 15 July 1975.
67. NLI, BFP, MS 37,075/1. Note dated 21 May [1975].

68. NLI, BFP, MS 37,075/1. Addition to the above, magenta ink, dated 15 July 1975.
69. NLI, BFP, MS 37,075/1. Note dated 21 May [1975].
70. Steiner, p. 221.
71. Steiner, p.35.
72. Steiner, p. 223.
73. Roche, pp. 155–6.
74. Richard Pine, 'Brian Friel and Contemporary Irish Drama', *Colby Quarterly 27*, No. 4 (1991), pp. 190–201 (p. 5).
75. NLI, BFP, MS 37,075/8. Typescript of *The Game*.
76. Brian Friel, *Give Me Your Answer, Do!* (London: Penguin Books, 1997), p. 49. Further references in parentheses in the text as 'Friel, *GMYAD*'.
77. NLI, BFP, MS 37, 075/8. Typescript of *The Game*.
78. NLI, BFP, MS 37,075/6. Undated note towards *The Game*.
79. NLI, BFP, MS 37,075/1. Note dated 21 May [1975]. See also Sylvester, p. 120.
80. NLI, BFP, MS 37,075/1. Note dated 19 May [1975].
81. NLI, BFP, MS 37,075/1. Note dated 1 May 1975. See also James Plunkett, *The Trusting and the Maimed and Other Irish Stories* (New York: Devin-Adair, 1955). There may be something in the story's heavy-handed pigeon metaphor relevant to *Faith Healer*, though I suspect the link is name only.
82. NLI, BFP, MS 37,075/1. Note dated 5 May [1975].
83. NLI, BFP, MS 37,075/1. Note dated 7 May [1975].
84. NLI, BFP, MS 37,075/1. Note dated 18 May [1975].
85. NLI, BFP, MS 37,075/1. Note dated 13 June [1975].
86. Roche, p. 155.
87. Nicholas Grene, '*Faith Healer* in New York and Dublin', in John P. Harrington, ed., *Irish Theater in America: Essays on Irish Theatrical Diaspora* (New York: Syracuse University Press, 2009), pp. 138–146 (p. 140).
88. NLI, BFP, MS 37,075/9.
89. NLI, Correspondence of D.E.S. Maxwell, MS 36,252/2.
90. Nicholas Grene, 'Friel and Transparency', *Irish University Review 29*, No. 1, Special Issue: Brian Friel (1999), pp. 136–144 (p. 136).
91. NLI, BFP, MS 37,075/3.
92. NLI, BFP, MS 37,077/2.

93. Hayden White, 'Between science and symbol', *TLS*, 21 January 1986, pp. 109–110, (p. 109).
94. Proust, p. 191.
95. NLI, Brian Friel Papers, MS 37,100/1.
96. Friel, *Plays Two* (London: Faber and Faber, 1999), p. 264. Further references in parentheses in the text as 'Friel, *P2*'.
97. See Emmett O'Byrne, Aidan Clarke, and Judy Barry, 'Bagenal (O'Neill), Mabel', in the *Dictionary of Irish Biography*, October 2009, https://doi.org/10.3318/dib.006953.v1 [accessed 24 June 2022.] The *Dictionary of Irish Biography* also paints a less than rosy picture of their brief marriage, and notes that there is some dispute as to whether she died 'in virtual imprisonment at Dungannon or in refuge at Newry'.
98. Paul Veyne's *Writing History* (1984), C. Behan McCullagh's *Justifying Historical Descriptions* (1984), José Ortega y Gasset's *Historical Reason* (1984), and Dominick LaCapra's *History and Criticism* (1985).
99. See Hayden White, 'The Historical Text as Literary Artifact', in *The Norton Anthology of Theory and Criticism*, 3rd Edition, ed. by V. B. Leitch, W. E. Cain, L. Finke, J. McGowan, T. D. Sharpley-Whiting, and J. Williams (New York; London: Norton, 2018), pp. 1463–1480.
100. NLI, BFP, MS 37,100/1. Note towards *Making History* dated 21 November 1985.
101. White, p. 109. Compare with Friel's notes towards *Lovers: Winners*.
102. White, p. 110.
103. Brian Friel, 'Making a Reply to the Criticisms of *Translations* by J. H. Andrews (1983)', in Murray, ed., *Brian Friel: Essays, Diaries, Interviews*, pp. 116–119 (p. 119).
104. White, p. 109.
105. NLI, BFP, MS 37,100/1. Note towards *Making History* dated 1 October 1986. Friel returned to this note at an unspecified date and underlined it in green ink, adding a (possibly baffled) '?!'.
106. NLI, BFP, MS 37,100/1. Note towards *Making History* dated 29 March 1984.
107. Friel, 'Making a Reply to the Criticisms of *Translations* by J. H. Andrews', p. 118.

108. NLI, BFP, MS 37,100/1. Note towards *Making History* dated 20 February 1986.
109. NLI, BFP, MS 37,100/1. Note towards *Making History* dated 5 November 1984.
110. NLI, BFP, MS 37,100/1. Note towards *Making History* dated 18 January [1985]. Underlining in original; original underlining in red ink.
111. NLI, BFP, MS 37,100/1. Note towards *Making History* dated 18 January [1985].
112. NLI, BFP, MS 37,100/1. Note towards *Making History* dated 20 February 1986.
113. White, p. 110.
114. NLI, BFP, MS 37,100/1. Note towards *Making History* dated 20 February 1986.
115. White, p. 109.
116. NLI, BFP, MS 37,075/1. Note dated 21 May [1975].
117. NLI, BFP, MS 37,075/1. Addition to the above, magenta ink, dated 15 July 1975.
118. NLI, BFP, MS 37,134/1. Undated note towards *Give Me Your Answer, Do!*. See also Eamon Duffy, *The Stripping of the Altars: Traditional Religion in England 1400–1580* (1992).
119. See Friel, *Give Me Your Answer, Do!*, pp. 70–71.
120. NLI, BFP, MS 37,134/1. Note towards *Give Me Your Answer, Do!* dated 26 June [1995].
121. NLI, BFP, MS 37,134/1. Addendum to the above, dated 1 July [1995].
122. NLI, BFP, MS 37,134/1. Undated note towards *Give Me Your Answer, Do!*.
123. Douglas Johnson, 'Getting to know the General', *TLS*, 28 July 1995, p. 30.
124. NLI, BFP, MS 37,134/1. Addendum to undated note towards *Give Me Your Answer, Do!*, dated 25 May 1996.
125. NLI, BFP, MS 37,134/1. Undated note towards *Give Me Your Answer, Do!*. Underlining in original; original underlining in red ink.
126. Brian Friel, 'Extracts from a Sporadic Diary: *Give Me Your Answer, Do!* (1995–96)', in Murray, ed., *Brian Friel: Essays, Diaries, Interviews*, pp. 166–172 (p. 168).

127. NLI, BFP, MS 37,134/1. Note towards *Give Me Your Answer, Do!* dated 23 June [1995].
128. I am grateful to Laurence Price for his theological insights into the relationship between orthodoxy and orthopraxis at this juncture, and indeed for expanding my vocabulary.
129. Friel, 'Self-Portrait', p. 38.

CHAPTER 3

A Story Told Through People: Friel's Embodied Intertexts

Friel's creative encounters with Bacon's interviews lend themselves particularly well to a practice-focused approach to his archive as a record of the 'how' of influence. Here, I will be extending this approach to ideas of embodiment and synthesis, focusing exclusively on another landmark Friel play, *Translations* (1980), by way of a case study. Specifically, I will be exploring the extent to which Friel's plays, as stories 'told *through people*'[1] (my italics), embody his various syntheses of ideas through the contouring of theatrical space by bodied speakers. Put simply, how does Friel's mixing of source materials manifest itself as the words and actions of speaking bodies on a stage that is, by definition, only the visible dimension of a much wider continuum? To what extent is a play like *Translations* greater than the sum of its parts? And how do Friel's intertexts function once they become speakable lines? These lines of inquiry will each by underpinned not only by Friel's creative process as revealed by the Brian Friel Papers but also by two different approaches to embodiment that draw on Vimala Herman's cognitive poetics and Diana Taylor's performance studies scholarship. Both are in many ways an extension or formalisation of ideas that can be found in Friel's own thinking. By establishing some theoretical touchstones that are compatible with Friel's process, my aim is not to complicate but rather to bolster an approach to Friel's plays that considers embodiment both thematically and in the context of literary

© The Author(s), under exclusive license to Springer Nature Switzerland AG 2023
Z. Kuczyńska, *Brian Friel's Models of Influence*, https://doi.org/10.1007/978-3-031-17905-1_3

influence. Key to the chapter is the first detailed analysis of the influence of a second Steiner text on the play—*In Bluebeard's Castle: Some Notes Towards the Re-definition of Culture* (1971). This book, I want to suggest, had a profound effect on the play's development, not only in and of itself but as part of a wider synthesis of source materials.

Embodiments

The primary approach to embodiment that informs this chapter is based on the idea of theatrical deixis. This is a cognitive poetics-based approach that considers embodiment in the context of 'theatre, as the art of [...] the transformation of space'. In her article 'Deixis and Space in Drama', Vimala Herman suggests that deixis—a kind of verbal pointing used to indicate personal, spatial, or temporal relationships relative to the speaker—'*presupposes a corporeal context of utterance with corporeal bodies and channels of communication open for use*'. This is because deixis '*uses the body of participants in speech events as the primary point for calculations of space*'[2] (italics in original). In this context, not only is language embodied (i.e. corporeally situated) as speech, but it also becomes a means of doing. Adopting Hanna Scolnicov's terminology, Herman goes on to argue that theatrical space as a whole can be seen as a continuum within which '[t]he deictic relationship can contour the visual, spatial field of the stage as other spaces [...] in order to transform one space into another imaginatively'.[3] Crucially, for Herman, deixis also 'expands the visual field of the on-stage world into off-stage spaces, as extensions of it' through acts of bodied speech: 'Off-stage space thus becomes part of the same, unbroken space and is made continuous with it'.[4] To this end, she adopts Scolnicov's recharacterisation of onstage and offstage as 'theatrical space within' and 'theatrical space without', respectively.[5] Embodiment, then, in the context of Herman's explorations of deixis within a continuum of theatrical space, is a means of approaching the way in which Friel's influences, as intertexts, function not merely as quotations but also as ways of transforming theatrical space. This will become apparent in my approach to the mapping process of *Translations* in particular, which is staged in part as a series of deictic naming events by bodied speakers.

A secondary definition of embodiment used in this chapter draws on performance studies, specifically Diana Taylor's conception of the embodied archive. For Taylor, the archive consists not only of supposedly enduring artefacts but also of practices that are usually categorised in terms of ephemerality. The latter are fundamentally embodied practices, insofar as they require the presence and participation of living bodies. These repeated and repeatable acts are known as the 'repertoire', and include practices like storytelling, dance, and song. Key to Taylor's argument is that the acts that make up the repertoire are both ways of knowing and ways of transmitting knowledge. Performance can, therefore, be understood as an embodied archive, where the body is both a site and a means of transfer, particularly with regard to cultural memory and identity. Taylor's anti-colonial perspective challenges the largely Western imperialist assumption that performance does not remain, and functions as a riposte to 'the centuries-old privileging of written over embodied knowledge'[6] that grants 'only the literate and powerful [...] social memory and identity'.[7] This perspective will inform aspects of my discussions around the naming and recording processes of the Ordnance Survey in the play.

Friel's sources

Translations (1980) is one of Friel's best-known, most politicised plays. The first play to be produced by the Field Day Theatre Company, it is primarily an exploration of the erosion of the Irish language under British colonial rule and, by extension, the role that language plays in cultural collapse. Set in 1833 in a hedge-school in Co. Donegal, it stages the arrival of the map-making British officers of the Ordnance Survey in a culturally rich Irish-speaking community already threatened by emigration, material poverty, and famine. The master of the hedge-school, Hugh Mor O'Donnell, is a polyglot, a poet, a classicist, and a drunk; he is also one of the play's most perceptive commentators. His son Manus, accidentally lamed by his father as a baby, assists in the running of the hedge-school in a monitor-like role; as the play opens, he is teaching Sarah, who has long been unable to speak, to say her own name. Hugh's other son, Owen, returns home in the pay of the Survey, employed as a translator. It is Owen who facilitates the task of incurable romantic and budding Hibernophile Lt. George Yolland, anglicising and then standardising Irish place-names and entering them into a Name Book that will formalise them for use in the mapmaking process. Initially, the sappers meet with a mostly pranksterish resistance (some of the locals steal some of their equipment). Things get serious, however, when Yolland's blossoming romance with hedge-school pupil and aspiring emigrant Maire is cut short by his abduction at the hands of the Donnelly twins, whose menacingly offstage presence is associated with the secret agrarian societies of the time. Yolland's commanding officer, Captain Lancey, orders violent retribution; Sarah loses her speech; Owen realises his complicity too late; Hugh resolves to learn the new nomenclature of his parish as he ruminates on the downfall of ancient civilisations.

As a play underpinned by multiple texts, only two of which are regularly given sustained critical attention, *Translations* is certainly ripe for analysis as an example of the ways in which Friel combined his sources. Many of these are common knowledge, thanks in part to extracts from Friel's 'sporadic diary' for the play published in 1999 as part of a volume of essays, diaries, and interviews edited by Christopher Murray: 'I keep returning to the same texts: the letters of John O'Donovan, [Thomas] Colby's *Memoir [of the City and North Western Liberties of Londonderry]*, *A Paper Landscape* by John Andrews, *The Hedge-Schools of Ireland* by [Patrick John] Dowling, [George] Steiner's *After Babel*'.[8] The latter is perhaps the play's most famous intertext; instances of direct quotation from and close paraphrases of *After Babel* in *Translations* have been well documented.[9] There is, however, at least one major source for *Translations* that has been relatively ignored: a second Steiner text, *In Bluebeard's Castle*, which is acknowledged only in passing by Martine Pelletier[10] and, later, Murray.[11] In addition to this, it should be of no surprise that the *TLS* also raises its ubiquitous head in Friel's notes. Indeed, Roy Foster's 1976 review of the play's other well-known intertext, *A Paper Landscape*, appears to have informed Friel's reading of its historical figures to an extent. A further additional minor source would appear to be Brian Bonner's *Our Inis Eoghain Heritage: The Parishes of Culdaff and Cloncha* (1972), given that Friel makes reference in his notes to Bonner's characterisation of Urris as 'a sort of "Poteen Republic", where the King's writ had no effect'.[12]

Broadly speaking, Friel's major sources for *Translations* can be divided into two categories. The first is historical context, combining nineteenth-century documents (Colby and O'Donovan) and twentieth-century scholarship (Dowling and Andrews); the second concerns theories of language and culture (the two Steiner texts). Of Friel's documented historical source materials,[13] three are concerned with the persons and institutions involved in the mapping of Ireland by the Ordnance Survey between 1824 and 1846. In *A Paper Landscape: The Ordnance Survey in Nineteenth-Century Ireland* (1975), J.H. Andrews gives a general (and largely sympathetic) account of the mammoth undertaking that was the mapping of Ireland at six inches to the statute mile. The 'dominant character of the narrative'[14] is one Thomas Colby, 'a vigorous and hard-working officer' in the Royal Engineers who 'had established a reputation as an expert in trigonometrical surveying, field astronomy, and base measurement' and who 'had inherited [from his predecessor] the custom that the senior officers of the department should be primarily men of science' (Andrews, *APL*, 20). It is he who, according to Andrews, was most likely responsible for steering the government in the direction of a military rather than a civilian mapping operation. However, unlike some of the more cynical characters in *Translations*, Andrews makes a point of crediting Colby 'with [no] more than the average Englishman's prejudice against the Irish' (Andrews, *APL*, 21) in his preference for his own officers over Irish mapping expertise: 'In any country, so far as Colby was concerned, the ordnance knew best' (Andrews, *APL*, 20–21). It was also Colby who 'insisted that his officers should keep their own records of every name, first as commonly spelt and then in its various deviant spellings with the authority for each'. Moreover, 'each officer was to keep a journal of the scientific, economic, and historical facts that came to his attention'—the 'kernel' (Andrews, *APL*, 56) of an ill-fated project culminating in Colby's *Memoir*. Friel, by his own admission, had been 'fascinated' by Colby prior to his having read *A Paper Landscape*, partly due to 'the fact that he had one hand'.[15]

Similarly compelling for Friel, or so it would seem, was another prominent figure in Andrews's book—an officer named Thomas Aiskew Larcom. '[N]either bluff soldier-man nor soulless bureaucrat but a master of human relations' (Andrews, *APL*, 186), Larcom was the 'officer in charge of publication from 1828' (Andrews, *APL*, 114) and 'responsible for some far-reaching reforms in the treatment of place-names' (Andrews, *APL*, 119):

> His instinct was to polish and to civilise[.] [. . .] In matters of orthography, however, Larcom was in sympathy with the etymological trend and even took the drastic step of trying to learn the Irish language himself. [. . .] His own solution of the orthographic problem was to retain the field name-books with their variant spellings, and to adopt not necessarily the commonest version but the version which came nearest to the original

Irish form of the name. This was an attractive compromise between the empirical and the antiquarian. It was rational, scholarly, and practical. It also showed a well-intentioned deference to the Irishness of Irish place-names. (Andrews, *APL*, 122)

Again, it should be noted that there is little in Andrews's reading of Larcom as an officer of the Survey that suggests unusual anti-Irish sentiment—quite the contrary, in fact. Larcom's Irish teacher was none other than distinguished Irish-language scholar John O'Donovan, who was later hired by the Survey as a lexicographer to 'hear the names pronounced and interpreted by Irish-speaking residents and to study them in the context of local topography and antiquities' (Andrews, *APL*, 123). Among the other historical figures in *A Paper Landscape* are some familiar surnames. One is (William) Yolland, 'another officer of outstanding scientific ability who joined the Survey in London in 1838'. The other is not one but two men named Lancey: a Captain T.F. Lancey who was one of Colby's more outspoken critics (Andrews, *APL*, 64), and a Lieutenant W. Lancey who once wrote to Larcom from Co. Donegal to say he felt somewhat pressed for time on the memoir project (Andrews, *APL*, 152). Neither the Yolland nor the Lancey of *Translations* appear to share anything other than a name with these historical figures.

Friel's other source materials relating to the Survey are not twentieth-century histories but contemporary accounts. Colonel Thomas Colby's *Memoir of the City and North Western Liberties of Londonderry* (1837) is, in many respects, an attempt to put into documentary form the larger part of an iceberg of which a map is only the tip. '[A] map', according to the book's Preliminary Notice, 'is in its nature but a part of a Survey, and [...] much of the information connected with it, can only be advantageously embodied in a memoir, to which the map then serves as a graphical index'.[16] According to Colby's preface, it was Larcom's idea 'to draw together a work embracing every species of local information relating to Ireland'; it was Larcom, too, who had 'charge of the execution of the work'.[17] Although the book is attributed to Colby, the preface makes clear that the memoir is essentially a collaborative work, with different persons responsible for different sections. However, as the different sections are not assigned individual or even multiple authors, it is impossible to say with any clarity who is writing at any given time from the text alone. Nevertheless, speaking in a Frielian vein—i.e., as a non-historian with an anti-colonial perspective—the memoir gives a revealing insight into the animating values of the Survey. It is possible from the outset to see how colonial attitudes are embedded even in its apparently benevolent commitment to 'purposes of public utility'. For instance, on the one hand, it is undeniable that the Survey's combination of 'minute' topography and 'information collected with similar minuteness' was in many ways a genuine attempt to meet at least some local needs: 'The direction in which a rail road or canal should be made might be indicated by maps, but the necessity for making it must be sought in the objects to be attained by it when made'. At the same time, there is an unmistakable note of imperialism in the means by which those 'objects to be attained' were to be ascertained. Indeed, the wording of the memoir strongly implies that the gathering of local knowledge was also in part a rejection of *undesirable* local knowledge that did not help to further a narrative of progress: 'in order that the present condition of the country might be exhibited in every useful light, it was necessary to divest History of fable and error, and to hold up the past as a beacon and guide to the future'.[18] Thus the tone of the memoir becomes dismissive where it speaks of 'foolish legends [...] current among the peasantry'[19] even as it brightens with curiosity over the shared Celtic origins of the names 'London' and 'Derry'.[20] Meanwhile, the 'Irish annals of Derry, preceding its occupation by the English', are taken as 'saddening illustrations of the insecurity of life and property, and the amount of misery and confusion, which were the inevitable results of such a social system'.[21] (It hardly takes a great leap of the imagination to arrive from here to Owen's apologist take on the anglicisation of 'place-names that are riddled with confusion'.[22]) Fascinatingly, it may well have been from the memoir that Friel first gained a sense of the centrality of place-names. Indeed, the standardisation process is posited as 'a basis for historic inquiries' and thus an entry point into the memoir project itself:

> The mode of spelling the names of places was peculiarly vague and unsettled, but on the maps about to be constructed, it was desirable to establish a standard orthography, and for future reference, to identify the several localities with the names by which they had formerly been called; and as the townland, and other divisions under various denominations, have existed over the whole of Ireland from the earliest times, it soon became apparent, that a sufficient extension of the original orthographic inquiries, *to trace all the mutations of each name, would be, in fact, to pass in review the local history of the whole country.*[23] [My italics.]

In other words, the history of place-names was a gateway both to local history and to an imperialist narrative, in which the history of Ireland as an independent country was made continuous with its colonial future by means of a story of improvement.

Although Friel considered Colby's *Memoir* to contain some 'excellent etymological examples',[24] there is a significant amount of material relating to the day-to-day process of gathering information on Irish place-names to be found in the letters of John O'Donovan. MS 37,085/6 comprises a Donegal County Library photocopy of the 1946 typescript copy of *LETTERS Containing information relative to the ANTIQUI-TIES of the COUNTY OF DONEGAL Collected during the progress of the ORDNANCE SURVEY in 1835*. In these occasionally 'wild'[25] letters, John O'Donovan writes to his unnamed superior (presumably Larcom) as he travels around Ireland hearing the pronunciation of Irish place-names. O'Donovan writes with the effusiveness of a scholar in his element, pausing on occasion to make observations on the decline of the Irish language, evidence of which he was confronted with as he went about his task. In one example of this, O'Donovan is 'totally disappointed' to have arrived in 'the Parish of Raw-Moghy (Rath Mo-Eochaidg) to hear the names of that Parish pronounced' only to find that 'the old language and traditions are extinct in the district' (O'Donovan, 75). Elsewhere, he notes that 'the disappearance of the Irish language from the district extending around the Town of Letterkenny, and the consequent loss of traditions' (O'Donovan, 65) has hampered him in his task: 'for with that language, the remembrance of things old vanish' (O'Donovan, 68). This is in some respects an extension of his musings on the differences between spoken variants of Irish: 'so local and unfixed is the Irish Language, and so must every language be as long as its preservation depends upon the memory of the peasantry' (O'Donovan, 20). These passages have all been marked by Friel.

O'Donovan's letters are also a rich content source for Owen's dialogue as he goes about his naming task. As Friel would later make clear, Owen's character owes a significant debt to O'Donovan, even if his specific role in the Survey bears a greater similarity to a man named Edward Quin, mentioned in a passage that was also marked by Friel:

> He has been employed by Lieutenant Vicars to give the Irish names of places about Ballyshannon, and has saved me a good deal of trouble—I wish you could induce Mr. Vicars to take him to his next district, and

keep him employed writing in the Name Books, and taking down the names from the pronunciation of the Country people. (O'Donovan, 150)

Notable examples of the naming process marked by Friel include a letter written from 'Buncranagh' on 26 August 1835, in which O'Donovan observes that '[t]he name Strawbreaga is very much corrupted, and I think that we should restore the proper spelling' (O'Donovan, 14). This chimes with dialogue in which Owen distractedly tells Manus about 'The Murren' as 'a corruption of Saint Muranus' and suggests that they 'go back to the original' (Friel, *Pl*, 430–1). Saint Muranus himself appears later in the same letter in the context of 'the old Church of Fathain Mura' (O'Donovan, 15) in the parish of Upper Fahan. The letter also invokes the authority of 'the old Irish inhabitants of Clonmany and Clonca' who state that 'the true name is Traigh Breige, that is, the deceitful or lying strand' (O'Donovan, 14)—a possible inspiration for the name given to the play's offstage purveyor of poitín Anna na mBreag, which 'means Anna of the Lies' (Friel, *Pl*, 417). Elsewhere, O'Donovan shows an amused delight at Columb's 'foresight of futurity' in predicting that 'two guns shall be mounted on the pig's back'—a prophecy that apparently came to fruition when 'a Martello Tower was erected on this pig-resembling place called Muc-amish' (O'Donovan, 22). Here, hedge-school pupil Doalty's own rhyming prophecy of St Columcille comes to mind: 'The spuds will bloom in Baile Beag/Till rabbits grow an extra lug' (Friel, *Pl*, 395).

What is particularly striking about these letters, however, is that—like the Owen of the first two Acts—O'Donovan does not suffer from a sense of divided loyalties. This emerges most vividly in another passage marked by Friel, in which O'Donovan acknowledges his tendency to write with a fervour and occasional lyricism that might not have been entirely appropriate for reporting back to his boss:

> Though my letters are wild as the mountains in which they were written, still do I feel myself very sober in thought, and exceedingly (excessive) in love with truth *even to the prejudice of all national feelings*. But when you consider the subject and difficulty of my task—that of seeking through the dim vista of tradition some faint glimmerings of truth—and the incoherency of rude tales which I have attempted to digest, you will perhaps feel convinced that I could not be at all times serious or sober in expression. (O'Donovan, 143, my italics)

In other words, O'Donovan considers himself devoted (perhaps obsessively) to the uncovering of empirical truths, to the point where they outweigh national concerns. This same letter also contains a fascinating insight into O'Donovan's views on the validity of written versus embodied knowledge (in this case in the form of oral history). These can be encapsulated by his own choice of 'vulgar and common place proverb', again underlined by Friel: 'Vox audita perit, lit[t]era scripta manet'. (The spoken word vanishes; the written word remains.) As will become apparent in later chapters, this tension between the written and the spoken word is just one iteration of what performance scholar Diana Taylor calls 'the rift [...] between the "archive" of supposedly enduring materials (i.e., texts, documents, buildings, bones) and the more ephemeral "repertoire" of embodied practice/knowledge (i.e., spoken language, dance, sports, ritual)'.[26]

Dowling's *The Hedge Schools of Ireland* (1935) is unrelated to the Survey, but provides a kind of political template for Friel's engagement with mapping. Dowling portrays the hedge-schools as the remnants of a Bardic educational tradition 'gradually absorbed into the peasantry',[27] having been deliberately stamped out for political gain by the occupying English. Unapologetically anti-colonial, the book makes its position on the English language clear: that it was a force for cultural and political aggression and, above all, suppression. It was also, as Hugh observes in the play, a language of commerce: 'English they used in business affairs, while Irish was the language of the home and the fields' (Dowling, 72). Irish-language education, meanwhile, is hailed as an act of resistance. Indeed, at one point, Dowling quite literally describes the hedge-schools as having facilitated 'a kind of guer[r]illa warfare in education' (Dowling, 48) in the face of systematic anti-Catholic legislation and the establishment of 'rival instrumental establishments intended mainly to wean the people from the customs, the language, and [...] the religion of their country' (Dowling, 33). For Dowling, the teaching of history in particular laid 'the foundations of discontentment and of disaffection to constituted government' (Dowling, 85). Consequently, the hedge-schoolmaster appears as a kind of revolutionary figure, whose politics were shaped by his (and only very occasionally her) circumstances:

> National history cannot be read without forming prejudices of some kind; and this is more true of a subject race which can only find in its history an account of its past glory, its wrongs and its present plight. No one has yet

discovered a conquered race that is entire in its loyalty to its conqueror. Minor illegalities among a free people are merely punishable by law; but when committed by a subject people, they are regarded as open defiance and disloyalty. This point of view must not be overlooked when forming a judgment of the character and political outlook of the Irish schoolmaster. (Dowling, 110–111)

This makes for a fascinating comparison with the Survey's relationship with the beacon-like past that lights the way to the future, as in Colby's memoir. Indeed, to place Dowling in dialogue with Colby is to enter into Orwellian territory: 'Who controls the past controls the future: who controls the present controls the past'.[28]

Despite the fact that hedge-schools were no longer illegal by the time in which *Translations* is set, then, it is clear that Dowling's portrayal of the hedge-school as a site and a means of resistance continues to animate the play. Likewise, the fact that *Translations* takes the view that the passing of the hedge-schools '[severed] the last link with the ancient Gaelic schools of Ireland' (Dowling, 153)—and, by extension, its culture—can be attributed squarely to Dowling. In addition to a political stance, *The Hedge Schools of Ireland* also provided Friel with a wealth of practical details, including some notable examples of the behaviours of individual schoolmasters. The emphasis on classical education, the idea of the poet-schoolmaster, the satires composed against rival schoolmasters (Dowling, 95), the monitor system, and the general learning conditions are all to be found in Dowling. Notable borrowings include Hugh's 'Pentaglot Preceptor' (Friel, *Pl*, 418), which was a real volume by a schoolmaster named Patrick Lynch (Dowling, 140–141), and Jimmy Jack's cries of 'Thermopylae!' in the face of the British army—a scene that surely owes something to Dowling's inclusion of a political speech of Waterford schoolmaster James Nash: 'every potato field shall be a Marathon, and every boreen a Thermopylae'.[29] Hugh's idiosyncratic way of speaking to his pupils, meanwhile, is in some respects a caricature of a caricature—specifically '[William] Carleton's caricature [of a schoolmaster], Mat Kavanagh': 'You literati will hear the lessons for me, boys, till afther I'm back again; but mind, boys, absente domino, strepuunt servi—meditate on the philosophy of that [...] and [...] I'll castigate any boy guilty of misty manners on my retrogradation thither'.[30] The scattershot Latin, the parentheses, and the use of five syllables where two will do are all unmistakeably Hugh.

Friel's source materials for theories of language and culture are both texts by George Steiner—a scholar whose lengthy prose might well be assessed by Yolland and Owen's verdict on that same prose placed in Hugh's mouth: 'He's an astute man'. 'He's bloody pompous'. 'But so astute' (Friel, *P1*, 419). As has already been indicated, the influence of *After Babel* has been well covered over the past few decades of Friel scholarship, most comprehensively by Helen Lojek; I have no intention of reinventing the wheel in this respect. However, to save the reader the task of wading through Steiner's bulky and occasionally problematic tome, I will provide as brief a summary as possible of the ideas it contains that are most relevant to *Translations*. Key among these is that, in addition to there being no earthly possibility of a perfect translation from one language to another, translation within the same language is likewise impossible outside the confines of a brief chapter in Judeo-Christian mythology before the fall of the Tower of Babel.[31] This is partly because language is 'literally, at every moment, subject to mutation',[32] and partly because there is no language in which a signifier maps fully onto its signified: 'We mean endlessly more than we say' (Steiner, *AB*, 281). In this respect, all human understanding is an act of translation where language is concerned: to use a phrase of Steiner's that clearly resonated with the man who wrote *Philadelphia, Here I Come!*, 'all translation "interprets" between privacies' (Steiner, *AB*, 198). Other resonant ideas include the creativity of falsehood, the coexistence of material poverty and linguistic riches, and the close relationship between linguistic and cultural collapse. *After Babel* is also notable for its highly spatialised metaphors, which makes it well suited to a play about map-making. In addition to the oft-quoted 'linguistic contour[s]' of 'the changing landscape of fact' (Steiner, *AB*, 20), *After Babel* contains multiple examples of a cartographical turn of phrase. Steiner waxes lyrical about the invention of enduring classical metaphors as 'new mappings of the world' that 'reorganize our habitation in reality' (Steiner, *AB*, 23); he glosses Sapir-Whorf-style linguistics by explaining how '[t]he linguistic worldview of a given community shapes and gives life to the entire landscape of psychological and communal behaviour' (Steiner, *AB*, 87); he invokes 'Wittgenstein's use of "mapping"', whereby 'different linguistic communities literally inhabit and traverse different landscapes of conscious being' (Steiner, *AB*, 89). Other notable but less frequently noted borrowings include the terms 'exogamy and endogamy' (Steiner, *AB*, 301), the idea of '*erosive* standardization' (Steiner, *AB*, 31)[33] (my italics), the question of 'the status of the word "always"' (Steiner, *AB*, 145), and the translator as a potentially untrustworthy go-between (Steiner, *AB*, 252). There are also two key moments in *Translations* that are, to my knowledge, not generally spoken of in relation to *After Babel*, but which bear pointing out at this stage for later analysis. The first is the moment when Owen finally, explosively, tells Yolland '*My name is not Roland!*' (Friel, *Pl*, 421). This is, to my mind, a playful subversion of one of the examples Steiner gives of the significance of naming oneself. 'I am Roland'—presumably a reference to Browning's 'The Dark Tower'—is, for Steiner, indicative of 'the perilous gift a man makes when he gives his true name. To falsify or withhold one's real name', Steiner continues, 'is to guard one's life, one's *karma* or essence of being, from pillage or alien procurement' (Steiner, *AB*, 225). The second is the famous love scene between Maire and Yolland, in which they ultimately fail to understand one another beyond the fact of their mutual attraction: she wants to go; he wants to stay. This can be traced, I would suggest, to Steiner's outdated (sexist) musings on binarily gendered language, during the course of which he supposes that '[t]he two language models follow on Robert Graves's dictum that men do but women are' (Steiner, *AB*, 41) and, unfortunately, keeps going. In the example relevant to Maire and Yolland, Steiner proposes that, '[u]nder stress of hatred, of boredom, of sudden panic, great gaps open' between men and women: 'It is as if a man and a woman then heard each other for the first time and knew, with sickening conviction, that they share no common language, that their previous understanding had been based on a trivial pidgin which had left the heart of meaning untouched' (Steiner, *AB*, 44). He goes on to cite the example of Racine, whose every play, he suggests, contains 'a crisis of translation: under extreme stress, men and women declare their absolute being to each other, only to discover that their respective experience of eros and language has set them desperately apart' (Steiner, *AB*, 44–5). This is not a discovery that Maire and Yolland ever make, but the audience certainly does. Happily, Friel does not stress what Steiner would see as the gendered dimension of their fundamental misunderstanding.

The second Steiner text that underpins Friel's approach to cultural collapse in *Translations* is the much neglected (but much slimmer) *In Bluebeard's Castle: Some Notes Towards the Re-definition of Culture* (1971). Given that Steiner's arguments in this work are not common knowledge, and that I intend to draw extensively on Friel's engagement with it, a fuller summary is necessary here. Partly by way of a riposte to

T.S. Eliot's post-war essay *Notes Towards the Definition of Culture* (1948), Steiner argues that 'a contemporary defence of culture as "a way of life" will [...] have a void at its centre'.[34] Instead, he suggests that it is 'a certain view of the relations between time and individual death' that is 'central to a true culture' (Steiner, *IBC*, 70–1). In the case of what he terms a 'classic' civilisation, this relationship is a gamble on what he calls transcendence. By this, he means the 'axiomatic [notion] in classic art and thought, of sacrificing present life, present humanity, to the marginal chance of future literary or intellectual renown' (Steiner, *IBC*, 72). In other words, for Steiner, the thing that defines a 'classic' culture is taking a punt at immortality—living, as it were, for tomorrow; a desire to endure. (Or, as Lee Edelman would have it, a fundamentally heteronormative 'reality based on [...] reproductive futurism'.)[35] In this, Steiner suggests, language is key. Indeed, he contends that 'the very verb-systems of Indo-European languages are "performative" of those attitudes towards act and survival which animate the classic doctrine of knowledge and of art. What the poet terms "glory"', he continues, 'is a direct function of the felt reality of the future tense'. For Steiner, then, privileging the future and privileging the role of language go hand in hand in 'classic' cultures:

> Thus the time-death copula of a classic structure of personal and philosophic values is, in many respects, syntactic, and is inherent to a fabric of life in which language holds a sovereign, almost magically-validated role. Diminish that role, subvert that eminence, and you will have begun to demolish the hierarchies and transcendence-values of a classic civilization. (Steiner, *IBC*, 88)

By this we are to understand that to devalue the centrality of language within a 'classic' culture is to destabilise its relationship with time and death and, by extension, the values upon which it is structured. Steiner claims to see this devaluing, moreover, in the counter-cultures of his own time: '[t]he mumble of the drop-out, the "fuck-off" of the beatnik, the silence of the teenager in the enemy house of his parents, are meant to destroy'. (What would he have made of Gar Public?) Pausing only to take another swipe at 'murderous' Cordelia and make some ableist generalisations about autistic children, Steiner goes on to declare that '[d]eliberate violence is being done to those primary ties of identity and social cohesion produced by a common language'. Interestingly, Friel appears to have been more taken with Steiner's characterisation of the deliberately silenced than his defamation of the deliberately silent. The idea that '[w]e empty of their humanity those to whom we deny speech' (Steiner, *IBC*, 89) might well be applied to Sarah's loss of speech at the end of the play.

The book concludes with Steiner supposing that the way forward for a Western post-culture that has lost its 'kinship between speculative thought and survival' is simply to carry on regardless, even unto destruction: 'If a *dur désir de durer* was the mainspring of classic culture, it may well be that our post-culture will be marked by a readiness not to endure rather than curtail the risks of thought'. Hugh's resigned determination to move forward in another language springs to mind here. As Steiner puts it, in an observation that wouldn't have been out of place in Hugh's dialogue, '[t]o be able to envisage possibilities of self-destruction yet press home the debate with the unknown, is no mean thing' (Steiner, *IBC*, 106). Tellingly, Steiner rejects outright the exploration of existing non-Western cultural alternatives to the 'classic' gamble on transcendence. This is largely due to a set of generalised, racist assumptions. Indeed, Steiner sees what he calls the 'questing compulsion' of 'Western man' as something that is 'imprinted on the fabric [...] of our cortex' that 'evolved' due to 'an adequate climatic and nutritive *milieu*'. What Steiner sees as its 'partial absence [...] from less-developed, dormant races and civilizations does not', in his view, 'represent a free choice or feat of innocence' but rather 'the force of adverse ecological and genetic circumstance'. In other words, he sees 'Western man' as being quite literally more highly evolved (Steiner, *IBC*, 105). Furthermore, these unspecified non-Western cultures—called 'primitive societies' by Steiner—are deemed unsuited to the task of the pursuit of future knowledge due to their having 'chosen stasis or mythological circularity over forward motion'. In words cited by Hugh in *Translations*, these cultures are seen to have 'endured around truths immemorially posited' (Steiner, *IBC*, 104).

There is a lot to unpack here, not least Steiner's Eurocentric, fundamentally racist view of what a 'true' or 'classic' culture is. Key to understanding (if by no means accepting) Steiner's terms is his view of the history of Western civilisation between the nineteenth century and the dawn of the 1970s. For Steiner, mid-late twentieth-century Western culture is not a culture at all, but rather a 'post-culture' that has been forced to reimagine itself for the worse in the wake of the atrocities of World War II, and the Holocaust in particular: 'In locating Hell above ground, we have passed out of the major order and symmetries of Western civilization' (Steiner, *IBC*, 48). This sense of post-cultural anxiety is heightened, Steiner suggests, by comparison with 'the "myth of the nineteenth century" or the "imagined garden of liberal culture"' (Steiner, *IBC*, 14). In some respects, this is the temporal equivalent of the other man's grass always being greener. In other respects, however, this is due to a phenomenon that Steiner expresses in terms that are almost identically expressed by Hugh in the closing scenes of *Translations*: '[i]t is not the literal past that rules us' but rather 'images of the past' (Steiner, *IBC*, 13). (It is of note that Friel replaces 'rules' with 'shape[s]'; the addition of 'embodied in language' (Friel, *Pl*, 445) is Friel's own elaboration.)

But where did these 'inhuman [...] crises [...] that compel a redefinition of culture' originate? According to Steiner, 'the long peace of the nineteenth century' (Steiner, *IBC*, 17) itself was to blame, or rather the ennui that set in after a period of revolutionary change followed by a 'brutal deceleration of time and radical expectation' (Steiner, *IBC*, 22). Indeed, Steiner's version of the nineteenth century is one in which '*ennui* was breeding detailed fantasies of nearing catastrophe' (Steiner, *IBC*, 26), as expressed in the 'ultimately destructive ripostes [...] of Romanticism' (Steiner, *IBC*, 24). He goes on to characterise '[t]he genocide that took place in Europe and the Soviet Union during the period 1936–1945' as a kind of cultural suicide constitutive of 'an attempt to level the future—or, more precisely, to make history commensurate with the natural savageries, intellectual torpor, and material instincts of unextended man': 'We can interpret it as a voluntary exit from the Garden and a programmatic attempt to burn the Garden behind us' (Steiner, *IBC*, 42).

Steiner's classic culture, then, is essentially a temporally forward-looking Western European culture that, to his mind, ended itself in a perverse act of wish fulfilment around the time of World War II. A post-culture, by contrast, is characterised by 'stoic or ironic pessimism' that comes with the post-war knowledge of 'the inhuman potentialities of cultured man'. This goes somewhat further than the idea, familiar to scholars of Adorno, that there can be no poetry after Auschwitz. Indeed, for Steiner, what he saw as Western culture's collective ignorance that it could be capable of genocide on the scale of the Holocaust was 'an enabling programme for [pre-Holocaust] civilization'. In other words, ignorance was bliss. This is where things get problematic again and not a little messy: there is a nagging implication that Steiner is unwilling to fully accommodate the coexistence of two facts that should by no means be mutually exclusive. The first is the scale and horror of the systematic extermination of Jewish people during World War II and its undeniable impact on post-war culture on a global level. The second is that white Europeans had shown that they were clearly capable of either directly causing or systematically allowing the deaths of millions of subjugated people throughout the nineteenth century without causing any major disruptions to the 'order and symmetries of Western civilization' (Steiner, *IBC*, 48). On the contrary, that these people were killed or allowed to die was in the interests of maintaining and even furthering that same order. It is true that Steiner acknowledges that 'colonialism and the rapacities of empire' were enabling factors in what he calls 'the cultural predominance of the West'. However, he sees this as part of a different discussion altogether—that of 'the true nature of the relations between the production of great art and thought on the one hand and of régimes of violent and repressive order on the other'. Personally, I don't see the equivalence between the flourishing of Western art and literature against a backdrop of colonial subjugation, on the one hand, and the extent to which 'Stalinism [might be] the necessary condition for a Mandelstam' (Steiner, *IBC*, 54), on the other. For my taste, this is altogether too close to the kind of 'planetary imagination'[36] that does not interrogate the validity of asking the question: 'What kind of world are you willing to make, or at least tolerate, in order to get the kind of world that you want to make?'[37] Moreover, though it would be unfair to say that Steiner's view of colonialism is entirely apologist, he is also flamboyantly critical of what he calls the 'penitential hysteria' of those who 'have morally indicted the brilliance of their own past', sounding more and more like the kind of complacent neoliberal commentator who feels threatened by calls to rethink the uncritical commemoration of slave traders, brutally imperialist monarchs, or racist ex-Prime Ministers.[38] Nor are Steiner's objections a critique of white guilt: on the contrary, he sees white westerners' capacity to '[turn] in penitence to those whom they once enslaved' as 'a characteristically Western, post-Voltairian act' that is ultimately to their credit. Rather, for Steiner, to 'placate the furies of the present' by 'demean[ing] the past' is to 'soil that legacy of eminence which [...] we are invited to take part in, by our history, by our Western languages, by the carapace and, if you will, burden of our skins' (Steiner, *IBC*, 55). Steiner's choice of vocabulary at this juncture is hard to swallow: the echoes of Kipling are unmistakeable.[39]

That Friel was able to translate all this toxicity into something profoundly humane seems hard to believe, but translate it he did. If I were to be uncharitable, I would say that Friel's ability to sidestep Steiner's highbrow white supremacism owes something to what we would at the time of writing call a lack of intersectional thinking. Ireland's postcolonial status is complicated to say the least, and any attempt to connect the Irish experience of British colonial rule with a more global postcolonial discourse in which structural white supremacism looms large is to walk a fine line between productive solidarity and a potentially reductive overidentification. A similar but more actively harmful phenomenon can be observed in some of the more uninformed comparisons between the civil rights movements in Ireland and the USA. Indeed, in some cases, acknowledgement of a common experience of disenfranchisement has been problematically entangled with the unfounded equation of indentured servitude with chattel slavery, fostering a myth of Irish slavery. In short, there are instances where shared suffering results not in solidarity but in an unwillingness to recognise one's complicity in other kinds of suffering. It is an attitude perhaps best expressed in a scene from the first season of popular police procedural drama *Line of Duty*, in which the leader of an anti-corruption unit, accused by his subordinate of racial bias in his pursuit of a black officer with suspiciously good crime figures, invokes his experience as a Catholic officer in the Royal Ulster Constabulary: 'Don't you talk to me about victimisation. Nobody's blacker than me, son'.[40] Consequently, it would appear that Friel saw no issue with equating aspects of Irish-language culture with Steiner's euphemistic 'primitive' cultures of stasis that 'endure around truths immemorially posited' (Steiner, *IBC*, 104). If colonising cultures and 'classic' cultures are roughly equivalent, it would make sense for Friel to emphasise the difference in temporal outlooks between coloniser and colonised by depicting his hedge-school characters as having embraced 'mythological circularity' rather than forward motion. This is arguably what Friel achieves through the character of Jimmy Jack, who speaks of the protagonists of the Odyssey and the major Irish myth cycles as though they were all to be found drinking poitín at Anna na mBreag's. The complexity of the different cultural and temporal models evoked by Friel, however, suggests something far more interesting: a synthesis of source materials to which *In Bluebeard's Castle* is essential but that ultimately allows for a much more nuanced portrayal of cultural collapse than Steiner's. In the analysis that follows, the development of the characters of Yolland and Hugh will illustrate the process by which Friel came to create a play that dramatises the dying days of an Irish-speaking culture, using borrowed terminology but very much on its own terms.

The enterprise of consciousness

The question of how Friel combined his different sources is difficult to answer in terms of establishing a concrete timeline in which different influences acquired different weightings. This is largely because the chronology of Friel's encounters with his major source materials cannot easily be deduced from the available manuscripts: many of Friel's early notes for *Translations* are either entirely undated or omit the year in which they were written. The earliest fully dated note in MS 37,085/1 is from 22 November 1978. However, it was not until almost a year later on 5 November 1979 that, after several stops and starts, Friel was able to make the following note in his sporadic diary: 'The play, named *Translations*, completed'.[41] Between these certainties, there is a folder full of notes: some are loose; others are collated (by Friel) into various dated and undated booklets. Among the undated booklets are Friel's notes on both Steiner texts, *A Paper Landscape*, and *The Hedge Schools of Ireland*. There is, however, Friel's own account of the genesis of the play, first published in *The Crane Bag* in 1983 following a seminar at St. Patrick's College, Maynooth; it was later reprinted (rather tellingly) as 'Making a Reply to the Criticisms of *Translations* by J.H. Andrews' in 1999. Andrews, although decidedly tone deaf in places, concedes that the play is ultimately 'an extremely subtle blend of historical truth and—some other kind of truth'.[42] Friel, meanwhile, is genial but quietly defensive: 'Drama is first a fiction, with the authority of fiction'.[43] According to Friel, 'various nebulous notions' around the themes of the play had been 'visiting [...] and leaving' him '[f]or about five years' prior to writing *Translations*. 'During that time', he claims, he 'made two accidental discoveries': firstly, that his great-great-grandfather had been a hedge-schoolmaster who was 'fond of a drop'[44]; secondly, that he was living just across the river from the 'the first trigonometrical base for the ordnance survey',[45] led by one Colonel Thomas Colby. This, he claims, led to his reading of Dowling, Colby's *Memoir*, and the letters of John O'Donovan. In 1976—most likely, I would conjecture, by way of Roy Foster's review in the *TLS*—Friel encountered *A Paper Landscape*[46]:

> And suddenly here was the confluence—the aggregate—of all those notions that had been visiting me over the previous years: the first half of the nineteenth century: an aspect of colonialism; the death of the Irish language

and the acquisition of English. Here were all the elements I had been dallying with, all synthesized in one very comprehensive and precise text.[47]

Friel goes on to sketch his various abortive attempts to dramatise *A Paper Landscape* before '[f]inally and sensibly' abandoning it and 'embarking upon a play about a drunken hedge-schoolmaster'.

Although Friel's account seems reasonably plausible, it should nevertheless be taken with a pinch of salt. He was, after all, trying to vindicate himself and mollify Andrews by downgrading *A Paper Landscape* to a useful metaphor gratefully acknowledged, whilst simultaneously downplaying 'the tiny bruises inflicted on history in the play'.[48] By Friel's account, the reason that Colby, who had so fascinated him early on, ultimately appears only 'as a minor character called Captain Lancey', is essentially personal: apparently he simply gave up trying to remake history and wrote about his great-great-grandfather instead. Similarly, he claims to have abandoned a fuller portrayal of O'Donovan due to a sour taste left by 'a short-lived delusion' that O'Donovan was a perfidious 'quisling' (i.e. a collaborator) that was a result of 'the political situation in the North' being 'particularly tense about that time'. In other words, that O'Donovan instead 'appears [...] as a character called Owen'[49] is again portrayed as a consequence of his personal circumstances, i.e. living in the shadow of sectarian violence. Moreover, his characterisation of *Translations* as a play about a drunken hedge-schoolmaster, though true insofar as he grew increasingly convinced that the story should grow out of the character of the master,[50] has a hint of calculation in its self-deprecating, understated tone.

It is unsurprising, then, that Friel's account makes no mention of Steiner in the development of the play from an historical drama to something more character-driven. The seminar was, after all, concerned mostly with the play's historical contexts and the relationship between fiction and history. Furthermore, if Friel was constructing a defence against historical inaccuracy based on the personal, he was unlikely to bring Steiner into the mix. He may not even have had a strong sense of the role of Steiner's thinking in the development of his characters. However, there is sufficient archival evidence to suggest that *In Bluebeard's Castle* in particular played an important part in transforming Friel's characters from historical figures to something greater than the sum of their parts. In the case of George Yolland, the naively romantic Hibernophile, Friel's notes show a gradual but significant change in his approach to staging a British presence in nineteenth-century Ireland. This is roughly analogous to a shift away from the officers of Colby's *Memoir/A Paper Landscape* and an attendant move not so much towards the personal but rather towards a view of the nineteenth century more heavily influenced by Steiner.

Ironically for a play in which a name is never 'only a name' (Friel, *Pl*, 408), this development is often made difficult to track by 'the number and kind of name changes'[51] that appear in Friel's largely undated notes as he rebalanced the different elements of his work in progress. Examples of these changes include Hugh's two sons, who at one stage appear to have been encapsulated in a single character called Manus, who 'does an O'Donovan job'[52] whilst at the same time fulfilling the role of the lamed hedge-school monitor. Indeed, this only son of Hugh was still in play in an early handwritten draft of Act 2 Scene 1, functioning as a kind of Owen prototype with more Manus-like personal circumstances (and indeed Manus's disability).[53] Ultimately, Manus the Monitor, the Master's son, became two sons. The lame scholar who finds himself in a love-triangle with Maire was arguably merged with aspects of a largely undeveloped and mostly redundant[54] character called Felim—a Dowling-style hedge-school monitor who is 'precise', 'measured', and 'will succeed the master'[55]; the O'Donovan aspect of his character became Owen. The name Owen, meanwhile, is recycled from a character who, even in some of the earlier typed drafts, formed a kind of double-act with Doalty; the two occasionally feature in lists of dramatis personae as the Donnelly twins. In Friel's character notes for 'Doalty + Owen', the latter is described as a 'political theorist' in possession of 'knowledge of what the naming means', which he then '[a]rticulates [...] to Manus', i.e. the O'Donovan type.[56] It is to Manus proper, however—and, to a lesser extent, Yolland—that this political awareness is ultimately reassigned once the double-act is broken up. Confused? You should be: it's confusing.

A more superficially straightforward switch occurred in the case of Lieutenant George Yolland. That his name was changed from 'Lancey' can be attributed relatively simply to Friel's sense that 'Lancey's name [is] wrong'[57]—a note that appears in the front of a notebook in which he drafted and redrafted versions of Act 1. Nevertheless, the change does necessitate a little guesswork in places, and it can be slightly jarring at first to see Friel mulling over, say, the possibility of Maire being left pregnant by 'Lancey' in his notes.[58] What is clear, however, is that Yolland evolved out of what had been the dominant influences of Colby's *Memoir* and, increasingly, *A Paper Landscape* on in terms of the representation of the British. As Friel's own account of the composition process would suggest, there was a stage during which *Translations* was more obviously an attempt to dramatise *A Paper Landscape*. There are remnants of this phase of the play's development in an undated note headed 'Larcom's Story', in which a hedge-schoolmaster appears as a possible narrator:

> Caught between Colby + the local field-workers—all of whom are caught in turn between other pieties + pretenses [*sic.*].
> Art—politics—physical achievement—the end of a society—language.— 19th Century British drive—the exchange of cultural values of two totally different orders[.]

Though there is some ambiguity as to whether it is the schoolmaster or Larcom who is caught between Colby and the local field-workers, the heading 'Larcom's Story' is certainly suggestive in this respect. What is particularly fascinating about this passage is that it is indicative of the influence of Roy Foster's unmistakeably revisionist view of the Ordnance Survey as exemplifying 'two-way' 'cultural traffic', which is somewhat at odds with the play's ultimately anti-colonial stance. Foster's influence is also discernible in Friel's characterisation of Colby and Larcom: where Foster writes of Colby appearing 'alternately as an invincibly narrow-minded military commander and as a scientist of vision' in contrast to the 'dedicated and likeable [...] passionate [...] Hibernophile' Larcom,[59] Friel writes of '[Colby's] militarism ameliorated by Larcom, the Hibernophile'.[60] When Friel abandoned the idea of dramatising *A Paper Landscape*, however, what appears to have happened is that these contrasting attitudes were inherited by the characters who were to become Lancey and Yolland. Indeed, in an undated note headed 'Royal Engineers', in which Friel considered scaling down what was potentially a cast of multiple British characters to a representative binary, the two types bear a striking resemblance to Foster's characterisation of the clashing military and 'literary'[61] attitudes of Colby and Larcom, respectively:

> Perhaps the British presence in the area represented by only one or two men (an officer + an ordinary sapper); who live in a tent; who represent both British attitudes—the stern/militaristic + the enlightened officer.[62]

Though these attitudes undoubtedly went on to inform the Lancey and Yolland of the finished play, however, there is evidence in Friel's notes to suggest that Yolland in particular began to leave his assorted historical counterparts further and further behind. In fact, thanks to Friel's synthesis of sources, Yolland's status as an enlightened officer becomes less a redeeming feature than a key part of his complicity in what Friel would refer to in his notes as 'a domination by enlightenment'.[63]

In an undated page devoted to one 'George Lancey'—the Larcom figure who would become George Yolland—it is clear that this prototype of the young lieutenant still had one foot in *A Paper Landscape*. This Yolland prototype appears to be a combination of the '[h]uge, bubbling [...] lover's enthusiasms' and '[e]nraptured' Hibernophilia of the character's final incarnation and a Larcom-style zeal for the task to which he has been appointed: 'My aim—elegance, euphony, clarity, good taste, modern usage'. Unlike his counterpart in the finished play, this young officer is less concerned with looking backwards to Eden than looking forwards to Utopia: 'We're a pair, Manus! I'm no soldier! You're no farmer! We'll make a new world!' ('Manus' here refers to the O'Donovan type.). The 'William Yolland' who was to become Captain Lancey, meanwhile, is described in the same booklet as possessing 'a concept of himself as a participant in the enormous + exciting task of fashioning an Empire i.e. spreading a splendid modus vivendi + admirable vision'. What is significant here is that the contrast between the two earlier versions of these men is the nature of each man's undeniable passion for the job: the 'practical enthusiasm' of Colby/William Yolland/Captain Lancey is a foil to the 'spontaneous + ill-focused' zeal of Larcom/George Lancey/Lieutenant George Yolland, whose 'capacities for enthusiasm are available for whatever is at hand'.[64] By the time the play was finished, however, much of the Yolland prototype's more fervent dialogue relating to his job with the Survey was reassigned to the final version of Owen. In a note dated 9 May (year not given), for instance, an unnamed 'Lieutenant' is given the following speech:

> Let's be very precise about what we're doing: we're not killing Gaelic + replacing it with English. We are not standardizing. We are not rechristening. What we are doing is rescuing names (1) from confusion + finally oblivion + (2) giving them a permanence—their Gaelic permanence—your permanence—in English form; not English.

That this Lieutenant is a Yolland prototype is suggested by Friel's additions in red pen—'with Manus somewhere in 2–1'—which indicates a Larcom-type/O'Donovan-type scene in Act 2 Scene 1, at a time when the O'Donovan type was called Manus rather than Owen. However, the version of this speech that appears in the finished scene has Yolland take the exact opposite view:

> Owen   We're making a six-inch map of the country. Is there something sinister in that?
> Yolland Not in—
> Owen   And we're taking place-names that are riddled with confusion and—
> Yolland Who's confused? Are the people confused?
> Owen   —and we're standardizing those names as accurately and as sensitively as we can.
> Yolland Something is being eroded. (Friel, *Pl*, 420)

In other words, the final version of Yolland is fundamentally in disagreement with his more Larcom-like predecessor: the early Yolland sees the new names as giving permanence; the new Yolland sees the new names as eroding that permanence, albeit in ways he cannot quite articulate. Significantly, Yolland's talk of cultural erosion is a further instance of Friel's redistribution of dialogue. Indeed, an earlier draft of one of Hugh's most iconic speeches from Act 2 suggests that it was he who originally introduced the idea of erosion when speaking of the relative opulence of the Irish language:

> It is our response to mud cabins and a diet of potatoes; o[u]r only method of replying to . . . inevitabilities. Manus is content with that response. Owen thinks we are in stasis. I don't know. Perhaps we are already eroded.[65]

This would eventually be replaced by one of the play's most famous borrowings from *After Babel*: 'a civilization can be imprisoned in a linguistic contour that no longer matches the landscape of... fact' (Friel, *Pl*, 419).

The difference between 'we' and 'something' in terms of cultural erosion is vast and should not be overlooked: Hugh's choice of pronoun indicates that he is speaking as a member of a culture in crisis; Yolland's altogether shiftier pronoun positions him as an outsider who cannot get a fix on the object of the sentence. Moreover, when Hugh says 'we', he is the centre of a field of deictic reference that anchors him in place and opens up onto a vast 'theatrical space without'[66] that encompasses the whole of Ballybeg and beyond; when Yolland says 'something', he is anchored to nowhere. As other examples will make clear, Friel's embedding of Steiner's words in his play—in this case a variant on 'erosive standardizations' (Steiner, *AB*, 31) as found in *After Babel*—is more than a parroting of ideas: who says what and when is key to the creation and transformation of theatrical space. It is also essential to some of the detoxification of Steiner's more problematic ideas. Just as Yolland's sense of cultural erosion differs from Hugh's, so Hugh's evocation of *In Bluebeard's Castle* and its talk of so-called 'primitive' cultures in 'stasis' (Steiner, *IBC*, 104)—i.e. cultures whose values and temporal outlooks are not derived from a colonial model of progress—is fundamentally altered by his speaking as a member of such a society. Caught between the subjective certainties of his sons' cultural commentaries, this earlier Hugh's pomposity is tinged by genuine uncertainty. In many ways, the phasing out of this more honest Hugh is a loss to the play, insofar as his uncertainty underlines his position as someone whose cultural identity is being mapped out without his input.

To return, as Hugh might say, to Yolland, it seems clear to me that his development is more than a matter of his being assigned more political awareness than his Larcom-like predecessor. Rather it is indicative of the same alteration of temporal outlook indicated by Yolland's forward-looking, utopian zeal being replaced by a lazy fetishisation of what he sees as a more ancient way of life. Certainly, what passes for political awareness in Hugh's dialogue becomes tinged with a sense of infatuation with an idealised, bucolic past when reassigned to Yolland. He has a burgeoning sense of cultural erosion, but his appreciation of what that culture is bears more than a passing resemblance to an attitude that, for Steiner, contained within it the seeds of annihilation on an unprecedented scale. Specifically, Yolland's development is symptomatic of his having adopted some of the characteristics of Steiner's ennui-driven generation of Romantics in *In Bluebeard's Castle*. This is particularly evident in Yolland's speech in Act 2 Scene 1, in which he tells Owen of his family and how he came to work for the Survey. Yolland's father, for instance, embodies all the characteristics of what Steiner calls '*l'an un*' (Steiner, *IBC*, 18)—attributes he shares with Lancey:

> Born in 1789—the very day the Bastille fell. I've often thought maybe that gave his whole life its character. [. . .] He inherited a new world the day he was born—The Year One. Ancient time was at an end. The world had cast off its old skin. There were no longer any frontiers to man's potential. Possibilities were endless and exciting. [. . .] The Apocalypse is just about to happen[.] (Friel, *P1*, 416)

That this chimes so neatly with *In Bluebeard's Castle* is no accident. On the contrary, Friel's notes show that he regarded this Steiner text as providing a 'good description of the sense of the new dawn, of the future tense just being minutes away, of the world shedding its [...] skin, of the quickening of the pace of time felt, of the acceleration of the rhythm of consciousness, of endless + exciting possibilities':

> Could Yolland or Colonel—at first, in a long opening speech—personify this? This is why the country is being mapped. This is why English is vital. Etc. etc. Ancient time is at an end.[67]

This note indicates a merging of the colonialism of Colby's *Memoir* with Steiner's thinking on the character of nineteenth-century Europe. Though only a generation removed from people like the real Colby, the fictional Lancey, and indeed his father, Yolland is very much the embodiment of the 'ultimately destructive ripostes [...] of Romanticism' (Steiner, *IBC*, 24) in response to a 'brutal deceleration of time and radical expectation' (Steiner, *IBC*, 22). Indeed, his enthusiasm for rural Irish life is suggestive of a 'Romantic pastoralism' which 'is as much of a flight *from* the devouring city as [...] a return *to* nature' (Steiner, *IBC*, 24). His sense of 'experience being of a totally different order' (Friel, *P1*, 416), moreover, hints at 'Romantic exoticism, that longing for *le pays lointain*' (the faraway land), which is 'a hunger for new colours, new shapes, new possibilities of nervous discovery' (Steiner, *IBC*, 24). For Yolland, Baile Beag is indeed 'Eden' (Friel, *P1*, 422), and while he personally may not have burned the garden behind him when he left it, the play still ends with the smell of burning tents and the threat of famine in the air. This is in line with Friel's growing sense that the play was to do with *cultural* collapse, effectively combining Steiner and Dowling:

> I get a sense that what the play is really dealing with is the end of a culture (not a nation); the final stages of a Gaelic aristocracy; the beginning of standardisation in education + thought.

Certainly, for Friel, it was important that it be made clear that this was an 'enterprise [that] ends in a FAMINE'.[68]

The difficulties of establishing a timeline notwithstanding, Yolland emerges from Friel's notes as a more complex character than his frequent staging as a well-meaning stooge would suggest. Growing out of the idea of the enlightened officer in an age where enlightenment was often a euphemism for the imposition of the values of the coloniser, he also encapsulates a series of complex ideas drawn from across Friel's reading. Chief among these is the idea that it is not necessary to subscribe wholeheartedly to colonial values to do harm within the context of a colonial enterprise. This is something that might well emerge from an anti-colonial reading of Colby's *Memoir*, or indeed by bringing Andrews's characterisation of the British officers into dialogue with Dowling's views on the role of the English language in what Steiner would call 'erosive standardization'. It also emerges from a detoxification of *Bluebeard*, adopting its ideas of a failed narrative of progress as the basis of the inhuman, whilst avoiding Steiner's racism when it comes to a portrayal of cultures that do not share the transcendence values that come with such a narrative. Yolland may not care for the Survey, but his Hibernophilia is at least in part symptomatic of an attitude to perceived otherness that is an extension of the kind of existential boredom that, for Steiner, is the root cause of cultural collapse on a global scale. In this sense, he is less a Hibernophile than a Xenophile, perpetually enraptured with the new: he does not feel like he has stepped 'back into ancient time' (Friel, *P1*, 416); he feels like he is experiencing something radically *different*. Yolland is, fundamentally, 'a decent man' (Friel, *P1*, 422), but he still manages to bulldoze his way through a series of complex interpersonal and intercultural relationships he doesn't fully understand, and all in the name of a love of the exotic.

Crucially, as we have already seen with some of Yolland's dialogue, Friel's combination of sources is not only a reshuffling of ideas but also an at-times dramatic recontextualisation of speech. In this, the body is key: those who deliver borrowed words do so as bodied speakers in theatrical space, and a recontextualisation of words can change the dynamics of that space. This is particularly apparent in Friel's depiction of the process of recording entries in the book of names. This prop has only a superficial significance as a symbol of the imposition of the language of the coloniser upon the landscape of the colonised. Rather the book of names is a written record of transformations of theatrical space in a language that excludes the residents of Ballybeg from exercising their agency as bodied speakers. Through his use of staging in the naming scenes, Friel makes it clear from the outset that the naming of a place is fundamentally a speech act which 'occurs [...] as a corporeal event'[69] within a continuum of theatrical space, using the body of the speaker as the 'primary reference point' for the calculation and transformation of space. Indeed, he ensures that, interrupted though they are by the frequent comings and goings of Hugh, Manus, and various other locals, Owen and Yolland are the only two people ever onstage when a place is actively named. In the spoken act of naming, therefore, Owen and Yolland alone are the primary points of reference: they alone are able to transform theatrical space because they are at 'the *deictic centre* of speech' (italics in original).[70] For instance, when Yolland cries '[w]elcome to Eden', he indicates a deictic relationship between his own body and the ground on which it stands, which he names 'Eden' (Friel, *PI*, 422). This is what Herman, glossing Karl Bühler, refers to as 'deixis *am phantasma* modes as "transposed" types [that] can bring other deictic contexts located via imagination or memory, into the corporeal context of utterance [...] as if present and visible within it'.[71] The act of welcome implies that Yolland's occupancy of the theatrical space within is an ownership that predates the arrival of Manus, who at this point has just entered to find Owen and Yolland in a state of drunken euphoria. Owen's confirmation—'Eden's right!'—is both an affirmation that he shares this space and its ownership with Yolland, and that Eden is restricted to their immediate bodily surroundings in that it is characterised by acts of naming carried out by an exclusive 'we':

Owen   [...] We name a thing and—bang!—it leaps into existence!
Yolland Each name a perfect equation with its roots.
Owen   A perfect congruence with its reality. (Friel, *PI*, 422).

This dialogue, transposed almost word for word from *After Babel* (Steiner, *AB*, 58), is rendered demonstrably able to reconfigure the power dynamics of theatrical space when spoken aloud on a stage. Steiner's mostly impersonal prose, attached to the personal pronouns of *Translations*, allows Yolland and Owen to transform the theatrical space within to an Eden, while the theatrical space without is conjured into being through its being renamed.

This moment was particularly telling in Adrian Dunbar's direction in a 2013 production of the play at Derry's Millennium Forum, where his use of stage space highlighted Owen and Yolland's agency in the naming process. In this production, for the duration of Act II Scene 1, there was a washing-line onstage with a tent-like construction hanging from it, into which Yolland (Paul Woodson) disappeared periodically, most notably for the entire 'Tobair Vree' sequence (Friel, *Pl*, 420–1). Yolland was onstage and spoke, but only his legs were visible, sticking out of the 'tent'. Though he was, technically, onstage, he performed partial bodily absence, complementing perfectly his half-hearted, reluctant, mulish responses to Owen's insistence on the obscurity of the name Tobair Vree. It was only the shock of Owen's outburst that his name was not in fact Roland—arguably another Steiner moment—which caused Yolland's head to pop out of the 'tent' in surprise, followed shortly by the rest of his body. It was then as a fully active bodied speaker at the deictic centre of speech that Yolland was able to revel in the agency he shared with Owen as an active participant in the naming process, leading directly to his welcoming of Manus to 'Eden' (Friel, *Pl*, 422). By the end of the play, the exchanges between Owen and Hugh highlight the full extent to which the 'catalogue of names' as a document is emblematic of the lack of agency of the residents of Ballybeg, who have been excluded from the naming process. It is, fundamentally, the imposition of one form of archive over another—a privileging of the document that dooms Ballybeg's more performance-based form of archival memory— the spoken word—to oblivion.[72] Owen's telling apology—'nothing to do with us'—is an identification with his friends, family, and neighbours that comes too late. In this deictic context, 'us' is Owen, Hugh, and—by extension—the other residents of Ballybeg, but the damage done by the 'we' that is Yolland and Owen has already taken place.

This phenomenon of synthesis and embodiment through bodied speech is also apparent with the character of Hugh, who began to emerge as the dominant character of the piece as the play developed. Though his verbal tics are clearly lifted from Carleton, it is he and not any of the would-be historical figures who is ultimately granted the meatiest portions of Steiner's prose. This too is a product of Friel's move away from a more historical play. As a note dated 14 May makes clear, Friel had seriously considered giving Colby one of Hugh's most iconic speeches: 'Perhaps Colby will use the information in Steiner about (1) dying languages in small communities (2) the richness of the language is poor communities'.[73] He had also considered condensing similar ideas from Steiner in a speech given by the Monitor, by which it can be assumed he means the O'Donovan-type Manus who became two sons instead of one.[74]

That Friel considered multiple speakers as a means of embodying Steiner's ideas is highly suggestive: Friel, I would conjecture, wasn't just looking for a mouthpiece. Rather he was looking for ways in which Steiner's words as they are read might most effectively be translated into words as they are spoken by and through people. In Hugh's case, his embodiment of Steiner's words as a speaker in theatrical space places him at a cultural crossroads. Christopher Murray comes close to the crux of the matter when he says that 'Friel effectively divided Hugh in two', in that he is simultaneously 'a one-man chorus' whose 'knowledge of Steiner and of linguistics [...] ironically qualifies him as guide to the fall of a community' and a member of that community, with 'the ambivalence of a native Gaelic speaker towards the Ordnance Survey project'.[75] I would go further and suggest that Hugh also embodies the tensions between different possible characterisations of Irish culture, particularly in the context of Steiner. These are tensions, moreover, that are already brewing independently of the Ordnance Survey project. For Hugh, whose distaste for men like Daniel O'Connell and his advocacy for English is palpable, there is in fact a sense that his transcendence values are already being destabilised from within. Indeed, the idea that '[t]he old language is a barrier to modern progress' (Friel, *Pl*, 400) is one which privileges Steiner's 'classic' transcendence values over Taylor's 'repertoire' as a means of producing and reproducing cultural knowledge. More significantly still, Hugh is a means by which Friel is able to explore not only the crises of cultural identity that arise throughout the play, but also the degree to which it is possible to exercise forms of agency in the face of such crises. Steiner, in what is perhaps a casual choice of words, asserts that some cultures have '*chosen* stasis or mythological circularity over forward motion, and have endured around truths immemorially posited' (Steiner, *IBC*, 104, my italics). Through Hugh, Friel is able to emphasise this question of choice—though Hugh is perhaps one of the few residents of Ballybeg who is equipped to make one, given his multilingualism and high levels of literacy.

One of the most striking examples of this comes from late in the play, when Hugh recounts his abortive march to Sligo in the spring of 1798 as part of that year's Irish Rebellion against British rule.[76] Significantly, he does so using language borrowed from a passage in *Bluebeard*, in which Steiner evokes the quickening of 'the pace of felt time' that was 'unleashed' by the French Revolution:

> We lack histories of the internal time-sense, of the changing beat in men's experience of the rhythms of perception. But we do have reliable evidence that those who lived through the 1790s and the first decade and a half of the nineteenth-century, and who could recall the tenor of life under the old dispensation, felt that time itself and the whole enterprise of consciousness had formidably accelerated. (Steiner, *IBC*, 18)

Though Friel's notes suggest that 'Yolland—or Colonel' might 'personify this',[77] it is ultimately Hugh, and not one of the representatives of 'domination by enlightenment',[78] who speaks of '[t]he rhythms of perception' and '[t]he whole enterprise of consciousness accelerated', as he and Jimmy Jack marched forwards 'with pikes across their shoulders and the *Aeneid* in their pockets'. In other words, that they set out with the United Irishmen as part of a literal march of progress puts them in touch with a new sense of time—an alternative model of forward motion to that espoused by the colonising British (and, potentially, an alternative form of the transcendence values that go with it). In a rare moment for *Translations*, Irish culture is briefly posited as an extension of a larger, European 'classic' culture, not by virtue of a classical education, but through affinities between the attitudes stoking the French Revolution and the Irish Rebellion. Indeed, the classics here are not so much representative of Steiner's 'classic' cultures as they are metaphor for being caught at a crossroads. Hugh and Jimmy Jack embark on a military venture armed with a work of literature in which the heroes are the proto-Roman, proto-British Trojans; when they decide to abandon the march and return home, they identify instead as Greeks, 'homesick [...] like Ulysses' (Friel, *Pl*, 445), transitioning from the *Aeneid* in their pockets to Homer's *Odyssey*. Hugh's preference for Greco-Roman mythology is one that, whatever other significance it has, facilitates the expression of his having been caught between progress and stasis, expectation and memory, going and staying. And yet there is some agency to be recovered here, even though Hugh recognises the no-win nature of his current situation. That they got only as far as Glenties in 1798 before turning back to 'older, quieter things' (Friel, *Pl*, 446) represents an active decision to embrace their existing sense of time. It is a subtle affirmation of the fact that, for Hugh at least, the choice of 'mythological circularity over forward motion' (Steiner, *IBC*, 104) is a conscious one. This speech is almost immediately followed by Hugh resolving aloud to teach Maire English (Friel, *PI*, 446)—another, altogether braver choice for the present moment that is again a reworking of Steiner. This time, Steiner's statement in *After Babel* that 'all communication "interprets" between privacies' (Steiner, *AB*, 198) is recast as a question that casts it into doubt: 'I will provide you with the available words and the available grammar. But will that help you to interpret between privacies? I have no idea' (Friel, *PI*, 446).

Hugh's resolution to press on through the medium of English is all the more courageous given his realisation that his community is one in which language itself has become devalued, and can, therefore, provide no guarantee of survival. It is an attitude, in fact, that Steiner might have considered characteristic of a post-cultural society:

> If a *dur désir de durer* was the mainspring of classic culture, it may well be that our post-culture will be marked by a readiness not to endure rather than curtail the risks of thought.

For Steiner, this aspect of the post-cultural applies only to 'classic' Western cultures for whom language is a means of attempting to achieve a kind of afterlife. He juxtaposes this explicitly with societies that 'have endured around truths immemorially posited' (Steiner, *IBC*, 106). Through Hugh, Friel seems to suggest that the two are by no means mutually exclusive: Hugh may personally have made a choice to return to his own microcosmic mythological circularity, but in a wider context his is still a society that is affected by the devaluation of language. In other words, through Hugh, Friel seems to suggest that it is not only temporally forward-looking post-cultures but also temporally non-linear cultures in a state of collapse which must abandon their language-based transcendence values in favour of embracing the quasi-suicidal impulse to pursue future truths even unto their own destruction. And when language is devalued, it is not only the documentary archive that is destabilised, but also the embodied archive: neither can find meaning in the word 'always' because there is always the possibility that, even if a language continues to be read or spoken for centuries, it can be corrupted beyond its reliability as a form of transcendence.

Hugh's interactions with the name-book are particularly revealing. In the closing moments of the play, there are telling deictic relationships being established. Following Friel's stage directions, Hugh, '*Indicating the Name-Book*' (italics in original), determines: 'We must learn those new names'. In his scripted gesture, 'those' names are located unambiguously in the pages of the book through deictic referencing. Here, Hugh is establishing a spatial relationship not with the wider unseen parish offstage but with an onstage representation of the documentary archive: his determination to 'learn where we live' (Friel, *P1*, 444) is an acknowledgement that home also exists officially on paper. Prior to this, moreover, not only does Friel stage an archival encounter with a written document in which Hugh engages with practices of access, but he also stages a practice of memorisation that is the first step towards Hugh being able to participate in those iterative acts of knowing and transmitting knowledge that make up Taylor's repertoire. Hugh's gesture towards 'those' names, then, indicates a tangible relationship between the (Irish) names in his head and the (English) names on paper. It is a relationship between two repositories of transmissible knowledge—the document and the performing body—that might yet be bridged through bodily practices of learning, remembering, and transmitting. However, as his faltering final recitation makes clear, Hugh is not equipped to deal with the future he is trying to accommodate: he is trying to be a one-man repository of remembered knowledge for a community that is barely literate and officially powerless, and his memory is failing.

The disenfranchisement of the residents of Ballybeg is more than the imperialistic imposition of documentary archive logic (the book of names, the OS map) on a culture whose spokesperson, Hugh, claims to be given to more performance-based acts of transmission. By focusing on the Anglocentric renaming procedure itself as embodied practice—as an iterative process requiring bodily presence/participation—it is possible rather to speak of a double disenfranchisement. Indeed, the residents of Ballybeg (apart from the O'Donnell family) are not only excluded from the means of accessing the official record of the new colonial nomenclature of their own landscape, but also from the *process* of 'standardisation': they are denied access to both archival and embodied ways of knowing.

That Friel's characters embody his synthesis of Steiner in particular as bodied speakers as part of these processes transforms Friel's borrowings into something greater than the sum of their parts. Steiner's talk of '*erosive* standardization' (Steiner, *AB*, 31) is transformed from astute insider commentary from outside the standardisation process (Hugh's '[p]erhaps we are already eroded'[79]) to the half-formed misgivings of the subtly destructive Romantic outsider within it ('Yolland's [s]omething is being eroded' (Friel, *Pl*, 420)). Indeed, the recontextualisation of Friel's intertexts over the composition process effectively redraws the lines between not only endogamy and exogamy (themselves terms borrowed from Steiner) but also between spaces within a continuum of theatrical space. Eden is not offstage elsewhere but rather the ground on which Yolland and Owen stand in the moment of engaging with the process of renaming a given place. Steiner's images of the past that '[rule] us' (Steiner, *IBC*, 13) become images and facts 'embodied in language' that 'shape' (Friel, *Pl*, 445) us; his words are spoken by a man who indicates a book of names and identifies it as one of multiple places where Ballybeg exists in words. Indeed, it also exists as words spoken by those who remember them, and words spoken on a stage in order to indicate the wider imagined parish in the wings. Statements become questions as the ability of language to interpret between privacies becomes an area of doubt and uncertainty; in this way, they undermine Steiner's racist distinction between what he sees as civilised and primitive cultures by outlining how a devaluing of language affects the transcendence values of both.

Friel's synthesis of source materials in *Translations*, then, is a 'story [...] told through people'.[80] Both in the development of key characters as different sources gained more influence in Friel's mind, and in the way Friel's intertexts function as spoken words on a stage, it is clear that these borrowings are far from straightforward transpositions when it comes to their effect on the play in performance. Words in the mouths of the powerful mean different things to the same words in the mouths of the disempowered; the revolutionary spirit of the long eighteenth century has different connotations for the xenophilic young British officer than it does for the young Irish classicist of 1789; 'I am Roland' and '*My name is not Roland*' (Friel, *Pl*, 421) are superficially diametrically opposed but functionally the same.

On 3 May 1979, Friel wrote the following note to self: 'The play must grow out of the character of the master + his relationship with the others. If it doesn't, if it is a thesis about language or colonisation or famine, then scrap it'.[81] Though Friel's emphasis on the Hugh character became less pronounced over time, the idea of character-driven drama remained front and centre of Friel's process throughout his career. Where he lost sight of this, his plays faltered; where he kept this in mind, they flourished. What the composition process for *Translations* shows—and indeed the process for many of Friel's other successful plays—is that this does not mean he was not also, at some level, a playwright of ideas. It is true that Friel would chide himself, sometimes harshly, for neglecting to put people first. As he wrote whilst working on *The Mundy Scheme* (1969), which is notable for having a decent satirical notion at its core but being otherwise lamentable: '??? Isn't this ideas—not people ????'[82] Nevertheless, Friel's richest plays are where he allows his intellectual eclecticism to inform his writing in ways that are fundamentally character-driven, recontextualising ideas as spoken dialogue in the mouths of people whose interpersonal power dynamics are complex and mutable. There are many reasons why *Translations* is among Friel's most enduring plays; the combinations, recombinations, and transformations of his many and ideologically various sources as embodied by and through his characters is surely one of them.

Notes

1. Dublin, National Library of Ireland (NLI), Brian Friel Papers (BFP), MS 37,085/1.
2. Vimala Herman, 'Deixis and Space in Drama', *Social Semiotics 7*, No. 3 (1997), pp. 269–283 (p. 269).
3. Herman, p. 277.
4. Herman, p. 280.
5. Hanna Scolnicov, *Woman's Theatrical Space* (Cambridge: Cambridge University Press, 1994), p. 3, cited in Herman, p. 270.
6. Diana Taylor, *The Archive and the Repertoire: Performing Cultural Memory in the Americas* (Durham and London: Duke University Press, 2003), p. 8.
7. Taylor, p. xvii.
8. Brian Friel, 'Extracts from a Sporadic Diary (1979): *Translations*', in Christopher Murray, ed., *Brian Friel: Essays, Diaries, Interviews: 1964–1999* (London: Faber and Faber, 1999), pp. 73–79, (p. 74).
9. See Helen Lojek, 'Brian Friel's Plays and George Steiner's Linguistics: Translating the Irish', *Contemporary Literature 35*, No. 1 (1994), pp. 83–99.
10. Martine Pelletier, *Le Théâtre de Brian Friel: histoire et histoires* (Villeneuve d'Ascq: Presses Universitaires du Septentrion, 1997), p. 168.
11. Christopher Murray, *The Theatre of Brian Friel: Tradition and Modernity* (London: Bloomsbury, 2014), p.110.

12. Brian Bonner, *Our Inis Eoghain Heritage: The Parishes of Culdaff and Cloncha* (Baile Átha Cliath: Foilseacháin Náisiúnta Teoranta, 1972), p. 147. See also NLI, BFP, MS 37,085/1. Note towards *Translations* dated 16 May [1979].
13. It is always to be assumed that Friel's reading may have been wider than the archive suggests. For instance, J.H. Andrews mentions *Letters concerning information relative to the antiquities of the county of Donegal collected during the progress of the Ordnance Survey in 1835* (1928), edited by M. O'Flanagan. Andrews also mentions that 'Friel is known to have requested assistance from the map department of the National Library of Scotland'. See J.H. Andrews, 'Notes for a Future Edition of Brian Friel's "Translations"', *The Irish Review (Cork)* 13, Autobiography as Criticism (Winter 1992/1993), 93–106, p. 104.
14. J. H. Andrews, *A Paper Landscape: The Ordnance Survey in Nineteenth-Century Ireland* (Dublin: Four Courts Press, 2006), p. 19. Further references in parentheses in the text as 'Andrews, *APL*'.
15. Brian Friel, 'Making a Reply to the Criticisms of *Translations* by J. H. Andrews (1983)', in Murray, ed., *Brian Friel: Essays, Diaries, Interviews*, pp. 116–119 (p. 118).
16. Thomas Colby, *Memoir of the City and North Western Liberties of Londonderry: Parish of Templemore* (Dublin: Hodges and Smith, 1837), p. 7.
17. Colby, p. 6.
18. Colby, p. 7.
19. Colby, p. 26.
20. Colby, p. 17.
21. Colby, p. 24.
22. Brian Friel, *Plays One* (London: Faber and Faber, 1996), p. 420. Further references in parentheses in the text as 'Friel, *P1*'.
23. Colby, p. 8.
24. NLI, BFP, MS 37,085/1. Note towards *Translations* dated 27 May [1979].
25. *LETTERS Containing information relative to the ANTIQUITIES of the COUNTY OF DONEGAL Collected during the progress of the ORDNANCE SURVEY in 1835*, reproduced under the direction of Rev. Michael O'Flanagan (Bray, 1927), typescript copy made in the Courthouse, Lifford by Edward MacIntyre under the

supervision of Andrew MacIntyre (County Librarian), September 1946, p. 143, in NLI, BFP, MS 37,085/6. Further references in parentheses in the text as 'O'Donovan'.
26. Taylor, p. 19.
27. Patrick J. Dowling, *The Hedge Schools of Ireland* (Dublin: Talbot Press, 1935), p. 11. Further references in parentheses in the text.
28. George Orwell, *Nineteen Eighty-Four* (Oxford: Oxford University Press, 2021), p. 192.
29. Thomas Francis Meagher, *Meagher of the Sword: Speeches of Thomas Francis Meagher in Ireland 1840–1848*, ed. by Arthur Griffith (Dublin: M. H. Gill & Son, 1916), p. 287. Cited in Dowling, p. 113.
30. William Carleton, *Traits and Stories of the Irish Peasantry*, Fourth edition. Vol. II. (Dublin: William F Wakeman, 1836), p. 224. Cited in Dowling, p. 60.
31. See Genesis 11: 1–9.
32. George Steiner, *After Babel: Aspects of Language and Translation* (Oxford: Oxford University Press, 1976), p. 18. Further references in parentheses in the text as 'Steiner, *AB*'.
33. Steiner is speaking here of radio and television.
34. George Steiner, *In Bluebeard's Castle: Some Notes Towards the Redefinition of Culture* (London: Faber and Faber, 1971), p. 13. Further references in parentheses in the text as 'Steiner, *IBC*'.
35. Lee Edelman, *No Future: Queer Theory and the Death Drive* (Durham and London: Duke University Press, 2004), p. 4.
36. Lisa Messeri, *Placing Outer Space: An Earthly Ethnography of Other Worlds*, Experimental Futures (Durham: Duke University Press, 2016), p.12, cited in Fred Scharmen, *Space Forces: A Critical History of Life in Outer Space* (London: Verso, 2021), p. 9.
37. Scharmen, pp. 91–2.
38. I am thinking particularly of the spate of toppled and defaced statues of figures such as Edward Colston in Bristol, King Leopold II in Belgium, and Winston Churchill in London during the Black Lives Matter protests following the murder of George Floyd in Minneapolis by white police officer Derek Chauvin on 25 May 2020.
39. Rudyard Kipling's poem 'The White Man's Burden' (1899) exhorts imperialist colonial powers to take up what he sees as the moral obligation of 'civilising' people of colour.

40. Jed Mercurio, 'Episode 1', *Line of Duty*, BBC1, 26 June 2012.
41. Brian Friel, 'Extracts from a Sporadic Diary (1979): *Translations*', in Murray, ed., *Brian Friel: Essays, Diaries, Interviews*, pp. 73–78 (p. 77).
42. Brian Friel, John Andrews, and Kevin Barry, 'Translations and A Paper Landscape: Between Fiction and History', *The Crane Bag 7*, No. 2 (1983), 118–24 (p. 122).
43. Brian Friel, 'Making a Reply to the Criticisms of *Translations* by J. H. Andrews (1983)', in *Brian Friel: Essays, Diaries, Interviews*, ed. by Murray, pp. 116–119 (p. 119).
44. Friel, 'Making a Reply to the Criticisms of *Translations* by J. H. Andrews', p. 116.
45. Friel, 'Making a Reply to the Criticisms of *Translations* by J. H. Andrews', p. 117.
46. Friel makes reference to Foster's review in MS 37,085/1.
47. Friel, 'Making a Reply to the Criticisms of *Translations* by J. H. Andrews', p. 117.
48. Friel, 'Making a Reply to the Criticisms of *Translations* by J. H. Andrews', p. 118. Andrews didn't buy it: in the early 1990s, he would go on to publish a series of corrections to the play's inaccuracies in which he was far more vocal about 'the credulity shown by serious scholars in swallowing *Translations* as a record of historical truth or at any rate historical probability'. See Andrews, 'Notes for a Future Edition of Brian Friel's "Translations"', p. 93.
49. Friel, 'Making a Reply to the Criticisms of *Translations* by J. H. Andrews', p. 118.
50. NLI, Brian Friel Papers, MS 37,085/1. Note towards *Translations* dated 3 May [1979].
51. Anthony Roche, *Brian Friel: Theatre and Politics* (Basingstoke: Palgrave Macmillan, 2011), p. 137.
52. NLI, BFP, MS 37,085/1. Undated note towards *Translations* headed 'Manus (who does an O'Donovan job)'.
53. NLI, MS 37,085/2.
54. To a sparse, undated note headed 'Felim', Friel added in pencil 'WHY HAVE HIM?'. See NLI, MS 37,085/1.
55. NLI, BPF, MS 37,085/1. Undated note towards *Translations* headed 'Felim'.
56. NLI, MS 37,085/1. Undated note towards *Translations* headed 'Doalty + Owen'.

57. NLI, MS 37,085/2.
58. NLI, MS 37,085/1, pencil note dated 18 June [1979?].
59. Roy Foster, 'View from the Monument', *Times Literary Supplement*, 6 February 1976, p. 8.
60. NLI, MS 37,085/1. Undated note towards *Translations*.
61. Foster, p. 8.
62. NLI, MS 37,085/1. Undated; appears in a treasury-tagged booklet marked 'B', dated 'March–April 1979' but containing notes dated up to and including '12 May [1979]'.
63. NLI, Brian Friel Papers, MS 37,085/1. Undated note towards *Translations*.
64. NLI, MS 37,085/1. Undated note towards *Translations*. The 'Manus' referred to here is the O'Donovan type and Owen prototype mentioned in the same character booklet.
65. MS 37,085/2.
66. Scolnicov, p. 3, cited in Herman, p. 270.
67. MS 37,085/1. Undated note towards *Translations* in booklet titled 'Bluebeard's Castle'.
68. MS 37,085/1. Note towards *Translations* dated 24 April [1979].
69. Herman, p. 272.
70. Herman, p. 273.
71. Herman, p. 274.
72. See Taylor, above.
73. NLI, BFP, MS 37,085/1. Note towards *Translations* dated 14 May [1979].
74. NLI, BFP, MS 37,085/1. Undated note towards *Translations* in booklet labelled 'Steiner', p. 2.
75. Murray, *The Theatre of Brian Friel*, p. 113.
76. This may be a reference to the Battle of Collooney, which took place on 5 September 1798. Whether this spring march to Sligo was a mistake on Friel's part or another instance of Hugh's faulty memory is unclear.
77. NLI, Brian Friel Papers, MS 37,085/1. Undated note towards *Translations* in booklet titled 'Bluebeard's Castle'.
78. NLI, Brian Friel Papers, MS 37,085/1. Undated note towards *Translations*.
79. MS 37,085/2.
80. NLI, Brian Friel Papers, MS 37,085/1. Undated note towards *Translations*.

81. NLI, BFP, MS 37,085/1. Note towards *Translations* dated 3 May [1979], bracketed in green pen.
82. NLI, BFP, MS 37,062/1. Undated note towards *The Mundy Scheme*. Blue felt tip pen, outlined in a box.

CHAPTER 4

Form and Core: Brian Friel and Denis Donoghue

Friel's enduring popularity also owes a great deal to the subtlety of his experimentation in his mature work. Where the composition processes of earlier plays such as *The Loves of Cass McGuire* (1966) were more overtly indebted to the Pirandellian wing of the early twentieth-century avant-garde, Friel's later plays are notable for wearing their formal experiments lightly. However, whilst Friel's dramatic works remain character-driven and accessible on the whole, it would also be true to say that not since his first pre-*Philadelphia* forays into drama has there been an unambiguously naturalistic original Friel play. This, I would suggest, is due to the idiosyncrasies of a composition process in which the relationship between what Friel called the 'core' of a given play and its form was consciously explored, often giving rise to experimentation. Here I examine the genesis of two of Friel's less successful plays, *The Communication Cord* (1982) and *Wonderful Tennessee* (1993). Although discussed and indeed revived less frequently than other plays, these are notable for two things. Firstly, they are prime illustrations of the way in which Friel worked to give the core of a play formal expression through subtle innovation (and indeed what happened when he failed to be true to his own process). Secondly, they are both heavily indebted to the works of scholar and literary critic Denis Donoghue, whose status as one of Friel's major literary influences is revealed by the contents of the Brian Friel Papers. In this way, the writing

© The Author(s), under exclusive license to Springer Nature Switzerland AG 2023
Z. Kuczyńska, *Brian Friel's Models of Influence*,
https://doi.org/10.1007/978-3-031-17905-1_4

of these plays gives a crucial insight into a vital aspect of Friel's creative practice whilst recovering a major source for his work.

WHERE IS THE CRISIS?

Although I use the terms 'form' and 'core' in this chapter, Friel's own vocabulary for the crux or animating theme of a given play and its manifestation as theatre changed over the years. In Friel's earlier plays, this relationship was relatively unarticulated. Nevertheless, he had an early habit of writing important insights about a play in capital letters and occasionally (if not explicitly) suggesting appropriate related formal devices or '[t]echniques'.[1] For instance, his notes for *Philadelphia* contain the following upper-case statement:

> EVERYBODY
> WANTS
> SOMETHING
> ―――――――――――――――――
> TRIES TO STATE IT.
> ―――――――――――――――――
> CAN'T.
> ――――――――――――――――― [2]

This is something close to the heart of the matter, and is intimately linked to the device of Gar Private, who makes manifest that which cannot be stated by Gar Public. Similarly, Friel's notes for *The Loves of Cass McGuire* contain capitalised statements such as:

> WE LIVE AMONG STRANGERS WHO NEVER SUSPECT THE TRUTH.
> AND WHICH—DREAM OR ACTUALITY—IS THE TRUTH?[3]

Elsewhere in the MS, Friel writes down what he sees as the two 'THEMES' of the play in red ink:

> THE NEW IRISH—TALBOT PARK—THE BEGINNINGS OF SPIRITUAL WANT.
> THE REALITY OF DREAMS—(BECAUSE OF THE IMPOSSIBILITY OF LOVE).[4]

This idea of the New Irish was one that plagued Friel throughout the sixties and which he never dealt with entirely successfully. The New Irish, or so Friel thought, had made 'substantial progress on the material plane' at the cost of 'a corresponding diminution in feeling, perception + sensitivity'.[5] This feeling would find its most scathing expression in *The Mundy Scheme* (1969), a play that suffered when Friel apparently failed to take his own advice when the composition process caused him to observe: 'It seems that an obstacle arises when you try to write without love—or at least without concern'.[6] In the case of *Cass*, Friel did, in fact, heed his own warning:

> Do not write about the New Irish
>   if you do not understand them.
> Do not write about the New Irish
>   if your purpose is to expose them.
> Do not write about the New Irish
>   if you do not love them.[7]

Cass's Irish family in their comfortable home consequently took a back seat. However, the second theme was one that appears to have driven some of Friel's thinking about form. It is true that many of his ideas for the play owe a great deal to Pirandello: 'The writer creates these characters, but once they are written—as in SIX CHARACTERS—they have a life of their own'. Nevertheless, there is also an extent to which Friel's thinking on dreams and reality informed some of his more overtly non-naturalistic ideas for staging: 'What about masks for the dream people—cast economy + also conveying the concept that all our dreams are the same'.[8]

Perhaps the first early play in which Friel successfully matched the play's core themes with their formal expression was *Lovers: Winners* (1967). It is in these notes that Friel asks himself not what the 'core' of the play is but rather the following: 'If conflict is the essence of drama where is the conflict here?'[9] This refers somewhat clunkily to the Aristotelian idea that 'agon' (ἀγών) or conflict is a driving narrative force. Elsewhere in the MS, he asks himself again: 'What is the crisis? What conflict?' Answering his own question, Friel writes, in a passage subsequently marked 'N.B.':

> The crisis of acceptance; the turmoil of fusing fact + fancy into a liveable whole; the crisis of making-do + of making believe that making-do is great.

The courage + spirit that such a synthesis requires. The almost breaking down – and laughing instead.[10]

Although Friel flirted extensively with a more Pirandellian approach in his notes, this 'synthesis' of 'fact + fancy' was ultimately given formal expression by Friel's use of Ardnageeha, 'the Hillside where the young couple have always gone', as 'the anchor location' of the play. From here, Mag and Joe 'talk sporadically; and reflect; and look into the future; and wonder what is happening now down in the town'.[11] In this respect, Ardnageeha anchors the two teens in the here and now as their imaginations take them forwards and backwards in time and space and into flights of 'fancy'. This grounding function is the key to its significance, and it is for this reason perhaps that Friel's stage directions recommend a non-naturalistic approach to the play's *only stage furniture*: '*I would suggest a large pentagonal platform, approached by four or five shallow steps all round*'.[12] Indeed, the hillside location is the site of what Vimala Herman (glossing Karl Bühler) calls '"transposed" types' of deixis that are capable of 'bring[ing] other deictic contexts located via imagination or memory, into the corporeal context of utterance [...] as if present and visible within it'.[13] It is the place from which bodied speakers are able to effect imagined transformations of space. Hence Mag and Joe's cathartic, crazy '*pantomime*',[14] in which the story of the signing of the lease of their new flat—which looks out into the yard of a slaughterhouse—turns into a play-acted killing spree in which the two teenagers gun down an absent cast of authority figures. Joe, dragged from his school life, takes aim at 'a bullock that looks like the president of Saint Kevin's' as he cries 'Drag 'em away!'; Mag, anticipating a c-section, sets her sights on '[a] sheep the image of Sister Paul' and roars 'Slice 'em open!'.[15] '*Ardnageeha, the hill that overlooks the town of Ballymore*',[16] becomes the flat with the '[f]inest view in town'[17]; the town becomes the slaughterhouse yard. Thus Friel's choice of staging allows for the play's driving conflict to be expressed insofar as it provides a location in which the two teenagers attempt 'to fuse fact + fancy into a liveable whole'.[18] This conflict is exacerbated by the presence of the play's two Commentators, whose allegedly factual account of proceedings cannot ultimately be reconciled with the action that takes place on Ardnageeha.

By the early 1970s, Friel had begun to write in terms of a play's core rather than its conflict alone, though the two were still demonstrably related in his mind. For instance, when making his notes for *Volunteers*

(1975), Friel writes: 'the dramatic friction must come from the interaction of site-workers among themselves + with management. And the development (?) of character will be seen only in this context'. The note continues: 'And could this core find its centre on the discovery of a skeleton?'[19] However, Friel would not be consistent in using this term until his plays of the early 1980s, when he began to think in terms of a play's 'core'. (In later plays, he would also refer to the play's 'spring' or 'engine'.)[20] In Friel's notes for *The Communication Cord* (1982), for instance, Friel was explicit in his aims:

1. To establish a strong thematic core
2. To illustrate it with a theatrical device.[21]

In these two statements, I would suggest, lies a key aspect of Friel's artistic practice, and one that can be applied to ways of working that are observable throughout his writing career.

THE COMMUNICATION CORD

The Communication Cord (1982) is not one of Friel's strongest plays. Functioning on a surface level as an attempted antidote to the pieties heaped on *Translations* (1980), it was hailed in the first instance as a 'wickedly funny farce'.[22] By the time of its Hampstead revival of 1983, however, it was being dismissed as 'a play that sets up a huge mechanical contrivance to make some fairly basic points about the sentimental plundering of the Irish past'.[23] Both reviews do the play's complexity an injustice, particularly regarding Friel's use of source materials that blended contemporary linguistic theory with literary essays on language and communication. Indeed, Friel's influences included a review of Erving Goffman's *Forms of Talk* (1981) in the *TLS* by Roy Harris (featuring a line from the other Francis Bacon); a review of George A. Miller's *Language and Speech* by Stuart Sutherland; David Mamet's essay 'A National Dream Life'; and Denis Donoghue's *Ferocious Alphabets* (1981). Nevertheless, 'contrivances' do abound, thanks chiefly to Friel's painting-by-numbers approach to farce.

The play's protagonist, Tim Gallagher, is '*a junior lecturer without tenure in a university*',[24] who is writing a thesis on 'Discourse Analysis with Particular Reference to Response Cries' (Friel, *CC*, 18), thereby providing a convenient mouthpiece for Harris's glossing of Goffman. Tim, we learn, is making use of his friend Jack's restored thatched cottage for an hour in order to impress his girlfriend Susan's father, Senator Doctor Donovan—another New Irish authority figure in the mould of *Philadelphia*'s Senator Doogan. The cottage is '*accurate of its time (from 1900 to 1930)*' to the point of being '*too "authentic"*' and '*is in fact a restored house, a reproduction, an artefact of today making obeisance to a home of yesterday*' (Friel, CC, 11). However, this simple ruse is complicated by the fact that Tim's ex-girlfriend, Claire Harkin, is already in the cottage when they arrive. This snag is unbeknownst to Jack, who expects to be entertaining a French woman named Evette later that evening (hence the necessity of Donovan's visit being a brief one). Other come-and-go characters move the farce towards its chaotic conclusion. One is Barney the Banks, a German stereotype who owns and lives in a caravan nearby. Jack impersonates Barney later in the play, intending to impress the Senator further by offering him a fortune to buy the house. Another is Nora Dan, '*[a] country woman who likes to present herself as a peasant*' (Friel, CC, 22) and who is '[c]onvinced this house is legally hers' (Friel, CC, 21). Over the course of the evening, as mistaken identities proliferate, the characters become hapless victims of their location. Following multiple malignant cascades of soot from the fireplace and an ongoing problem with a lamp-extinguishing draught, first Donovan and then Jack become clamped in the cow chains which are a period feature of the cottage; Nora Dan sprains her ankle and confines herself to the cottage. At the end of the play, Claire and Tim literally bring the house down with a rekindling embrace as they lean against an unstable roof support, presumably killing or seriously injuring those who are left inside.

This ruined farce has little warmth for its characters and even less mercy. It is this deficit of character-driven drama perhaps that makes *The Communication Cord* an unappealing play that sits slightly awkwardly on its intellectual foundations. In the words of the renaissance philosopher Francis Bacon, as quoted by Harris, 'talk [is] but a tinkling cymbal, where there is no love'[25]; it feels as though there's little love lost between Friel and his creations in *The Communication Cord*. Nevertheless, the composition process of the play is useful for highlighting Friel's methodology in terms of the relationship between form and core, in spite of (and even perhaps because of) his apparent failure to honour his own process in this case. In fact, the play's problems arguably stem from Friel's commitment to a predetermined form before having determined the play's core.

In a stark contrast to plays like *Faith Healer* (1979), whose characters and formal devices emerged from the process of Friel's engagement with his source materials, in turn generating a thematic core that was greater than the sum of its parts, *The Communication Cord* was already more or less bound to a form before Friel had a clear idea of the core of the play. Indeed, what emerges from Friel's composition process for this play is a picture of an incomplete synthesis of source materials, producing a fragmented thematic core inhabiting an inhibiting structure.

For all its thematic richness, *The Communication Cord* is a play that ultimately suffered from Friel having put the cart before the horse. This is evident from the play's relatively short composition process. On 16 October 1981, Friel floated two ideas for a new play. One was 'The O'Neill idea', which presumably became *Making History* (1988) some years later; the other was a plot in which '[t]wo couples—univ. lecturer + wife and their friends' are 'renting again the Donegal cottage after 7 years and digging up (never doing it) the time capsule'.[26] A third option was added to the mix on 8 November 1981: 'Lough Derg notion. (With day/night?)'[27] This would ultimately become *Wonderful Tennessee*, a play that was almost ten years in the making. The 'day/night' to which Friel refers becomes clear in a subsequent note from the same day, in which he considered an extension of the cottage plot: 'Using, perhaps, the Chinese technique of day/night—light/darkness. (Read Shaffer's "Black Comedy").'[28] Here, Friel makes reference to Peter Shaffer's one-act farce of 1965, in which the lighting scheme is reversed so that a previously darkened stage is plunged into full illumination during a power cut. Less than a week later on 13 November, Friel was seriously entertaining the possibility of utilising the conventions of farce as a means of providing a structure for the play, as is evident from his quoting a fragment of the entry on farce from *The Reader's Encyclopedia of World Drama*: 'Somebody has to be somewhere shortly.....—visitors are due to arrive—people will meet who mustn't meet... the hero gets pulled desperalety [*sic.*] into a catastrophe...'[29] This source would go on to inform his entire approach to farce.

The trouble with Friel's recourse to the *Reader's Encyclopedia* to generate a form is not one of snobbery but rather one of his having failed to answer some of the important questions that he himself had raised before moving forward. On 10 November 1981, Friel asked himself:

> What is the drama of the situation?

> What has it to do with the cottage, the attempts at resuscitating [*sic.*] a culture, at journeying into the past, at the past stalking the present?[30]

On the next page of this treasury-tagged booklet of notes, Friel asked himself a follow-up question: 'What is the relationship between the Now and the past?'[31] Three days later, however, having consulted the *Reader's Encyclopedia*, Friel's focus had shifted from 'core' concerns to formal elements: 'As of now there is no central reason why the characters are all here—no wound-up clock on the point of alarm'.[32] In other words, he was looking for character motivations that would satisfy what he understood to be the conventions of farce rather than developing the play's core. In this case, it is clear from Friel's notes on the *Reader's Encyclopedia* that he was looking for a way to engage with farcical time:

> Most farces grow to a chase or a rush. Time is of the essence; the exact time nearly always figures in the action. Somebody has to be somewhere shortly. An important visitor may walk in at any second or, worse, two visitors who must on no account meet (they invariably do.) The hero gets pulled desperately into a catastrophe.[33]

Hence some of the rather clumsy exposition early in the play in which Jack goes through 'the timetable' of the evening with Tim: 'Mess it up and we're all in trouble'. This also accounts for much of the action of the play, which relies heavily on the timing of its entrances and exits. For instance, the Donovans mustn't meet Claire, who inconveniently keeps leaving her underwear to dry by the fire whilst Tim is out of the room, to his increasing chagrin; when the inevitable happens, Tim improvises and tells them that Claire is Evette Giroux, only for the real Evette to turn up towards the end of the play. There are also some tantalisingly underdeveloped peculiarities about the use of a form reliant on clock-time set in a reproduction cottage in which the clock is 'stopped' (Friel, *CC*, 17). Beyond the useless time-piece being listed as part of the inventory of the house, however, this is not something that Friel explores at great length in the play. On 23 November, Friel seemed to realise his play was essentially hollow at heart: 'The play has no centre'. Further down the page, he brought himself back to the fundamentals:

1. To establish a strong thematic core
2. To illustrate it with a theatrical device.[34]

4 FORM AND CORE: BRIAN FRIEL AND DENIS DONOGHUE

By the following day, however, the situation remained unchanged: 'THE CORE IS STILL MISSING'.[35]

This is not to say that Friel's decision to write a farce was an arbitrary one, despite his reliance on farcical conventions from very early on in the process. As late as January 1982, Friel was still giving serious thought to the 'fundamental question'[36] of whether the play ought to be a comedy or a farce. As he was demonstrably aware, Friel's indecisiveness would have a significant impact on two key elements of the play: the nature of the characters, and the role of the house. The *Reader's Encyclopedia* entry seemed to indicate to Friel that a farce is peopled with types rather than with characters:

> Characters: not so much villains + saint-martyrs as amoral mixtures of innocence + roguery; ordinary people caught up in extra-ordinary goings-on. They may have an objective (for coming together) but the exigencies of the plot force them to postpone it, sometimes indefinitely . . . .
> They are mankind as primitives or as baffled children who act on impulse. They are not equipped for reflection
> They do not appear to lead self-conscious, independent lives nor to think interesting thoughts[37]

By 7 January 1982, Friel was still undecided, but clearer on the implications of his choices: 'If [it is a] comedy [...] the 4 must become characters + not types. And more characters would be introduced'. The plot would also have revolved around a scenario more like the dress function for which the Donovans are meant to be headed after visiting the cottage.

If Friel saw the difference between farce and comedy as the difference between types and characters, he also saw it as the difference between a location and a symbol. Friel had been interrogating the significance of the restored cottage almost from the very beginning of the writing process, and continued to do so for several months. For instance, on 7 December 1981, Friel asked himself the following questions:

> Is the cottage central to the plot?
> Why is it? Why not a town-house, a mews-house?
> Has this location a social/ironic element?[38]

He elaborated in a further note from the same day's work:

> Is the cottage merely a convenient location or is it symbolic? And if symbolic, symbolic of what?—a "tradition" to be used, a butt of satire, a piece of merchandise, a malign place that reduces all the characters?[39]

On 5 January 1982, Friel developed this idea of malignity:

> The house must be malevolent.
> [...]
> Part of the comedy must reside in the assumption of the characters that they have an affinity to + a dexterity with this kind of house; and in the accidents/violence resulting from that facile (cultural?) assumption[.]

This is effectively the essence of Senator Doctor Donovan, whose sentimental pantomime of milking a cow—'a little scene that's somehow central to my psyche' (Friel, *CC*, 60)—ends with him chained to a post and unable to free himself. Two days later, in a note to which he went on to refer himself in addenda to the notes that questioned the house's symbolism, Friel concluded that the house would indeed be central in its symbolism in either genre:

> In the farce situation (and maybe the comedy?) the house represents a morality, a moral structure that exacts vengeance for acts committed against its (outdated) standards etc. etc.[40]

This is observable in the finished play, and is articulated by Tim when he and Claire discuss some of the more malevolent habits of the house: 'Did you ever have a sense that a place hates you? [...] Maybe it's because I feel no affinity at all with it and it knows that. In fact I think I hate it and all that it represents. And it senses that'. In fact, Tim is convinced that the fireplace 'attacks' him every time he goes near it, calling it 'the willing, the conniving instrument of a malign presence' (Friel, *CC*, 43).

This is again derived from the *Reader's Encyclopedia*, satisfying one of the conventions of farce there listed in a very literal sense. Indeed, it is apparent from his transcribed notes that one of the ways in which Friel understood farce was as a genre that 'strives to reduce the pillars of society to ruins'.[41] Thus not only is a member of the Seanad Éireann reduced to the posture of a chained animal, but the literal pillars and posts of a house that represents the moral standards of an outdated and glorified past are physically brought crashing to the ground. However, as Stephen Daldry's ubiquitous 1992 production of Priestley's *An Inspector Calls*

(1945) will attest, bringing the house down has a lot more metaphorical weight behind it when the play in which it happens does more than a superficial job of exposing the cracks in the pillars. There are many reasons why Friel, a middle-aged man writing his second play for Field Day at the height of the hunger strikes, may not have felt like taking more of a serious swipe at the pillars of Irish society. Moreover, as Peter Kemp's review of Michael Frayn's *Noises off* (1982) puts it in a clipping from the *TLS* that Friel saved from an issue dated 5 March 1982:

> With the weakening of traditional sources of embarrassment, such as rigid standards of respectability, comes a corresponding weakening of the sense of comic outrage when such codes are breached. Accordingly, contemporary farce inhabits a never-never world of anachronistic primness or it tries to give a new dimension to the formula by technical ingenuity.[42]

Nevertheless, there remained greater challenges to the more dangerously outmoded mores of Irish society to be mounted in the early 1980s than implied casual sex and an irreverence for the romanticised past.

By 10 January 1982, Friel had decided on 'a comedy with farcical elements, dealing with characters, not types'.[43] In practice, this meant that Friel would be guided by the conventions of farce whilst keeping the characters as people rather than stock figures (though arguably they lean rather heavily towards the latter in the finished play). This is clear from a note from 9 January 1982 in which he made himself a checklist of generative questions comprising many of the elements of farce gleaned from the *Reader's Encyclopedia*:

(a) How is time of the essence?
(b) Who [...] will arrive at any minute? Who must never meet whom?
(c) How does the hero get pulled into catastrophe? Why is the plot anarchic?
(d) How are the pillars of society reduced to ruins?
(e) Does it grow into a chase or rush?
(f) What are the fresh complications, the uncovered secrets, the surprising revelations, the co-incidences, the accidents, the new arrivals, the sudden departures[?]
(g) Whose is the mistaken identity[44]

This is a departure from Friel's usual questioning habits insofar as he is using the conventions of farce, as gleaned from an encyclopaedia and the lighting scheme from a famous farce from the 1960s, to generate a play. The action emerges from the answers to these questions of form rather than from a core that was insubstantial if not actually missing.

What then was the core of the play, and what did it have to do with Friel's source materials? Friel's notes are not particularly illuminating in this respect. The source materials are present, but there is not the same level of direct or inferred engagement in evidence in the extant archive materials as might be found in the composition processes of other plays. Nevertheless, it is possible to see these influences at work. For instance, Harris's *TLS* review of Goffman manifests itself in the profession of Tim Gallagher, who is writing a thesis on the subject of 'Discourse Analysis with Particular Reference to Response Cries' (Friel, *CC*, 18). Significantly, Friel does not appear to have gone on to read the relevant essay in Goffman's book, engaging instead with the wording of the review. Certainly, Tim's initial explanation of the nature of response cries a propos of Jack's 'God' (Friel, *CC*, 19) is taken directly from Harris's definition of 'exclamations [...] which apparently get "blurted out" as involuntary reactions'.[45] Similarly, a passage underlined by Friel in which Harris identifies Goffman's 'analysis of man as a communicator' as belonging to 'that dominant twentieth-century trend which seeks to explain the individual as being simultaneously creator and creation of his own communicational possibilities'[46] reappears almost word for word in Tim's dialogue. And yet, despite Friel's demonstrable pilfering, there is an extent to which his understanding of Goffman's ideas as extrapolated from Harris's review is more of a misunderstanding. For instance, Friel was clearly taken with the idea that '[e]veryday social interaction is explained dramaturgically in terms of certain *communicational* "roles" which individuals learn to play—for the benefit of audiences which include themselves' (my italics).[47] However, though Harris's wording is once again embedded in Tim's dialogue (Friel, *CC*, 19), Friel appears to understand the idea of 'playing roles' not in terms of speaker/listener (to give one example) but rather figuratively, as a form of 'pretence' (Friel, *CC*, 20). Tim's overall argument, moreover, though resembling Goffman's at certain points, draws on a vocabulary that is very different from either Goffman or Harris. Tim, growing ever more animated, argues that response cries are a means of elevating an exchange of information to 'something much more important—conversation' (Friel, *CC*, 19), insofar as a response cry may be interpreted as 'desire to share [...] experience' (Friel, *CC*, 20). The conclusion of Goffman's essay on response cries, meanwhile, suggests that 'conventionalized expressions [...] must be referred to social situations, not conversations': 'even though these interjections come to be employed in conversational environments, they cannot be adequately analyzed without reference to their original functioning outside states of talk'. Both Tim and Goffman are expressing roughly the same idea—that '[o]ur blurtings' are an 'invitation into our interiors'[48] and therefore ought to be understood as social rather than exclusively linguistic phenomena. Nevertheless, Goffman and Tim (or rather Friel) are clearly using the word 'conversation' to mean almost entirely opposite things.

There is a very good reason for this: Friel was not getting his ideas about conversation from Goffman/Harris. Rather Friel was drawing on a book by Denis Donoghue, *Ferocious Alphabets*, which had been published in the autumn of 1981 and which Friel had quite possibly already read by the time he came across Harris's review of Goffman. (Friel had written 'Denis Donoghue' and 'Steiner' in pencil at the top of the *TLS* review.) Friel's notes on *Ferocious Alphabets* suggest that he was particularly inspired by Donoghue's distinction between communication and conversation. Indeed, for Donoghue, 'conversation is radically different from communication in the sense proposed by [Roman] Jakobson and [I. A.] Richards',[49] whose theories place an emphasis on 'the unit of communication' (Donoghue, *FA*, 42). '[T]he unit', glosses Donoghue, 'is the message: the question is how to deliver the message intended [...] without loss or obfuscation' (Donoghue, *FA*, 42–43). Conversation, on the other hand, is 'so different' from communication in Donoghue's view that he 'think[s] of it as communion rather than communication':

> The crucial difference is that in conversation there is no unit; and even if there were, it would not be a message or signal to be delivered. What happens in a conversation? Each person describes or tries to make manifest his own experience: the other, listening, cannot share the experience, but he can perceive it, as if at a distance. Compete proximity is impossible. What makes a conversation memorable is the desire of each person to share experience with the other, giving and receiving. All that can be shared, strictly speaking, is the desire: it is impossible to reach the experience. But desire is enough to cause the reverberation to take place which we value in conversation. (Donoghue, *FA*, 43)

It is no surprise that the bulk of this passage appears in Friel's notes: it forms a significant part of what is arguably the closest thing to a core *The Communication Cord* has. It also resonates with and extends the thinking Friel had been doing around language whilst writing *Translations*. That play ended with an act of courage—the determination to endure in another language despite serious reservations about its capacity for interpretation 'between privacies'.[50] *The Communication Cord*, however, draws on Donoghue's more positive approach to the idea that 'we mean endlessly more than we say'[51]—one that celebrates the possibility of sharing the *desire* to share an experience, even if the experience itself cannot be shared.

The intellectual foundations of *The Communication Cord*, then, are not Goffman's ideas in and of themselves but rather Goffman (as glossed by Harris) through the lens of Donoghue. This is particularly clear in Tim's dialogue relating to his research, which functions in the first instance as a gloss of the passage from *Ferocious Alphabets* above:

> You ask me what my thesis is about. You ask me that question every so often and I tell you every time. Information requested; information transmitted; information received. But by the very fact of asking me as often as you do, you do something more than look for information, something more than try to set up a basic discourse; you desire to share my experience. [. . .] And because of that desire our exchange is immediately lifted out of the realm of mere exchange of basic messages and aspires to something higher, something more important—conversation. (Friel, CC, 19)

Here it is abundantly clear that Tim's definition of a conversation—a word that Goffman uses to mean the very opposite of a social situation—comes directly from Donoghue. It is a definition, moreover, that lends itself particularly well to Friel's more figurative interpretation of what is meant by social or communicational *roles*. Donoghue's conversation is not just a shared desire for a shared experience; it is also a space, and therefore ripe for translation into the fundamentally spatial world of theatre. This is particularly evident where Donoghue cites and then expands upon Barthes's *Fragments d'un discours amoureux*: 'The perfect interlocutor, the friend, is he not the one who constructs around you the greatest possible resonance? Cannot friendship be defined as a space with total sonority?'[52] Moreover, it is a space that, like theatre, privileges words as bodied speech: 'voice is the most acceptable epitome of presence' (Donoghue, *FA*, 44). Indeed, for Donoghue, 'the sound of the voices' (Donoghue, *FA*, 45) in conversation is equivalent to the unit of speech in communication. Thus '[i]n conversation, the validity of the words is not their exact correspondence to the objects or situation to which they refer, but their continuous participation in communication: the words enact desire' (Donoghue, *FA*, 44).

It is this idea of the voice as a unit of conversation through which Friel can be seen to interpret Goffman's response cries. In a continuation of the scene in which Tim expounds on his thesis, Jack utters his own response cry of 'God' (Friel, *CC*, 19); Tim's interpretation of that cry indicates that he understands it in the context of Donoghue's conversational units:

> Does your "God" say: I never knew that before? Does it say: This is fascinating—please continue? Does it say: Yes, I do desire to share your experience? Does it say: Tim, you're boring me? (Friel, *CC*, 19–20)

Thus response cries in *The Communication Cord* function as a means of 'sustain[ing] the occasion' (Friel, *CC*, 92) of conversation. This is the key, moreover, to the ending of the play, in which Claire and Tim take Donoghue's ideas to parodic extremes. I use such words advisedly: Donoghue suggests that 'an ideology of conversation [...] could be parodied by asserting that in a conversation what is said doesn't matter so long as the saying keeps the occasion going' (Donoghue, *FA*, 46). Significantly, this is precisely what happens when Tim suggests that what is important is 'the reverberations' generated by a given occasion, 'saying anything, anything at all, that keeps the occasion going' (Friel, *CC*, 92). (This is surely a deliberate echo of Maire and Yolland in *Translations*, who encourage one another to say 'anything at all'[53] in their respective languages.) In the light of Friel's source materials, we can therefore see how the ending of the play parodies the ideology at the heart of its intellectual foundations even as it reasserts it by echoing Donoghue's language: 'desire is enough to cause the *reverberation* to take place which we value in conversation' (Donoghue, *FA*, 43, my italics).

I have been at pains to stress that *The Communication Cord* is a play that suffered from Friel's having put its textbook farcical form before its nebulous core, within which the ideology of conversation dances uneasily with the increasingly violent consequences of the present's warped relationship with the past. Friel's synthesis of Donoghue and Goffman is mostly told rather than shown, and what might have been a fascinating exploration of farce in the context of the ideology of conversation (or indeed the temporality of farce in dialogue with the dysfunctional temporality of the house) never quite gets free of its own machinery. In many ways, the play ends by enacting its own failings. As Friel observed on 23 November, '[r]omance isn't adequate' when it comes to providing the core of a play that 'has no centre'.[54] It is somehow appropriate, then, that the play ends when Tim suggests that 'silence is the perfect discourse' (Friel, *CC*, 92). He and Claire stop each other's mouths in a kiss that destroys the set as they lean against a beam supporting the roof, in an affront to the outdated morality of the malevolent house. Having reduced the ideology of conversation to a parody of itself, Claire and Tim press forward into silence. The house, having survived the play's proliferation of miscommunications, having survived being transformed into the resonant space of communion, cannot sustain a conversation in which the desire to share an experience is replaced with wordless romantic desire. (Perhaps Steiner's doom-laden vision of a post-culture characterised by bloody-minded silence is part of the background noise in this scene.)[55] The physical structure collapses, whether in a final act of spite on its part or else having been 'reduced to ruins' by the action of the play.[56]

For all its failings, however, *The Communication Cord* remains a significant work beyond its being a cautionary tale about the pitfalls of committing to a form too early in the composition process of a play. First and foremost, it represents Friel's first major documented engagement with the work of Denis Donoghue, whose *Ferocious Alphabets* facilitated a significant development of Friel's Steiner-influenced thinking around language and communication. The reverberations from this creative encounter can be felt in Friel's subsequent memory plays, in which the felt impossibility of sharing an experience is attenuated by the creation of resonant spaces in which to share the desire instead. It happens in the dances of *Dancing at Lughnasa* (1990), where music functions in much the same way as the *sound* of voices in conversation, replacing the unit of speech. *The Communication Cord* is also vital in establishing Friel's intellectual trajectory in terms of ideas around presence, absence, voice, and sound. Without acknowledging Donoghue's influence in this respect, there is little to connect Friel's early, radio-like experiments with disembodied speakers and recorded sound in *Aristocrats* with later plays like *Performances,* in which soundedness is a means of creating resonant spaces in which the desire to share an experience can be acknowledged. In order to explore this trajectory fully, however, the influence of a second Donoghue text must be acknowledged: *The Arts Without Mystery*. This work, derived from Donoghue's Reith Lectures of 1982, would help Friel to recontextualise the ideas around language he had begun to explore in *The Communication Cord* in the light of the relationship between a problem and a mystery. It would also inform the core and form of a play that was almost ten years in the making: *Wonderful Tennessee*.

WONDERFUL TENNESSEE

The onstage cast of *Wonderful Tennessee* comprises three married couples: Berna and Terry, Angela and Frank, and Trish and George; they are celebrating Terry's birthday. Among them are two sets of siblings: Berna and Angela, and Trish and Terry. Berna is a barrister and psychiatric patient; Angela teaches Classics. Trish is permanently disorientated; Terry is generous but secretly broke, and has obtained the right to buy the island; both are 'neurotic [...] about not having children'[57] with their respective partners. Frank is writing a book on time, supported by Angela and by handouts from Terry. George, a musician, is dying of cancer, communicating mostly through pertinent songs played on his accordion. The six arrive in Ballybeg at '*a remote pier in north-west Donegal*' (Friel, *P2*, 344), where they wait for Carlin the boatman to ferry them to the island where they plan to spend the night: Oileán Draíochta, 'Island of Otherness; Island of Mystery' (Friel, *P2*, 369). Carlin never arrives. Instead, they pass the night telling stories and singing songs, consciously and unconsciously recreating the island's rituals on the pier. At the end of the play, Terry reveals the extent of his financial difficulties and admits that he will not be buying the island after all. As the minibus arrives to take them home, they vow to return next year.

Despite its sparse plot, *Wonderful Tennessee* is a play that took more than a decade to come to fruition. Friel's notes for *Wonderful Tennessee* in MS 37,123/1 date back to 16 November 1983, but as we have already seen, there is prior mention of the 'Lough Derg notion'[58] in Friel's notes for *The Communication Cord* on 8 November 1981. In his note of 1983, Friel writes of his as yet untitled, unwritten play, that '[its] core—not necessarily its manifestation—would be the mystical-symbolic notions of pilgrimage: both an element in and a definition of life'.[59] However, though he revisited the idea briefly in 1988, it was not until 1990 that Friel began to work on his pilgrimage play in earnest. By this time, it had acquired not only significant philosophical baggage, but also the remains of a time play that never bore fruit. This development was thanks largely to two texts first published in 1983, on which Friel drew heavily. The first is David S. Landes's *Revolution in Time: Clocks and the Making of the Modern World*; the second is Denis Donoghue's *The Arts Without Mystery*, comprising his 1982 Reith Lectures for the BBC with additional notes and extended commentaries. It was through the influence of Donoghue in particular that Friel came to find a form that would best express the play's core, by focusing not only on the 'mystical' aspect of pilgrimage but also on pilgrimage as an aspect of the mysterious itself.

Friel's interest in the notion of pilgrimage in a specifically Irish context is reflected in the contents of MS 37,123/1. This folder includes a souvenir booklet from Doon Well (a holy well in Donegal) and a review by Deasún Breatnach of two books on Celtic mythology: Miranda Green's *Symbol and Image in Celtic Religious Art* (1989) and Peter Berresford Ellis's *The Celtic Empire* (1990). The souvenir booklet may well have been obtained on 28 June 1990, when Friel drove to Doon Well only to find that it was '[n]ot at all the place I remembered'.[60] The idea of pilgrimage alone, however, was proving insufficient to say the least, as Friel's brief and desperate typed diary entry of summer 1990 will attest: 'Pilgrims. Pilgrimage. I feel I'm hanging—'.[61] In the next entry, Friel appears to change tack: 'Back to the play about TIME. A time-salesman going round Donegal?' The entry continues:

> TIME play incorporated into Pilgrimage play?
> A philosophical clock-salesman making the pilgrimage. Why?
> "Do we know what time is?
> More important: can we measure it accurately?
> And once we can measure it: now we must obey it."[62]

If Friel had written notes towards a time play prior to this entry, he did not archive them. However, subsequent diary entries strongly suggest that Friel's source for this time play was most likely Landes's *Revolution in Time*, which Friel went on to cite in the same note.[63] Certainly, the question 'Do we know what time is?' echoes Landes's evocation of St. Augustine's famous meditations on the nature of time. Moreover, the notion of the imperative to 'obey' measurable time is one that Friel borrows directly from Landes, transcribing the relevant passage in his diary entry for 1 August 1990:

It was this possibility of widespread private use that laid the basis for *time discipline* as against *time obedience*. [. . .] It is the mechanical clock that made possible, for better or worse, a civilisation attentive to the passage of time, hence to productivity and performance.[64] (Italics in original.)

Significantly, the distinction between obedience to the 'summon[s]' of 'public clocks' and the emergence of a collective work ethic from the discipline of private time management through the use of portable, personal time-pieces is not one that Friel makes in *Wonderful Tennessee*. This, as I will go on to suggest, may be due to the stronger influence of Donoghue on Friel's perception of clock time.

Friel's initial approach to blending the pilgrimage play with the time play appears to have hinged on the relationship between time measurement and colonialism. Throughout July 1990, Friel's diary entries betray a particular interest in the figure of Matteo Ricci,[65] a Jesuit missionary who features fairly prominently in *Revolution in Time*. Fascinatingly, Friel went so far as to draw a comparison between Ricci in mid-sixteenth-century China and the nineteenth-century Ordnance Survey mapping expedition in Ireland which forms the background to *Translations*: 'Ricci [...], with his clocks and dazzling machines, was a kind of Colby in Ireland'.[66] That said, Friel's notes on 'TIME and Pilgrimage'[67]—begun on 4 July 1990, on the same day that Friel decided to merge these two notions—suggest that the time-salesman was to be one of several pilgrims 'who moves in + out of the action'[68] rather than the play's protagonist. Consequently, Friel's consideration of form at this stage was dictated less by Landes's ideas about the significance of the invention of mechanical clocks than by the idea of pilgrimage itself. In other words, Friel's sense of the core of the play was still the specific mystery of pilgrimage rather than the nature of the mysterious itself. Hence Friel's diary entries from July 1990 contain references to various storytelling forms, including the recurring possibility of *Under Milk Wood*[69] and, some days later, Chaucer's *Canterbury Tales*. Indeed, as Friel mused in his diary entry for 19 July 1990, the idea of storytelling as a form struck him as particularly appropriate insofar as 'whatever about the mystical-symbolic, whatever about redemption through suffering, whatever about the curative power of language, the play—the drama—survives as a story, as story-telling, as a fictional narrative'.[70] However, though storytelling would indeed be central to the finished play, it is not to Chaucer or Thomas that *Wonderful Tennessee* owes the manner in which its stories are told, but rather to the work that determined its philosophical foundations: Donoghue's *The Arts Without Mystery*.

A slightly extended print version of Donoghue's 1982 Reith Lectures, *The Arts Without Mystery* arose from a wish 'to talk about the arts in relation to the mystery that surrounds them, not as a problem to be cleared up but as the very condition in which they appear at all'.[71] 'A work of art is in some sense mysterious', claims Donoghue, but he sees 'no evidence, in contemporary criticism, that the mystery is acknowledged or respected' (Donoghue, *TAWM*, 7). Donoghue's definition of the mysterious is grounded in Christian Existentialist thought, building on foundations laid down by French philosopher Gabriel Marcel (1889–1973). Specifically, Marcel's *Being and Having* (1933) makes the distinction between the mysterious and the problematic, in a passage quoted by Donoghue:

> A problem is something met with which bars my passage. It is before me in its entirety. A mystery, on the other hand, is something in which I find myself caught up, and whose essence is therefore not to be before me in its entirety. [. . .] It is a proper character of problems [. . .] to be reduced to detail. Mystery, on the other hand, is something which cannot be reduced to detail.[72]

There is a fair amount of elision here, which I have reproduced for the sake of demonstrating the aspects of Marcel's thinking deemed most relevant to Donoghue's argument by Donoghue himself. However, for the purpose of additional clarity, I would reinstate Marcel's further characterisation of the mysterious as a zone in which 'the distinction between *in me* and *before me* loses its meaning'.[73] The mysterious, then, is that which cannot be entirely separated from the self, and which therefore cannot be fully explained. And if it cannot be explained, then it must be accommodated by other means. Indeed, for Marcel, in Donoghue's own neat summary, '[t]he gist of the matter is: a problem is something to be solved, a mystery is something to be witnessed and attested' (Donoghue, *TAWM*, 12).

This key idea of witness is an active and multifaceted one. In the English edition cited by Donoghue, 'witness' is a translation of what Marcel calls 'témoignage'[74] in the original French, suggesting something akin to the idea of testimony; 'attestation' (already a loan word from the French) is a little more complex. Helpfully, Marcel expands on this idea of attestation by noting that it incorporates 'not only witnessing' (as in bearing witness/testifying) 'but also calling to witness'[75]—'non seulement témoigner, mais prendre à témoin'.[76] This can be simplified, however, by thinking of witness and/or attestation not as esoteric concepts but rather as practical methods of *acknowledgement*. Indeed, Marcel stresses that 'it is an essential part of a mystery that it should be acknowledged'[77]; Donoghue, taking his cue from Marcel, likewise states that 'mystery is to be acknowledged, not resolved or dispelled' (Donoghue, *TAWM*, 11).

Onto this distinction between the mysterious and the problematic, Donoghue maps three pairs of corresponding juxtapositions: Jacques Lacan's distinction between desire and need; Friedrich Nietzsche's distinction between the Dionysian and Apollonian; and Susanne K. Langer's distinction between lived time and clock-time. Donoghue's glosses are succinct and illuminating, and are consequently reproduced here in full. (They are also essential reading for *Wonderful Tennessee*, insofar as they make their presence decidedly felt in the finished play, and were each transcribed by Friel during the composition process.) Donoghue begins with Lacan:

> What corresponds in the human psyche to mystery in the arts is what he calls desire, which is desire only because it is unconscious and ineffable. What he calls need is a drive that can be met, like hunger or thirst. It is a specific detail of compulsion; your body would protest if you didn't satisfy. But desire is lack, it can't be met, because it is categorical and therefore endless. It is the condition of life as such, not a particular craving that can be satisfied. The distinction corresponds to the one between mystery and problem. (Donoghue, *TAWM*, 72)

Thus need is to problem as desire is to mystery because, like a problem, need can be reduced to detail. Need can be met; a problem can be solved. Moreover, like a mystery, desire cannot be wholly disentangled from the self, and is thus a condition wherein 'the distinction between *in me* and *before me* loses its meaning'.[78] 'Desire attain'd is not desire'[79]; a mystery solved is not a mystery. Donoghue continues with Nietzsche:

> Dionysus is a god of nature, associated with forces biological and violent, orgiastic mysteries, with everything that refuses to be civilised. Apollo is the god of civilisation: if he were linguistic, he would be the perfectly formed sentence, self-possessed in its transparency. Dionysus wants not to possess himself but to lose himself in an ecstasy in which he and nature are

one and the same: the methods of ecstasy are intoxication, sexuality, the Dionysiac music and dance, the dithyramb in which the barriers between man and nature are overwhelmed. [. . .] Dionysus is wild, god of a maddened group, people who drive themselves out of civilisation by wine, drugs, dismemberment. Modern versions of Dionysus include the forces active in bullfights, cockfights, rock concerts, wrestling, charismatic revival meetings. (Donoghue, *TAWM*, 83-4)

For Donoghue, then, Apollo is a god of 'culture as [a series of] techniques for managing natural impulses' as though they were solvable problems, whereas Dionysus is a god of 'aesthetic forms as ways of acknowledging natural or primitive impulses' (Donoghue, *TAWM*, 83). In other words, Nietzsche's Dionysus satisfies Donoghue's demands that 'mystery is to be acknowledged, not resolved or dispelled' (Donoghue, *TAWM*, 11).

This is closely related to another key concept in *The Arts Without Mystery*: 'the managerial motive in language'. This, according to Donoghue, amounts to 'the insistence of those who use it that there is nothing it cannot name' (Donoghue, *TAWM*, 96). Thus those critics Donoghue terms 'zealots of explanation' who 'want to deny the arts their mystery, and to degrade mystery into a succession of problems' (Donoghue, *TAWM*, 12) are, in his view, guilty of managerial motives: 'It is the aim of management to accommodate every apparent contradiction within a standard diction by neutralising the offensive words' (Donoghue, *TAWM*, 96). The Dionysian, then, is to the Apollonian as 'characteristic revival meetings' are to 'the perfectly formed sentence' (Donoghue, *TAWM*, 84): one uses language to acknowledge experience whilst the other uses language in an attempt to manage it. This distinction between management and acknowledgement is similarly evident in Donoghue's gloss of Langer:

> Clock-time is time as pure sequence, its events are indifferent in themselves, and their sole relation to one another is that of succession. Lived time differs from clock-time by virtue of the feelings, interests, and so forth which give it its character. We don't live by the clock. But music "makes time audible. And its form and continuity sensible".[80]

In other words, for Donoghue, clock-time is a managerial form of time insofar as its function is one of empirical measurement and sequential ordering; lived time, meanwhile is analogous to the subjective human experience of time. Lived time, then, is something that cannot be measured but only attested. Crucially, however, there are means of acknowledging lived time through aesthetic forms—in this case, music. Indeed, Friel's additional research suggests that he saw lived time in a broader context of carnival and spectacle. This is clear from his quoting of Octavio Paz's essay 'The Day of the Dead' in his notes: 'Time is no longer succession, and becomes what it originally was + is: the present, in which the past + future are reconciled'.[81]

The theoretical concept of time in *Wonderful Tennessee* therefore emerges as a combination of Donoghue and Landes. In addition to drawing on Donoghue's gloss of Langer's distinction between clock-time and lived time as manifestations of manageable problems and attestable mysteries respectively, Friel also incorporated some of Landes's thinking on the history of time measurement into the idea of clock-time in particular. This is clear from the development of the character of Frank, whose slightly murky origins lie in what were initially two different types of pilgrim: 'the time-man' and 'the Chronicler'. The time-man is a development of the time-salesman character Friel mentioned in his diary entry for 4 July 1990. This character began to take on characteristics highly reminiscent of Donoghue's gloss of Langer. This is particularly evident from a juxtaposition of notes in MS 37,123/3. On 6 August 1990, Friel transcribed the definitions of clock-time and lived time from *The Arts Without Mystery*; on 13 August 1990, underneath this note, Friel added a snippet of dialogue with commentary:

> "What may be experienced—remembered in a sort of way—is lived time, not clock-time[.]" He carries in his case the accoutrements for two kinds of life: watches that obey Apollo and icons that bow before Dionysus? And of course his lute/lyre.[82]

At this stage in the play's development, then, one of the pilgrims is a man who sells watches and plays a musical instrument—two ways of marking two different kinds of time. (Confusingly, there is also an artist-musician pilgrim, who plays either the ukulele or the accordion, floating around Friel's notes at this time.) The Chronicler, meanwhile, is essentially the embodiment of what Donoghue would call the managerial motive. Hence in this piece of draft dialogue from 17 August 1990, a speaker known only as '<u>Young woman</u>' directs a Donoghue-inspired outburst at the likewise unnamed Chronicler:

> Look at the fucker (Chronicler)! Measuring. Mapping. Peering. D'you know why? Because he's terrified!—the fucker's terrified. God knows of what. But he thinks that if he can weight [*sic*] it + measure it + feel it—he thinks he can <u>tame</u> it. Because it affronts him. He can't stand it.[83]

On 29 May 1991, Friel annotated this speech with 'Angela talking about Aiden's book',[84] suggesting that Frank (at this point known as Aiden) had taken on the Chronicler's attributes.

By the time Aiden had become the Frank of the finished play, however, he had also taken on some of the characteristics of the time-man, to the extent that he was writing a book called '*The Measurement of Time and its Effect on European Civilization*' (Friel, *P2*, 395) and consequently tells stories on the subject of time itself. Unlike earlier versions of the time-man character, however, Frank does not comfortably embody the two kinds of life represented by Apollo and Dionysus. Rather he is a character acutely aware of the managerial aspect of his work on time, whilst equally aware of the indigence of language, which is the medium in which he works. This conflict gives him an appalling cynicism, as is evident from much of his dialogue concerning the book. For instance, his explanation of monastic apparitions as the products of sleep-deprived minds at continuous prayer ('Honestly! Medieval monks were always seeing apparitions') is followed by a glib dismissal of his own writing practice: 'How would I know? But there must be some explanation, mustn't there? The mystery offends—so the mystery has to be extracted' (Friel, *P2*, 399). Frank's explanation of the relationship between apparitions and the invention of time-pieces, moreover, is essentially a conversational paraphrase of Landes, who elaborates on the effect of time measurement on religious communities:

> Multiplication of simultaneous devotions—this was the way of salvation for all. Indeed, there were those who would have revived the Pauline ideal of continuous prayer (in relays presumably): thus Benedict of Aniane in the early ninth century and, even more, the monastery at Cluny in the tenth. (The latent purpose—or, if you will, the consequence—was, in conjunction with ascetic diet, to promote a state of light-headedness conducive to enthusiasm and hallucinations, or, euphemistically, to illumination and visions.)[85]

What is significant about Friel's use of this source material is that what follows Frank's spiel is a self-ironising critique of those 'modern critics' characterised by Donoghue as 'zealots of explanation' (Donoghue, *TAWM*, 12):

> TERRY Is that going to be in your book?!
> FRANK Maybe. Why not? Anything to explain away the wonderful, the mystery. (Friel, *P2*, 399)

Frank identifies in himself a managerial motive, recognising the impulse to treat the mysterious as a problem that can be reduced to detail rather than attested; to treat the mysterious as a need that can be met rather than as a desire that is a condition of being; to domesticate the Dionysian with Apollonian forms; to attempt to express lived time as clock-time.

In summary, then, Donoghue's schema, if put into a table, would look something like this:

	Management	*Acknowledgement*
Marcel	Problem	Mystery
Lacan	Need	Desire
Nietzsche	Apollo	Dionysus
Langer	Clock-time	Lived time

Problem-solving, the meeting of specific needs, Apollonian civilisation, and clock-time are all characterised by managerial motives. The active witnessing of mystery, unattainable desire, Dionysian ecstasies, and lived time, meanwhile, are all characterised by their unmanageability and can only ever demand acknowledgement. And running parallel to this schema is the idea of language as subject to managerial motives, wherein (in Donoghue's view) arts critics who do not acknowledge the mysterious believe there is nothing that cannot be explained away in words.

As one might imagine, this all had something of an impact on Friel, and at a time when inspiration was sorely needed at that. Indeed, Donoghue begins to appear prominently in Friel's notes around the beginning of August 1990, after a month of Friel's attempting to fuse the ideas of time and pilgrimage. As is clear from Friel's diary entry of 31 July 1990, he had been struggling up to this point: 'I have no idea at all of what the Pilgrimage play is about—so little do I know that I can't believe there may be a play there'.[86] The next day, on 1 August 1990, Donoghue makes his first unequivocally recognisable appearance in Friel's diary entries—not, at first, in his own words, but in two passages that informed the two central tenets of *The Arts Without Mystery*: 'one, that knowledge, the dominant force in our engagement with experience, cannot admit mystery or respect it; and two, that discursive practices don't recognise what can't be explained' (Donoghue, *TAWM*, 8). Friel transcribed these two passages as follows:

> St. Augustine. "Whatever is understood by knowledge is limited by the understanding of knowledge; even what can be called ineffable is not ineffable."
> [E. M.] Cioran: "The indigence of language renders the universe intelligible."[87]

To this Friel added, in his own words: 'Does the indigence of language make mystery possible—and intelligible?'[88]

For the playwright who incorporated Bacon, Steiner, and *Ferocious Alphabets* into his work with evident relish, it is unsurprising that Friel was intrigued by the possibility that it is the inadequacy of language (rather than its capabilities) that makes the universe intelligible as mystery. Certainly, Friel saw how this might relate to—and expand upon—his earlier notion of the play's core as 'the mystical-symbolic notions of pilgrimage'.[89] Indeed, following a note from much later in the process in which he adapted the Cioran quote to read 'The indigence of language makes mystery possible—maybe necessary', Friel went so far as to write: '*This* is probably the core of the play'[90] (my italics). This does not mean, however, that Friel decided to abandon language as a means of engaging with the mysterious altogether. It is true that Friel was eager to transcribe Donoghue's T. S. Eliot-inspired musings in which Donoghue 'find[s] it congenial to believe that there are moments at which language stands baffled, saying of that which it has just said that that is not it at all, not at all'.[91] It is also true that these words resonate within the finished play through the character of Frank, who delivers a speech in which he suggests glibly that the only way one could write down '[w]hatever it is we desire but can't express' would be in 'a book without words'. Indeed, Frank's fevered evocation of an experience for which there is 'no vocabulary' where 'language stands baffled' (Friel, *P2*, 398) is almost entirely Donoghue. Nevertheless, Friel arguably sought to use language in the play in a way that would attest to the mysterious, rather than abandoning language altogether as a tool of fruitless explanation.

In this, form is essential. What Friel had begun in the context of time and pilgrimage, he now developed using Donoghue's ideas. The finished product was not perhaps Friel's finest work, though I myself am fond of the play (having thoroughly enjoyed the Nottingham Playhouse revival I saw with my school library in 1999). Rose-tinted reminiscences aside, it is undeniable that even Friel had a sense that the play was 'perilously close to being a Theory Into Practice—Philosophy in Action—Religion Realised'[92] rather than character-driven drama. If the combination of a marriage of form and core with a story told through people is what makes Friel's most successful plays what they are, Friel was acutely aware of it. Certainly, though he had suggested that the play's core might be the Cioran quote on 22 January 1991, by the end of the month, Friel had serious doubts as to whether his characters were up to the play's 'very large and potent theme'. The realisations thereafter came thick and fast:

> That [the theme] requires very exact elements of form and language to release it, to fulfil it. That what has inhibited the play's development in the past has been the choice of the wrong people. That it must be encased in a musical sound that alternates between the sacred and the profane—but which must always haunt the action. That there must be a second music—*language forged into antiphonal expression that transcends individual, private, personal utterance and that assumes the responsibility and the terror of all the pilgrims.* That the tawdry experience, however, incomplete and ridiculous, will to some degree purge.[93] (My italics.)

On the question of the characters, Friel had already expressed his unease that 'the pilgrims I've chosen are not rich and complex enough in themselves' some months earlier:

> Uneasy that [. . .] their complexity isn't amenable to theatrical enquiry— that it is the material of the novelist. My people have to be explored by and reveal themselves by word and by action and by silence. And without character they have no characteristics.[94]

This sense of unease was still manifest in early February 1991, at which time Friel was still struggling to find characters that would be able to transform theory-in-practice into a play: 'It has no animating core—only an idea providing an outline. [...] (Are the characters too ephemeral, inadequate to the **idea** of the play? Don't know.)'[95] Whether or not Friel succeeded in finding a set of characters capable of animating the play's core is debatable. However, what is clear is that Friel was actively invested in finding a means of translating the ideas of Donoghue (and, to a lesser extent, Landes) into a form and a language capable of expressing the play's themes. And the characters, whilst often failing to exist beyond their being mouthpieces for Friel's research, are—at their most successful—crucial to the process not simply of parroting but rather of *performing* those ideas. Donoghue's influence in particular manifested itself in the finished play not only through the characters' dialogue but also through the play's use of games and storytelling as dramatic forms. This is perhaps best illustrated through focusing on two of the play's key elements that are also essential to theatre: time and space.

In order to evoke (rather than explain) lived time, Friel resorts to formal means that allow for its performance. That is to say that, in order for lived time to be experienced by an audience, it has to be something the characters can 'do'. This is partly achieved through the use of music throughout the play as what Cole M. Crittenden calls 'an art form in time'.[96] George's accordion may be a theatrical device for allowing him to 'speak' despite his bandaged throat, but it also provides two other functions. Firstly, it is an opportunity for Friel to stage 'a musical sound that alternates between the sacred and the profane'[97] and which taps into attestatory, Dionysian aesthetic forms; secondly, it is a means of making lived time 'sensible'.[98] A further way in which Friel facilitates the performance of a lived time that can be experienced and acknowledged is through the use of what we might call 'story time' (Friel, *P2*, 424). It can be no coincidence that three of the provisional titles for *Wonderful Tennessee* were 'WORDS IN THE DARK', 'STORIES IN THE DARK', and 'STORIES BEFORE DAWN'.[99] Indeed, this formal element of the play is crucial to recovering an attestatory function of language: each story both witnesses and calls to witness. Moreover, the act of storytelling is one that is deeply entrenched in the history of the philosophy of time, and is used by St. Augustine in his *Confessions* as a performative example of the subjective experience of time (i.e. lived time) as a threefold present. For Augustine, the human experience of time is not one of past, present, and future, but rather one of memory, present attention, and expectation. To illustrate this, he uses the example of a psalm recited by heart:

> The life of this act of mine is stretched two ways, into my memory because of the words I have already said and into my expectation because of those which I am about to say. But my attention is on what is present: by that the future is transferred to become the past. As the action advances further and further, the shorter the expectation and the longer the memory, until all expectation is consumed, the entire action is finished, and it has passed into the memory.[100]

To recite from memory as a bodied speaker is therefore to perform the way in which the action of remembering or of expecting effectively performs lived time.

A potent example of Friel's use of storytelling as a performance of lived time is Frank's tale of the dancing dolphin. Having '[w]asted' '[t]wo bloody spools' of film trying to 'capture' 'Oileán Draíochta emerging from behind its veil', he then sees 'suddenly—as if it had been a sign—a dolphin [that] rose up out of the sea'. It begins to dance 'with a deliberate, controlled, exquisite abandon':

> And for that thirty seconds, maybe a minute, I could swear it never once touched the water. A performance—that's what it was. A performance so considered, so aware, that you knew it knew it was being witnessed; wanted to be witnessed. (Friel, *P2*, 420–1)

Whereas photography, in Donoghue's view, 'appeases the desire to take immediate possession of our experience; not [...] as a whole but as the sum of its separately manageable parts' (Donoghue, *TAWM*, 102), Frank's narrative is an act of witness. Furthermore, insofar as to recite is to perform lived time, Frank—who cannot say for certain how long the dolphin danced—is able to experience the thing he has witnessed in what is quite literally 'story time'. Thus instead of a time-man whose watches and lute/lyre obey Apollo and Dionysus respectively, there is a chronicler who is simultaneously a photographer who tries to arrest the moment and a storyteller who performs lived time through storytelling.

Friel's use of space in *Wonderful Tennessee* is similarly influenced by Donoghue and also has a narrative element. The pilgrim-like partygoers' stories may function as an attestatory means of making lived time tangible, but they are also a means of the speakers establishing a complex deictic relationship between themselves and the mysterious as symbolised by the island. Like the mysterious itself, the island is not entirely exterior to the characters and cannot ever be before them in its entirety. As Friel observes in his notes, the Oileán Draíochta is 'maybe not posited any more in the place but refound in themselves'.[101] Indeed, in one of the blue A4 notebooks in which Friel began the drafting process, he wrote:

> The otherness, the mystery, the secret, that ineffable desire is not out there but WITHIN. Each of us has a private, interior island.
> [. . .]
> So each of the stories has to do with the private, interior island?[102]

Thus when the characters establish the deictic relationships between themselves and the island, they are unable to do so entirely satisfactorily, so that the spatiality of the play world is never quite defined. The island is shrouded in mist, or the characters are looking the wrong way; the boatman never arrives; they never set foot on the place.

A further means of establishing this mysterious deictic relationship is through Friel's recovery of the attestatory function of another managerial form. Friel subverts Donoghue's claim that 'there is no point in comparing the arts with games or even with language-games' on the grounds that '[a] game has rules which the players and spectators accept' and that therefore, [i]n an otherwise uncertain world, games are desirable because they provide the experience of certainty' (Donoghue, *TAWM*, 127). Rather Friel uses Angela's game of 'how close can you get without touching it' (Friel, *P2*, 415–6) as a further means of performing a relationship with the mysterious in *Wonderful Tennessee*. Indeed, it is a means of realising in objective, spatial terms the relationship between the self and the mysterious without attempting to explain it. The aim of the game is to throw stones as near to a bottle as possible without actually hitting it. It is a means of acknowledging an indexical relationship between the self and that which is desired without achieving direct contact: the intent and directionality of the thrown stones is an acknowledgement of the existence of the relationship without defining its limits. Just as 'the counters of common discourse'[103]—that is to say, language—can only attest to the mysterious, so the stones as the counters of the game can only attest to the presence of their target.

Friel's use of Donoghue, then, is not exclusively one of borrowed words but also one of form. It is true that Friel's characters remain underdeveloped in places, and there are times when the core of the play is more of a theory to be put into practice than a generative synthesis of source materials. Nevertheless, *Wonderful Tennessee* is an important example of how Friel attempted to stage the relationship between the self and the mysterious, employing the attestatory functions of what might otherwise be managerial forms. Language is a tool not for explanation but for attestation; clocks are replaced by music and story time; order gives way to chaos; the mysterious is desired but never attained. Crucially, these are not only ideas that are spoken but also performed through song, story, and games in a series of subtly experimental innovations; the form performs the core.

The composition processes for *The Communication Cord* and *Wonderful Tennessee* make clear that Denis Donoghue is a major influence for Brian Friel and should be considered as such within Friel studies. Neither play is considered to be a masterpiece within Friel's oeuvre, due partly to an incomplete synthesis of ideas that failed to generate a core capable of outgrowing its source material and partly due to insufficiently realised characters. In the case of *The Communication Cord*, moreover, Friel's choice to shackle himself to a predetermined form seriously hampered the play's development. Nevertheless, *Wonderful Tennessee* at least uses Donoghue's ideas to facilitate subtle formal innovations constituting a serious attempt to perform the distinctions between managerial and attestatory forms.

Donoghue's influence, I would suggest, also has further implications for Friel's intellectual trajectory over the years. *Ferocious Alphabets* represents a significant development of Friel's thinking around the relationship between signifier and signified. Donoghue privileges conversation (or 'communion') over communication, positing the creation of resonant spaces as a means of sharing a desire to share a common experience. Though it remains true that, in Steiner's words, '[w]e mean endlessly more than we say',[104] Donoghue opens up the possibility of using language as a means of connecting with others through enacting a desire to do so, simply by having conversations. *The Arts Without Mystery* is also key to Friel's move away from the relative pessimism of the ending of *Translations* in terms of language. Admittedly, it is difficult to ascertain the point at which Friel came into contact with this later work, which was first available in its radio broadcast Reith Lecture form as early as 1982 before its publication as a book in 1983. I will not therefore make any definitive claims as to how plays written between 1982 and 1993 might have been influenced by a text that only begins to appear in Friel's notes in August 1990. Friel's use of Dionysian forms in *Dancing at Lughnasa* (1990) is certainly suggestive, but the existence of a link between this seminal play and Donoghue's work is pure speculation on my part. What is clear, however, is that Friel's later thinking on language owes a significant part of its development to *The Arts Without Mystery*. Where Steiner highlighted what Cioran terms the indigence of language, Donoghue was instrumental in helping Friel to see that indigence as a key element of the mystery that is 'the very condition in which [the arts] appear at all' (Donoghue, *TAWM*, 11). Just as the inadequacies of language make it possible only to share the desire to speak, those same inadequacies make it possible to share only in the acknowledgement of a mystery. Moreover, this view of the arts—which include those art forms which, like theatre, possess a verbal element—is arguably key to late plays such as *Performances* (2003), in which the life versus work argument is effectively settled by an act of acknowledgement, i.e. listening to the work. This is also a development of Friel's engagement with Bacon, in which the role of chance in the context of artistic practice is explored: just as Bacon can only attest to his artworks as manipulated accidents, so the work of art in Donoghue's view defies complete explanation. As Friel's career progressed, he began to look at the idea of influence itself within his plays, in a way that—to my mind—resonates strongly with ideas Friel had gleaned from these two books by Donoghue.

Notes

1. Dublin, National Library of Ireland (NLI), Brian Friel Papers (BFP), MS 37,052/2. Undated note towards *The Loves of Cass McGuire*.
2. NLI, BFP, MS 37,048/1. Undated note towards *Philadelphia, Here I Come!* on onionskin paper in blue biro.
3. NLI, BFP, MS 37,052/2. Undated note towards *The Loves of Cass McGuire*.
4. NLI, BFP, MS 37,052/2. Undated note towards *The Loves of Cass McGuire*.
5. NLI, BFP, MS 37,052/2. Undated note towards *The Loves of Cass McGuire*.
6. NLI, BFP, MS 37,062/1. Note towards *The Mundy Scheme* dated 31 May [1968].
7. NLI, BFP, MS 37,052/2. Undated note towards *The Loves of Cass McGuire*.

8. NLI, BFP, MS 37,052/2. Undated note towards *The Loves of Cass McGuire*.
9. NLI, BFP, MS 37,054/1. Undated note towards *Lovers: Winners*, embellished with giant question mark.
10. NLI, BFP, MS 37,054/1. Undated note towards *Lovers: Winners*, to which Friel added 'READ THIS: (9 Nov 1966)' in green felt-tip pen.
11. NLI, BFP, MS 37,054/1. Undated note towards *Lovers: Winners*.
12. Brian Friel, *Lovers: Winners and Losers* (Oldcastle: Gallery Press, 2013), p. 11.
13. Vimala Herman, 'Deixis and Space in Drama', *Social Semiotics* 7, No. 3 (1997), pp. 269–283 (p. 274). See also Karl Bühler, *Sprachtheorie* (Jena: Fischer, 1934).
14. Friel, *Lovers*, p. 17.
15. Friel, *Lovers*, pp. 17–18.
16. Friel, *Lovers*, p. 11.
17. Friel, *Lovers*, p. 17.
18. NLI, BFP, MS 37,054/1. Undated note towards *Lovers: Winners*, to which Friel added 'READ THIS: (9 Nov 1966)' in green felt-tip pen.
19. NLI, BFP, MS 37,069. Note towards *Volunteers* dated 22 October 1973.
20. See, for instance, NLI, BFP, MS 37,134/1, note towards *Give Me Your Answer, Do!* dated 16 June 1995; NLI, BFP, MS 37,134/1, note towards *Give Me Your Answer, Do!* dated 7 February 1996.
21. NLI, BFP, MS 37,093/1. Note towards *The Communication Cord* dated 23 November [YEAR].
22. Eugene Moloney, '"Cord" that tilts the fun-bath over all', *The Irish News*, 13 September 1982, in NLI, BFP, MS 37,093/4.
23. Michael Billington, 'The Communication Cord', *Guardian*, 7 May 1983, in NLI, BFP, MS 37,093/7.
24. Brian Friel, *The Communication Cord* (Oldcastle: The Gallery Press, 1999), p. 11. Further references in parentheses in the text as 'Friel, *CC*'.
25. See Francis Bacon, 'Of Friendship', in *The Essays of Francis Bacon*, ed. with intr. and notes by Mary Augusta Scott (New York: Charles Scribner's Sons, 1908), pp. 117–129 (p. 118).
26. NLI, BFP, MS 37,093/1. Note towards *The Communication Cord* dated 16 October 1981. Struck through in pencil.

27. NLI, BFP, MS 37,093/1. Note towards *The Communication Cord* dated 8 November 1981. Struck through in pencil.
28. NLI, BFP, MS 37,093/1. Note towards *The Communication Cord* dated 8 November 1981.
29. NLI, Brian Friel Papers, MS 37,093/1. See 'farce', in *The Reader's Encyclopedia of World Drama*, ed. by John Gassner and Edward Quinn (New York: Dover Publications, 2002), pp. 262–265.
30. NLI, BFP, MS 37,093/1. Note towards *The Communication Cord* dated 10 November 1981.
31. NLI, BFP, MS 37,093/1. Undated note towards *The Communication Cord*.
32. NLI, BFP, MS 37,093/1. Note towards *The Communication Cord* dated 13 November 1981.
33. Gassner and Quinn, p. 264, cited in NLI, BFP, MS 37,093/1. Undated note towards *The Communication Cord*.
34. NLI, BFP, MS 37,093/1. Note towards *The Communication Cord* dated 23 November 1981.
35. NLI, BFP, MS 37,093/1. Note towards *The Communication Cord* dated 24 November 1981.
36. NLI, BFP, MS 37,093/1. Note towards *The Communication Cord* dated 7 January 1982.
37. Gassner and Quinn, p. 265, cited in NLI, BFP, MS 37,093/1. Undated note towards *The Communication Cord*. Underlining added by Friel in red ink.
38. NLI, BFP, MS 37,093/1. Note towards *The Communication Cord* dated 7 December 1981.
39. Ibid.
40. NLI, BFP, MS 37,093/1. Note towards *The Communication Cord* dated 7 January 1982.
41. Gassner and Quinn, p. 263, cited in NLI, BFP, MS 37,093/1. Undated note towards *The Communication Cord*.
42. Peter Kemp, 'Mixing mockery and homage', *TLS*, 5 March 1982, p. 252. See NLI, BFP, MS 37,093/1.
43. NLI, Brian Friel Papers, MS 37,093/1. Note towards *The Communication Cord* dated 10 January 1982.
44. NLI, Brian Friel Papers, MS 37,093/1. Note towards *The Communication Cord* dated 9 January 1982.

45. Roy Harris, 'Performing in words', *TLS*, 18 December 1981, 1455–1456 (p. 1455). See Friel, *The Communication Cord*, p. 19.
46. Harris, p. 1455. See also Friel, *The Communication Cord*, p. 36.
47. Harris, p. 1455.
48. Erving Goffman, 'Response Cries', *Language 54*, No. 4 (1978), 787–815 (p. 814).
49. Denis Donoghue, *Ferocious Alphabets* (London: Faber and Faber, 1981), p. 43. Further references in parentheses in the text as 'Donoghue, *FA*'.
50. George Steiner, *After Babel: Aspects of Language and Translation* (Oxford: Oxford University Press, 1976), p. 198; Brian Friel, *Plays One* (London: Faber and Faber, 1996), p. 446.
51. Steiner, *After Babel*, p. 281.
52. Roland Barthes, *A Lover's Discourse: Fragments*, trans. by Richard Howard (New York: Hill & Wang, 2001), p. 167. See also Donoghue, *Ferocious Alphabets*, pp. 43–44.
53. Friel, *Plays One*, p. 427.
54. NLI, BFP, MS 37,093/1. Note towards *The Communication Cord* dated 23 November 1981. Double underlining in original.
55. George Steiner, *In Bluebeard's Castle: Some Notes Towards the Redefinition of Culture* (London: Faber and Faber, 1971), p. 89.
56. NLI, Brian Friel Papers, MS 37,093/1. Note towards *The Communication Cord* dated 9 January 1982.
57. Brian Friel, *Plays Two* (London: Faber and Faber, 1999), p. 387. Further references in parentheses in the text as 'Friel, *P2*'.
58. NLI, BFP, MS 37,093/1. Note towards *The Communication Cord* dated 8 November 1981. Struck through in pencil.
59. NLI, Brian Friel Papers, MS 37,123/1. Note towards *Wonderful Tennessee* dated 16 November 1983.
60. NLI, BFP, MS 37,123/2. Typed diary entry towards *Wonderful Tennessee* dated 29 June 1990.
61. NLI, BFP, MS 37,123/2. Typed diary entry towards *Wonderful Tennessee* dated [3 July] 1990.
62. NLI, Brian Friel Papers, MS 37,123/2. Note towards *Wonderful Tennessee* dated 4 July 1990. Quotation marks added on 11 December 1991 in black ink.
63. '[T]he invention of the mechanical clock in medieval Europe [...] was one of the great inventions in the history of mankind—not

in a class with fire and the wheel, but comparable to movable type in its revolutionary implications for cultural values, technological change, social and political organisation, and personality'. David S. Landes, *Revolution in Time: Clocks and the Making of the Modern World* (Cambridge, Massachusetts; London, England: The Belknap Press of Harvard University Press, 1983), p. 6. See also NLI, BFP, MS 37,123/2. Typed diary entry towards *Wonderful Tennessee* dated 4 July 1990.
64. Landes, p. 7. See also NLI, BFP, MS 37,123/2. Typed diary entry towards *Wonderful Tennessee* dated 1 August 1990.
65. See Landes, pp. 38–40, 44–46.
66. NLI, Brian Friel Papers, MS 37,123/2. Typed diary entry towards *Wonderful Tennessee* dated 12 July 1990.
67. NLI, BFP, MS 37/123/3. Note towards *Wonderful Tennessee* dated 4 July 1990. Red ink.
68. NLI, BFP, MS 37,123/3. Undated note towards *Wonderful Tennessee* in 'TIME and Pilgrimage' booklet (begun 4 July 1990).
69. 'This becomes Under Milkwood. The characters all seated in a semi-circle of chairs. A verbal cantata. Very possible. Perhaps a try-out on radio?' NLI, BFP, MS 37,123/2. Typed diary entry towards *Wonderful Tennessee* dated 13 July 1990.
70. NLI, BFP, MS 37,123/2. Typed diary entry towards *Wonderful Tennessee* dated 19 July 1990.
71. Denis Donoghue, *The Arts Without Mystery* (London: The British Broadcasting Corporation, 1983), p. 11. Further references in parentheses in the text as 'Donoghue, *TAWM*'.
72. Gabriel Marcel, *Being and Having*, trans. by Katherine Farrer (Westminster: Dacre Press, 1949), pp. 100–101, cited in Donoghue, *The Arts Without Mystery*, p. 12.
73. Marcel, *Being and Having*, p. 100.
74. Gabriel Marcel, *Être et Avoir* (Paris: Fernand Aubier; Editions Montaigne, 1935), p. 138.
75. Marcel, *Being and Having*, p. 96.
76. Marcel, *Être et Avoir*, p. 144.
77. Marcel, *Being and Having*, p. 100.
78. Marcel, *Being and Having*, p. 100.
79. Sir Walter Ralegh, 'A Poesie to Prove Affection Is Not Love', in *The Poems of Sir Walter Ralegh: A Historical Edition*, ed. By Michael Rudick (Tempe, Arizona: Arizona Center for Medieval

and Renaissance Studies in conjunction with Renaissance English Text Society, 1999), p. 6.
80. Donoghue, p. 94. Susanne K. Langer, *Feeling and Form* (London: Routledge and Kegan Paul, 1953), p. 113, cited in Donoghue, *The Arts Without Mystery*, p. 94.
81. Octavio Paz, *The Labyrinth of Solitude: Life and Thought in Mexico*, trans. by Lysander Kemp (Middlesex: Penguin Books, 1985), p. 48.
82. NLI, Brian Friel Papers, MS 37,123/3. Note towards *Wonderful Tennessee* dated 13 August 1990.
83. NLI, Brian Friel Papers, MS 37,123/3. Note towards *Wonderful Tennessee* dated 17 August 1990.
84. NLI, Brian Friel Papers, MS 37,123/3. Note towards *Wonderful Tennessee* dated 29 May 1991.
85. Landes, p. 63.
86. NLI, BFP, MS 37,123/2. Typed diary entry towards *Wonderful Tennessee* dated 31 July 1990.
87. NLI, BFP, MS 37,123/2. Typed diary entry towards *Wonderful Tennessee* dated 1 August 1990. See also St. Augustine, *The City of God*, XII, 18 (Migne, *Patrologia Latina*, XLI), p. 368 and E. M. Cioran, *La Tentation d'Exister* (1956): *The Temptation to Exist*, tr. Richard Howard (Chicago: Quadrangle Books, 1968), p. 152, cited in Donoghue, *The Arts Without Mystery*, p. 8.
88. NLI, BFP, MS 37,123/2. Typed diary entry towards *Wonderful Tennessee* dated 1 August 1990.
89. NLI, Brian Friel Papers, MS 37,123/1. Note towards *Wonderful Tennessee* dated 16 November 1983.
90. NLI, Brian Friel Papers, MS 37,123/3. Note towards *Wonderful Tennessee* dated 22 January 1991.
91. Donoghue, *The Arts Without Mystery*, p. 132. See also NLI, BFP, MS 37,123/2. Typed diary entry towards *Wonderful Tennessee* dated 1 August 1990. See also T.S. Eliot's 'The Love Song of J Alfred Prufrock'.
92. NLI, BFP, MS 37,123/2. Typed diary entry towards *Wonderful Tennessee* dated 7 August 1990.
93. NLI, BFP, MS 37,123/2. Typed diary entry towards *Wonderful Tennessee* dated 31 January 1991.
94. NLI, BFP, MS 37,123/2. Typed diary entry towards *Wonderful Tennessee* dated 4 September 1990.

95. NLI, BFP, MS 37,123/2. Typed diary entry towards *Wonderful Tennessee* dated 7 February 1991. Bold type in original.
96. Cole M. Crittenden, 'The Dramatics of Time' *KronoScope* 5, No. 2 (2005), pp. 193–212 (p. 193).
97. NLI, BFP, MS 37,123/2. Typed diary entry towards *Wonderful Tennessee* dated 31 January 1991.
98. Donoghue, p. 94. Susanne K. Langer, *Feeling and Form* (London: Routledge and Kegan Paul, 1953), p. 113, cited in Donoghue, *The Arts Without Mystery*, p. 94.
99. NLI, Brian Friel Papers, MS 37,123/3. Note towards *Wonderful Tennessee* dated 31 January 1991.
100. Saint Augustine, *Confessions*, trans. by Henry Chadwick (Oxford: Oxford University Press, 2008), p. 243.
101. NLI, Brian Friel Papers, MS 37,123/3. Note towards *Wonderful Tennessee* dated 8 August 1990.
102. NLI, Brian Friel Papers, MS 37.123/4.
103. NLI, Brian Friel Papers, MS 37,123/3. Undated note towards *Wonderful Tennessee*.
104. Steiner, *After Babel*, p. 281.

CHAPTER 5

Influence as Model: Friel's Performing Muse

Thus far, I have focused on influence in Friel at the level of artistic practice, exploring how his eclectic sources of inspiration manifested themselves both as theatre and as ways of making theatre. Here, I turn to what was in many ways Friel's career-long preoccupation with the idea of influence itself at a thematic level. In the first instance, I want to shine a spotlight on one of Friel's last original plays, *Performances* (2003), which is also his most direct engagement with the idea of artistic influence. In previous decades, Friel had turned to artists like Francis Bacon and thinkers like Denis Donoghue to make plays whose cores were inextricably linked with the question of how artists make art, but whose plots—with the possible exception of *Give Me Your Answer, Do!* (1997)—remained only allegorically connected to this theme. Now Friel returned to familiar ground—the works of George Steiner—to stage what turned out to be his final debate on the process of artistic interpretation. At the same time, Friel was engaging with new sources that put the role of the artist's muse under scrutiny. This latter engagement with musedom is one that is enriching not only as part of our understanding of the play and its genesis, but also as a productive new lens for reading gender in Friel studies is a field when combined with certain elements of Steiner's writing on the interpretive power of performance. Indeed, this lens of what I have come to think of as Friel's 'performing muse' provides a useful framework within which to discuss gendered power dynamics in the

© The Author(s), under exclusive license to Springer Nature Switzerland AG 2023
Z. Kuczyńska, *Brian Friel's Models of Influence*,
https://doi.org/10.1007/978-3-031-17905-1_5

context of Friel's thinking around influence at the level of artistic practice. It is a lens, moreover, whose significance transcends the chronology of Friel's oeuvre, and which can be used to provide valuable insights into his other works. A prime case study in this respect is *Molly Sweeney* (1994)—a play that, partly by virtue of its having a sympathetic female lead, has already attracted a deal of highly gendered critical intervention. Building on existing feminist critiques of Friel's gender politics, I use the remainder of this chapter to show how an appreciation of Friel's 'performing muse' may provide the means of deconstructing some of the more unhelpful arguments around women's empowerment in Friel's works more generally. Specifically, I want to begin to move towards a discussion of how we talk about the creation of binarily gendered roles for the stage in a post-#MeToo, post-#WakingTheFeminists world.

Methodologically speaking, this chapter differs slightly from its predecessors by virtue of the relative poverty of the archive material pertaining to *Performances* in the Brian Friel Papers (Additional). This is partly to be expected, due to the fact that the play is a great deal shorter than Friel's only full-length original play of the 2000s, *The Home Place* (2005). However, though MS 49,252 is rich in holographic and typed drafts of the play, there is still very little by way of Friel's characteristic preparatory notes. The lengthy, questioning, and indeed revealing explorations we have come to expect from this part of Friel's process are therefore conspicuous by their absence. By necessity, then, my reading of Friel's engagement with his source materials for *Performances* is more speculative than it has been in other chapters. As such, it relies more on my own readings of those materials and their possible manifestation in the finished play than on a sense of how Friel's process itself might be said to bear the hallmarks of a significant creative encounter. Consequently, the question of the degree to which Friel was influenced by various source materials for the play is less prominent than with my readings of Friel's other creative encounters. Rather I am interested in showcasing the extent to which archival encounters might facilitate an imaginative leap in terms of a given critical approach. Certainly, my own encounter with both the archive material pertaining to *Performances* and the secondary reading it occasioned has brought about a significant alteration of the way in which I navigate my critical relationship with Friel's gender politics. It is in this spirit that I also supplement and extend my readings in this chapter with insights gleaned from two specific performances of the plays under discussion: Adrian Dunbar's 2013 production of *Performances*[1] and Andrew

Flynn's 2014 production of *Molly Sweeney*.[2] By reading archive, text, and performance into one another as part of an extended continuum of textuality, I hope to illustrate how taking a less chronological, more triangulated approach to meaning in Friel's plays might generate new critical perspectives on his work.

'HOW DARE YOU, MR JANÁČEK?'[3]

To arrive at a working understanding of what I mean by Friel's 'performing muse', it is necessary to start with Friel's engagement with traditional musedom. *Performances* is a play that deals with the idea of influence at the level of artistic practice head-on, and which takes a critical view of the relationship between artist and muse. As we will discover shortly, however, it is a form of criticism that is not unproblematic. The play stages a meeting between the long-dead Czech composer Leoš Janáček—the fact of whose death is established fairly casually near the beginning of the play—and PhD researcher Anezka Ungrova. Anezka is working on Janáček's second string quartet, known as 'Intimate Letters', and intends to argue in her thesis that the composer's passion for a much younger woman named Kamila Stösslová 'had a determining effect on that composition'. To achieve this, she draws on his many hundreds of letters to Stösslová to make her case for its being 'a textbook example of a great passion inspiring a great work of art' (Friel, *Performances*, 15). For Anezka, in other words, Janáček's work was created with the help of a muse. The dead Janáček of the play, however, reframes the relationship between artist and muse as one that is better understood as that between user and used. Much to Anezka's chagrin, Friel's Janáček dismisses the passion of which she speaks as a mere invention: 'dreams of music [...] transferred onto a perfectly decent but quite untutored young woman'. Instead, he insists that the music itself is 'the real thing', and that the intimate letters themselves are mere 'stammering pages' (Friel, *Performances*, 27) compared to the string quartet of the same name. The play ends with both the dead composer and the young researcher imploring one another simply to listen to the music—played by a live string quartet—in the belief that its performance will be their vindication.

Of the works that influenced Friel when writing *Performances*, some are better known than others. Moreover, the full extent of Friel's engagement with those sources is not immediately apparent from the available archive material. We ought therefore to begin with what we know before branching out imaginatively into the unknown. The biographical content of the play comes partly from a source readily acknowledged by Friel in the published text of the play—John Tyrrell's edition of *Intimate Letters: Leoš Janáček to Kamila Stösslová* (1994). This comprises an English language translation of what remains of the correspondence between the ageing Czech composer and the much younger woman he made his muse. It was suggested to Friel as a source of dramatic material by Michael Colgan, who was the Artistic Director of Dublin's Gate Theatre at the time. The correspondence is largely one-sided, due perhaps to Stösslová's insistence that Janáček burn the letters she had written. This imbalance is reflected in the play to the extent that, although her figure looms large, Kamila Stösslová herself never actually appears in the dramatis personae of *Performances*. In the absence of Stösslová's voice throughout the vast majority of Tyrrell's selection, Janáček's intense outpourings of unconsummated passion appear as much in love with their own fervour as with Stösslová. The letters themselves are in no small part dedicated to the writing of Janáček's second string quartet, completed in 1928, which he called 'Intimate Letters' in a deliberate acknowledgement of its unspoken subject matter. Tyrrell's edited selection, then, showcases a largely romantic view of musedom that, in a way that is exacerbated by the absence of Stösslová's replies, privileges the real Janáček's construction of the relationship between a passionate artist and 'his abiding muse'.[4]

The archive also suggests some additional, unacknowledged biographical source material. After reading and highlighting a *TLS* review[5] of Mirka Zemanová's *Janáček: a composer's life* (2002), Friel ordered his own copy on 25 September.[6] At first glance, it would appear that Zemanová's biography is the source of the play's acknowledgement of the possibility of the dead composer's having been 'a real pig' (Friel, *Performances*, 28) in life rather than the romantic figure of his correspondence. The book is heavy with implied criticisms of Janáček's behaviour where women were concerned. From the outset, Zemanová highlights 'his tendency to put women on a pedestal during the initial stages of a relationship, only to drop them later in favour of a new prospect'. So too does she point out the discrepancy between his treatment of fictional women and his conduct towards their real-world counterparts: 'while he glorified women on the stage, he was capable of emotional cruelty to them in life'.[7] Certainly, Zemanová's biography contains multiple examples of Janáček's abysmal treatment of his wife Zdenka, whom he married when she was still fifteen years of age (he being twenty-seven at the time). Whether refusing to see his daughter when she was born (Zemanová, 46) insisting that Zdenka—fresh from a suicide attempt triggered by his having blamed her for his creative impotence—invites his mistress Gabriela Horvátová to come and stay with her (Zemanová, 133), humiliating her in public (Zemanová, 219), writing to her after a dangerous and painful thyroid operation to demand that she apologise to Kamila Stösslová for offending her with her not-unfounded jealousy (Zemanová, 225), or just being brazenly emotionally unfaithful, the Janáček of Zemanová's biography leaves a skidmark of shoddy behaviour all over its pages. His conduct as a husband, whilst left refreshingly unexcused, is presented largely without comment from Zemanová. It is also almost entirely absent from Friel's play, which avoids the issue of the gender politics of Janáček's marriage altogether, despite the guiding focus of Paul Griffiths's review of Zemanová's book in the *TLS*. Indeed, with the exception of Griffiths's appraisal of Janáček as 'a bleak tyrant' in his personal life, Friel's highlights are mostly to do with Kamila Stösslová, apparently finding little of interest in the 'ultimately dismaying' 'record of the facts' of Janáček's marriage as summarised in the review. The question of 'why [Janáček] could extend his sympathy so abundantly to fictional characters but barely at all to his wife'[8] appears to have been of little interest to Friel, whose Janáček dismisses his wife as 'Moravia's supreme fantasist' (Friel, *Performances*, 10) in a cruelly ironic quip that goes unexamined by Anezka. Accordingly, the only other reference to Zdenka in *Performances* fails to mention even her name, instead referencing composer Antonín Dvořák's alleged response to being introduced to 'the new Mrs Janáček': 'In the name of God, Leos, you've married a child!'.[9]

Where Friel's play does deal with Janáček's problematic gender politics, however, is in connection to the idea of the muse in the context of the composer's creative process. Zemanová's biography touches on this theme in several places, noting that, whilst it would be a mistake to overstate the relationship between the life and the work, Janáček nevertheless showed a remarkable tendency towards 'creating [...] certain situations and then exploiting them'. His correspondence with Kamila Stösslová, she suggests, is symptomatic of a creative practice whereby he would deliberately maintain and cultivate a link between experience and inspiration (Zemanová, 5). She also alludes to Stösslová's reluctance to be a muse (Zemanová, 199), Janáček's awareness of his need for the 'made-up world'[10] that he had created around and through her, and the irony of a self-confessed fantasist deluding himself that a 'platonic' relationship based on '[unmistakably] erotic' (Zemanová, 224) feelings on his part was simply a case of 'perfectly ordinary sympathy'.[11] She also notes that the sublimation of sexual desire into a spiritual connection was firmly in the Petrarchan tradition, and that the Second String Quartet likewise constitutes the sublimation of an emotional life: 'love is undeniably the subject-matter of this work' (Zemanová, 239).

Friel's engagement with musedom itself in terms of the gendered conflict between his Janáček and Anezka—expressed in his notes as a 'soft, Romantic notion' (Anezka's research) that is subsequently 'attacked'[12] (by Janáček)—appears to come from somewhere quite different, however. Here, a more speculative approach becomes necessary, guided by the few archival breadcrumbs left by Friel. There is evidence for some additional minor sources beyond Tyrrell, Zemanová, and Steiner (of which more anon): the Škampa Quartet's 2001 studio recording of Janáček's String Quartets on the Czech record label Supraphon[13]; founding member of the quartet Milan Škampa's notes for the insert of the same CD[14]; and, in a zeitgeisty nod to the dawn of the age of Wikipedia, a print-out of what appears to be a now-defunct website accessed by Friel on 27 August 2002, which includes a brief biography of Janáček and a review of his chamber music at London's Wigmore Hall from the *Musical Times* of 1926.[15] Though informative even in their brevity, Friel clearly wasn't getting his ideas on musedom from here. There is, however, one additional source to consider: Francine Prose's *The Lives of The Muses* (2002).

This is a book with which the bulk of the play's commentary on musedom resonates fairly strongly, despite the evidence for Friel's having consulted his own copy being inconclusive. Friel had noted down the publication details of *The Lives of the Muses* on an undated card, along with the name of what was, at the time, merely an internet bookstore with no in-house means of sending its founder, Jeff Bezos, to space.[16] There is also some concrete evidence that Friel engaged with at least some of Prose's arguments. Indeed, MS 049,254/3 tells us that Friel had come across a review of Prose's book in the *New Yorker* a few days after having ordered Zemanová's biography. In a clipping from an issue dated 30 September 2002, Friel highlights a citation from *The Lives of the Muses* that subsequently reappears in one of his undated notes. It is a sentiment that is highly reminiscent of Friel's own version of Janáček, whose cynicism regarding the relationship between artists and muse is palpable: 'The power of longing is more durable than the thrill of possession'.[17] Friel also highlighted the reviewer's final assessment of Prose's book as having achieved a 'quiet reevaluation of the received notion that genius is solitary in nature'.[18] Here the archival trail, such as it is, runs out of crumbs. Though I believe there is a case to be made for the main body of Prose's work as a significant unacknowledged source for *Performances*, I think it would be more productive at this point to focus on *The Lives of the Muses* as having influenced my own reading of the play. Certainly, I have found that encountering Prose's take on the gender politics of musedom via the archive has given me a framework within which to articulate the things that—for want of a better way of putting it—bug me inordinately about a play of which I am otherwise fond. In other words, Prose's argument has allowed me to begin to answer the question of why I find a play in which the artist-muse model of inspiration is placed under an unflinchingly critical lens naggingly problematic.

The Lives of the Muses opens with a view of artistic inspiration that would surely have struck a chord with Friel. For Prose, the idea of the muse comes from the human 'desire to explain the mystery of inspiration', comparing it to the 'childish, suspect', but ultimately very human 'impulse to find out a magician's secrets'. However, in an uncanny echo of Denis Donoghue, 'one difference between magic and art is that magic can be explained'. Indeed, in Prose's view, '[t]o create *anything* is to undergo the humbling and strange experience—like a mystical visitation or spirit possession—of making something and *not knowing where it comes from*'[19] (italics in original). In this context, the muse emerges as one way of appeasing our desire to explain the inexplicable by functioning as part of a 'myth to help explain, or at least surround, the genesis of art'. Hence the divine Muses of antiquity, whose intervention helped make inspiration tangible without dispelling its mystery. However, as Prose goes on to say in her characteristically wry, pithy style, 'once the [pagan] gods stopped descending to earth to lecture shepherds and have sex with mortals [...] an alternate explanation for creativity' (Prose, 4–5) became necessary:

> Since a reversion to paganism was clearly out of the question, there was nowhere to go but down—from the divine to the mortal. And since falling in love is the closest that most people come to transcendence, to the feeling of being inhabited by unwilled, unruly forces, passion became the model for understanding inspiration.

Thus the creation myth surrounding the act of making art underwent a 'progression from the ethereal to the corporeal' (Prose, 5), resituating the divine inspiration of the Muse-goddess in the objectified body of a human muse.

The problem here, of course, is that this is more often than not a highly gendered model of inspiration that 'reinforce[s] the destructive stereotype of the creative, productive, active male and of the passive female, at once worshipped and degraded' (Prose, 9). Moreover, the woman-as-muse is expected simultaneously to fulfil the requirements of unattainable fantasy woman and to act in a caregiving role as '[n]urturer and diet police, understander and mirror' (Prose, 22), never too real to disrupt a generative state of desire but never too unreal to be beyond gendered expectations as to the division of domestic labour. Consequently, Prose's book works not only to highlight the misogynistic aspects of musedom but also to recover the personhood and agency of a varied selection of women whose 'mysterious role[s] in the process that turns experience into art' were not universal but rather symptomatic of each being 'a product of her time' who 'moved outside and beyond it' (Prose, 24). These women range from pre-Raphaelite icons like Elizabeth 'Lizzie' Siddal—the model and artist whose husband, Dante Gabriel Rossetti, violated her grave in order to retrieve a book of poems he had buried with her (Prose, 136)— to modern muses like Gala Dalí and Yoko Ono. Another woman who features heavily in Prose is Alice Liddell, the 'ideal child-friend'[20] of Charles Dodgson, a.k.a. Lewis Carroll. Tellingly, an earlier version of the critic-researcher character from *Performances* (here called Marie/Maria) makes reference to the pairing in the same breath as Dante and Beatrice, resulting in the following comic exchange:

JAN [...] Who was Alice?
MAR Alice in Wonderland.
J (NEVER HEARD OF HER) I see.[21]

In addition to recovering neglected biographical information, moreover, Prose's argument concerns itself with the possibility of a different gender politics of musedom with a more reciprocal power dynamic. In a deliberate challenge to Robert Graves's famously obnoxious dictum to the effect that women can never be true artists in their own right—'She is either Muse or she is nothing'[22]—Prose asks whether a relationship of mutual musedom is achievable. In the case of Yoko Ono, Prose observes that what began as 'a sort of job-sharing arrangement with her husband' became a struggle, 'even after death, over who was the real artist, and who was the muse' (Prose, 8), exacerbated by 'a mixture of jealousy, race and gender bias' (Prose, 20). Meanwhile, Prose considers the case of Suzanne Farrell and George Balanchine as proof that 'the roles of inspired and inspirer, artist and muse' can indeed be reciprocal. However, despite such collaborations '[producing] work that neither [artist] could accomplish alone' (Prose, 9), such reciprocity is rarely acknowledged in the context of a power dynamic where one party has the demonstrable ability to ruin the other's career, as happened when Farrell dared to marry a dancer of her own age and found herself 'not only ostracized and unemployed but unemployable' (Prose, 19).

How, though, might Prose's reading of the gender politics of musedom be seen to manifest itself in *Performances*? Or rather how does Prose's argument facilitate a productive problematisation of the play's gender politics? In the first instance, I suggest that Friel's characterisation of the dead Janáček resonates strongly with Prose's assessment of the relationship between artist and muse. It is true that Friel's Janáček's flippant characterisation of the artist as user can be attributed to Griffiths's review of Zemanová, in which the relationship between Janáček and Stösslová is called 'one of the most flagrant cases of the artist's use of other people for creative purposes'.[23] Most certainly true is the discrepancy between the Janáček of the play and the Janáček of the letters, from whose overblown lyricism Friel's Janáček distances himself with a ruthlessness he appears almost to relish. What makes a comparison between Friel's Janáček and Prose's argument irresistibly productive, however, is the implications of the extent to which it is Friel's Janáček—and not the bafflingly uncritical female researcher—who critiques his own process in the light of the warped gender politics of musedom. Indeed, what Anezka calls '[a]n outpouring of [...] passionate letters' constituting '[r]eaffirmations of [Janáček's] devotion'—sounding all the whilst less like a critical researcher than an incurable romantic—Janáček calls 'stammering pages' that are merely 'dreams of music [...] transferred onto a perfectly decent but quite untutored young woman' (Friel, *Performances*, 27):

> [I]n time the distinction between his dreams and that young woman became indistinguishable, so that in his head she was transformed into something immeasurably greater [...] The music in the head made real

[...] Came to know no distinction between the dream music and the dream woman! (Friel, *Performances*, 27–8)

In Friel's Janáček's assessment of his relationship with the woman he made his muse, then, his unrequited desire to possess Kamila Stösslová is analogous to his having created a piece of music that was 'the closest he ever got to the dream sounds in his head' (Friel, *Performances*, 28). This is strikingly similar to the passage in Prose's book in which Friel's highlighted quote from the *New Yorker* review can be found:

[T]he power of longing is more durable than the thrill of possession. [...] And unrequited desire may itself be a metaphor for the making of art, for the fact that a finished work so rarely equals the initial impulse or conception, thus compelling the artist to start over and try again. (Prose, 17–18)

The echoes of one of Friel's earliest plays, *The Enemy Within* (1962), are irresistible: 'to begin again—to begin again—to begin again!'.[24]

The implications of Friel's Janáček appropriating a feminist critique of his own artistic process by reframing unrequited desire as mere metaphor—whilst at the same time being an unrepentant misogynist—are certainly troubling. They become more so when considering the gender dimension of the debate at the heart of the play. It may well be significant, for instance, that the character of the PhD researcher Anezka was, in earlier typed drafts, a male student named Jan Mikota (named after the secretary to the real Janáček's Czech publisher)[25]:

Hat, coat, brief-case. He is in his twenties, a student at Prague University where he is working on a doctorate on Janacek's ~~late~~ \later/ work. He is a ~~nervous~~ \diffident/ and agitated young man and very eager to please. But even though he is patently in awe of Janacek he can be very determined, even ~~stubborn~~ \obstinate/, in his opinions.[26]

Originally, then, it seems, Anezka was another one of Friel's nervous young men in the mould of Tim Gallagher (the young academic from *The Communication Cord*), David Knight (the assessor from *Give Me Your Answer, Do!*), or even Casimir (the brittle young man of *Aristocrats* who likes to make a game of identifying works by Chopin when played by his sister on the piano). Her lineage is also that of the at-best ambivalent scholarly figure that crops up time and again in Friel's plays in a managerial (and therefore latently adversarial) role: David Knight, Tom Hoffnung of *Aristocrats*, and Lombard of *Making History* are among notable examples of the type.

Why, then, did Friel choose to gender-swap this particular iteration of these two familiar types? The archive is largely unhelpful here, but my own interpretation is that Friel may have done so in order to attempt to address the gender dimension of Janáček's use and abuse of Kamila Stösslová as a muse. After all, it makes at least some sense for it to be a young woman who takes the ageing composer to task, if only to make up for the absence of Kamila Stösslová onstage. This is something that came across particularly strongly in Adrian Dunbar's 2013 production of *Performances*. During the final, non-verbal segment of the play, the windows at the back of the set became periodically translucent as the fourth movement[27] of the 'Intimate Letters' Quartet was played onstage. They revealed Masha Dakič as Anezka progressing through the frames, gradually acquiring a 1920s costume in which she rotated slowly whilst reading a letter, hinting at a metamorphosis into Kamila Stösslová herself. In other words, *Performances* stages a debate about a highly gendered artist-muse model in which the gender dimension is *cosmetically* reproduced in the relationship between artist and critic. It certainly factored into Friel's notes, in which Anezka's remonstrations with her fallen idol—'How dare you, Mr Janáček? How dare you?' (Friel, *Performances*, 28)—are referred to in highly gendered terms as 'her scolding speech'.[28] In objecting to Janáček's Frank Hardy-esque characterisation of Stösslová as someone he had 'invented [...] as an expression of what was the very best in himself' (Friel, *Performances*, 28), then, Anezka is superficially in line with Prose, who is generally critical of the erasure of real-life women in favour of the fantasy constructions made of them by assorted male artists. Hence Anezka's assessment of Janáček's sense of having 'transformed an unsophisticated woman' into the dream woman in his head as 'cruel and heartless and deeply misogynistic' (Friel, *Performances*, 30)—something Friel's women rarely get to say outright.

Before we get ahead of ourselves in congratulating Friel on his progressive gender politics, however, I would draw attention to two major issues with Friel's characterisation of Anezka. Firstly, her objections are themselves problematically gendered; secondly, her critique of Janáček's behaviour towards Kamila Stösslová is based on an astonishing lack of critical thinking on her part, and is more the reaction of someone who has had her dreams of romance shattered than someone who has ever given the gender politics of musedom any serious consideration. The first issue becomes apparent even with the relatively scant archival material available. As Jan Mikota, the character was 'nervous-\diffident/' but 'determined' and occasionally 'stubborn \obstinate/ in his opinions'[29]; as Anezka Ungrova, the character is '*anxious, intense and earnest*' and '*very dogged in her questioning*' (Friel, *Performances*, 6). Similarly, it is highly unlikely that a male or masculine-coded character would be described by a septuagenarian male playwright in the early 2000s as a scold. Even her name is troubling in its implications: the name Anezka is one that crops up in Tyrrell's notes to Janáček's letters in the context of one Anežka Schulzová, who wrote the libretti to the last three operas of Czech composer Zdeněk Fibich, her former teacher and later lover. Potentially an example of an artist-muse relationship that became a productive collaborative relationship, the real Janáček dismissed her in his letters as the antithesis to his relationship with Kamila Stösslová: 'I found the charm of a body and a natural soul, he found a frump and the grammar of words'.[30] Indeed, in a far cry from Friel's Janáček, for whom 'the work's the thing', the real Janáček was fairly dismissive about the idea of producing with one's muse instead of reproducing: 'Fibich-Anežka were [...] warmed up by what they had forged [between them]—their work—librettos— and really didn't warm themselves! They had no children! But many stupid and unnecessary operas'.[31] It may well be significant, then, that the gender-swapped PhD researcher was initially renamed not only Anezka but Anežka *Schulzová*, after that collaborating muse the real Janáček had dismissed as 'a poor cripple' who 'lived in dry work' rather than being content to exist as a 'sacred fire' in which 'gold will get shaped into a ring and God knows what else'.[32]

Coincidence? Possibly. The same note in which Friel re-genders and renames Jan Mikota also has the names 'Clara Horvátová' and 'Marie Stejskalová' crossed out as alternatives, suggesting that Friel was using women mentioned in Janáček's letters to come up with names for a fictional Czech researcher. Gabriela Horvátová was a singer with whom Janáček had an affair prior to his obsession with Kamila Stösslová; Marie Stejskalová, meanwhile, was Janáček's maid, whose memoirs are quoted in Zemanová. Anezka's final choice of surname, meanwhile, comes from another singer: soprano Kamila Ungrová, who premièred the role of Jenůfa in Janáček's opera of the same name. However, it is difficult not to see a link between the real Janáček's dismissal of Anežka Schulzová's collaborative relationship with her composer and Friel's Janáček's dismissal of Anezka Ungrova's insistence on the importance of the letters: one has no time for 'the grammar of words'[33]; the other has no time for 'the people who huckster in words [who] merely report on feeling' (Friel, *Performances*, 25). It is true that this may have less to do with an unfavourable view of women of words in particular than with George Steiner's privileging of music over language (of which more presently). Nevertheless, there is something uncomfortable about Friel's choice to associate his Janáček's academic foil with a woman the real Janáček seemed to regard as the wrong kind of muse *whilst at the same time* making her naively uncritical until provoked into being a scold.

This brings us to the second major issue with Friel's characterisation of Anezka: the fact that, as a researcher, she is—to put it bluntly—not very good. This is partially a hangover from one of the few pieces of evidence in the archive to suggest that Friel envisaged other possibilities for the way in which the play's central conflict would play out:

Two possibilities:—
    Janacek proposes the soft, Romantic notion—"my little sun"—and this is attacked by the Critic.
        OR
    The critic proposes the soft Romantic notion—and this is attacked by Janacek: "She was useful for creative purposes."[34]

Consequently, Anezka's thesis, that Janáček's Second String Quartet is 'a textbook example of a great passion inspiring a great work of art' (Friel, *Performances*, 15), is at best naïve and unfocused. It not only fails to interrogate the gender politics of musedom but also ignores, say, Zemanová's take on the Janáček-Stösslová relationship when she claims that '[y]our biographers have *all* written of that relationship [...] as one of the great love affairs' (Friel, *Performances*, 10; my italics). However, Anezka's romanticism is also symptomatic of what Prose defines as a turn to passion for a model of inspiration in lieu of the divine inspiration of the Muse-goddess (Prose, 4–5). As we have seen, this desire to explain the inexplicable—to reduce the arts-as-mystery to a problem to be solved—is 'suspect' (Prose, 2) in its childishness, and can be associated with the managerial impulses explored in Donoghue's work.

Rather more puzzlingly, and less easily attributable to Friel's basic 'romantic versus cynic' model, many of the letters Anezka cites during the play are not from Tyrrell's edited selection at all. A notable example of this is a letter allegedly written on 1 February 1928, in which Janáček supposedly wrote: 'I've just completed the opening movement and it is all about our first fateful encounter and how you instantly enslaved me' (Friel, *Performances*, 12). The real Janáček's letter of 1 February 1928 as translated by John Tyrrell says no such thing. (Indeed, there are elements of Anezka's so-called letters that owe more to Milan Škampa's CD sleeve notes than to the timeline of the real Janáček's correspondence.) More significantly, this particular fictional letter can also be compared with examples given by Prose of the relationship between eighteenth-century diarist Hester Thrale and writer Samuel Johnson, who had been known to write to her in 'the language of bondage and restraint'.[35] Whether a case of wishing to avoid copyright issues, establishing Anezka as an unreliable scholar, incorporating other examples of the muse-artist relationship into his play, or merely having a little fun by indulging in what Christopher Murray calls 'Frielian pastiche',[36] it is unclear why Friel chose to exercise his artistic licence in this manner. Certainly, an audience without an encyclopaedic knowledge of the letters would hardly be in a position to notice that, when Friel's Janáček protests that he never wrote such a thing, or that Anezka has 'invent[ed]'[37] certain passages, he is technically telling the truth. It is therefore perhaps more likely that Friel was amusing himself rather than making a point. Nevertheless, the niggling if intriguing fact remains that many of the letters Anezka uses to undermine Janáček's cynicism are indeed inventions.

What is most problematic about Friel's portrayal of Anezka as a researcher, however, is that her eventual criticism of Janáček has very little to do with scholarly critique. Throughout the play, Anezka takes Janáček's letters almost entirely at face value, and is scandalised by Janáček's self-confessed cynicism and evident, apparently remorseless awareness of his having used Stösslová as a means to a creative end. Indeed, Anezka's shock appears to be genuine, insofar as it seems never to have occurred to her to read Janáček's letters through a feminist lens, or even a particularly critical one. In fact, what should have been Anezka's finest moment (and one that might well have resonated with a post- '#MeToo' audience) was edited out of the play:

ANEZKA (ANGRY BUT VERY CONTROLLED) That was an unworthy thing to say, Mr. Janacek. […] And arrogant and cruel. *Talent isn't a licence for cruelty*.[38] (My italics)

With this deletion in mind, it would certainly appear from the finished play that Anezka takes issue with Janáček's Prose-like assessment of 'unrequited desire' as 'a metaphor for the making of art' (Prose, 17–18) as much as if not more than his 'assaults on [Kamila's] life' (Friel, *Performances*, 30). Thus one major issue with *Performances* is that, despite the potential for a good production being able to convey 'a sharp awareness of the duality of the "Muse" as a concept' through emphasising Janáček's 'bewildering performance of obsession',[39] the woman who takes Janáček to task for his exploitation of Kamilá Stösslová is more upset by her idol falling off his pedestal than by his own pedestal sexism[40]: 'to shut out that love from the story of your lives or to talk about it just as a metaphor for your work [...] diminishes *you*' (Friel, *Performances*, 31; my italics).

Paradoxically, then, Anezka's criticisms of Janáček's sexist exploits and exploitations in the play are also a criticism of feminist readings of the artist-muse relationship that are based on a metaphorical understanding of the artist's passion for the muse, of which Prose's book is an example. In fact, I would suggest that, in Anezka, Friel has created a character who speaks not from a 'feminist viewpoint'[41] or even for the used Kamila Stösslová, but for the real-life counterpart of the user—the Janáček of the letters. The debate between Anezka and Friel's Janáček, then, in the light of Prose's work, is essentially a debate between the self-deluding Janáček of the letters, who is convinced of the sacredness and nobility of his actions, and a Janáček who is stripped of all pretence. Like the real Kamila Stösslová before her, Anezka is an idea made flesh—not the dream music but rather the stammering pages made carnal.

'Play—play—play',[42] O Muse...

In staging a conflict between romantic and critical views of traditional musedom in which the romantic is a critic and vice versa, Friel ultimately muddled Prose's feminist lens. Nevertheless, it would appear that, whatever the depth of his engagement with *The Lives of the Muses*, there is a clear debt to Prose in Friel's appropriation of her criticism that manifests itself in his Janáček's view of his own creative process. The fact remains, however, that the play ends not with the resolution of its central conflict but with the suggestion that the means of resolution lies with neither artist nor critic but with the performer. Indeed, the play ends with both composer and researcher entreating each other simply to listen to the music as a means of settling the matter. This facilitates an interpretation of the play that is more subtle and complex than what is more traditionally viewed as a pair of interrelated debates—'language versus music and life versus art'.[43] As Anthony Roche puts it: 'Less important here is the absolute equilibrium the writer has to negotiate between the life and the work, than the question of how the work survives the life'.[44] In other words, the play is, to a significant extent, about what George Steiner once called 'transcendence values'.[45] This becomes clearer when we bring Friel's acknowledged Steiner sources into play and—crucially—read them in the light of Friel's engagement with musedom. Specifically, it is my belief that Friel's incorporation of Steiner into a play that deals directly with a troubled artist-muse model of influence illuminates a Frielian phenomenon that is arguably observable in multiple plays: the 'performing muse' as a vehicle for transcendence.

Performances makes use of key ideas from two of George Steiner's works. The first, from *Real Presences* (1989), proposes that '[e]ach performance of a dramatic text or musical score is a critique in the most vital sense of the term', as 'an act of penetrative response which makes sense sensible'. In an extract particularly pertinent to *Performances*, Steiner goes on to assert that 'no musicology, no music criticism, can tell us as much as the action of meaning which is performance'.[46] In summary: 'in respect of meaning and of valuation in the arts, our master intelligencers are the performers'.[47] A secondary idea, that 'the most intricate organization of the reactions of feelings and of meanings known to us […] is that deployed in the string quartet',[48] is also to be found in *Real Presences*. Another key idea, from the much earlier collection of essays *Language and Silence* (1967), is focused on what Steiner sees as 'the deeper, more numinous code' that is music, in which artists whose medium is language hope to find a way of reconciling the meanings imparted to a given work by its creator(s) and its interpreters: 'It is in music that the poet hopes to find the paradox resolved of an act of creation singular to the creator, bearing the shape of his own spirit, yet infinitely renewed in each listener'.[49]

Friel's correspondence with Peggy Paterson (then drama editor at Faber and Faber) reveals that Friel sought permission from George Steiner to include his own paraphrases of some of Steiner's text in *Performances*.[50] These included the above from *Language and Silence* and the string quartet idea from *Real Presences*. The relevant permissions were duly granted on 27 February 2003, and Friel's paraphrases appear accordingly in the published text along with a deliberately vague acknowledgement of his debt to Steiner. (In a letter to Paterson dated 10 November 2002, Friel expressed a preference for 'dropping' the text altogether rather than 'getting into deep negotiation and making formal + precise acknowledgements', instead hoping 'to acknowledge G.S. in some kind of a general comment'.)[51] Once again, however, we find that Steiner's influence on Friel is more than a matter of borrowed words. Though Steiner's view of performers as 'master intelligencers' appears neither in the very sparse archive material pertaining to *Performances* nor in the play's dialogue per se, it is key to the action of the piece and arguably makes itself felt throughout.

This privileging of the interpretive act of performance goes beyond the play's title—a highly suggestive one that Friel selected in lieu of his first choice, 'The Real Thing', which he realised had already been taken by Tom Stoppard in his play of 1982. Nevertheless, the implied degree of equivalence between the two is illuminating: performance is not artifice but a real presence, as it were. And key to this, I would argue, is the real presence of the members of the string quartet onstage as bodied speakers. Though Friel understood that having the musicians 'struck dumb' might become necessary should they feel uncomfortable speaking lines, he felt that 'even in broken English, preferably in broken English', having them speak would 'add to the texture of the evening': 'it would be an advantage to have them—or even one of them—say something'.[52] This advantage is particularly apparent in the light of Steiner's claim that art is best interpreted by its performers. Friel lays the groundwork for this early in the play, in a series of casually interpretive remarks from the musicians. For instance, Ruth, the first violinist, gives PhD student Anezka her take on the opening bars of the first movement of the string quartet[53] as she plays them: 'Ta-ra-ra-ra—Ta-ra-ra-ra. "I'm my own man," that's what it says to me' (Friel, *Performances*, 12). That Anezka then contradicts Ruth's interpretation by citing what the audience assumes is an extract from Janáček's letters (see above) does not necessarily undermine Ruth's position as an interpreter. Instead, it emphasises that the performers' interpretations are not fixed readings but rather a series of renewals of meaning that exist in the moment of performance—'in the doing', as my own creative collaborators are fond of saying (see the following chapter). A similar and far more irreverent example can be found in John the cellist's musical joke about a flautato figure in the Second String Quartet, correctly identified by Anezka as a nightingale, to which Janáček ascribes a 'mourning [...]

lamenting' character. John then plays the figure again '*very slowly and woozily*':

> JOHN   And that, Maestro?
> JANÁČEK   (*to Anezka*) They're comedians, too. (*to John*) All right, what is it?
> JOHN   The same mourning nightingale on the way home from the pub. (Friel, *Performances*, 20–1)

Unlike Janáček, who wrote the music, and Anezka, whose ornithological insights we must assume are the fruits of her research, John's status as a performer allows him a flexibility of interpretation the other two lack. It is a particularly light-hearted example of Steiner's view of music in performance as being constitutive of 'an act of creation singular to the creator, bearing the shape of his own spirit, yet infinitely renewed in each listener'.[54]

I would also suggest, however, that Friel's musicians as speaking characters do more than put Steiner's words into action. They also fulfil a muse-like role, not as themselves but rather as bodied performers *for and through whom art is made*—transcendence made tangible. Apart from anything else, their behaviour is certainly suggestive of the caregiving aspects of musedom enumerated by Prose. Though the details of, say, Janáček's anti-rheumatic, anti-arthritic diet are gleanable from his letters[55] and from Zemanová's biography, it would seem to be from Prose that Friel conjures the image of the performer-as-muse ministering to the composer's needs beyond the grave. First violinist Ruth does Janáček's housework and D.I.Y. (Friel, *Performances*, 5;11); viola player Miriam grows flowers for his room and provides fresh lettuce for his diet from her garden (Friel, *Performances*, 5); Janáček even goes so far as to refer to the musicians as his 'life-support group' (Friel, *Performances*, 21). Indeed, the 'nurturing, sustaining, supporting' role of the muse—comprising activities that 'are traditionally considered to be woman's work' (Prose, 12)—is one that Prose emphasises, particularly (and perhaps most bizarrely) when it comes to micromanaging the artist's eating habits:

> Lou [Andreas-Salomé] had Rilke dining on groats and combing the forest for nuts and berries, Lee Miller put Man Ray on a bizarrely restrictive diet, Yoko introduced John to the joys of a strict macrobiotic regimen. (Prose, 22)

Hence Janáček's lettuce diet administered by Ruth and facilitated by Miriam's gardening abilities.

There is more to the musicians as Janáček's life-support system than their caregiving responsibilities, however. In fact, they are the only speakers in the play—including Janáček himself—who do not acknowledge the fact that the composer is long-dead. Their performances of his work, in which it is continually remade, are what keeps Janáček alive, so to speak. They are, to quote *Translations*, in the business of 'renewing those images'[56] through interpretive acts of performance, and thus are able to facilitate the artist's gamble on transcendence,[57] granting him a kind of immortality for as long as they continue to perform. It is this idea of immortality, I suggest, that situates the performers as muses in their own right. Though Friel's Janáček is adamant that the sublimated passion that undoubtedly informs his work is merely a means to an end—a way of channelling dream music—the Janáček of the letters is one for whom music is a means of immortalising his own emotions in a way that is characteristic of a certain kind of artist: 'even when the muse retains her strength and influence by remaining elusive or unobtainable, the male artist is generally less preoccupied by the challenge of staying fascinating or attractive to her than he is engaged by the evolution of his own feelings' (Prose, 12). Certainly, the real Janáček regarded the Second String Quartet as a means of immortalising his own longing, including his dreams of Stösslová being pregnant with his child—a recurring invention of the composer's that is alluded to by Anezka in the play. For the real Janáček, then, it is music as it is played that carries with it the promise of love undying: 'In that work I'll be always only with you!'[58] For Friel's Janáček, too, music as it is played is key to transcendence, despite his cynicism as to the true nature of his feelings for Stösslová. Nevertheless, he too seems to find inspiration in the idea of immortality, and continually chides Anezka for reminding him of the fact of his death. For Friel's Janáček, then, the String Quartet is also a means of immortalising his fantasy life, though here it is a dream of music rather than a dream of ideal womanhood. Although he does not compose for specific musicians, that he composes in order for his music *to be heard*—emphasised through his continued entreaties for Anezka to listen—suggests that for Janáček, the muse is embodied in those who are able to perform his work. Indeed, it is through the bodies of the musicians that Janáček's work is continually renewed and thus guarantees him a life beyond the grave. In short, immortality inspires, and it is only through the performing body that dreams of immortality can be in any way realised. It is a position that Friel, whose mistrust of directors, love of actors, and wariness of literary criticism, would have understood only too well in the context of his own work.

Reading *Performances* through the lens of Prose and Steiner allows us to see the play for the troubled but fascinating work that it can be as live theatre. Friel's Janáček is an artist who, like Frank Hardy before him, knows exactly what he's doing when engaging in acts of emotional cruelty, but who sees those acts as justified in the pursuit of his craft. His awareness of the problematic ways in which male artists abstract their female muses—in line with Prose's readings—undermines and defangs the researcher Anezka who, instead of taking him to task for being a delusional user, is reduced to shock and outrage in the wake of her own shattered romantic illusions. And into this exploration of the artist-muse relationship, Friel adds four real musicians with spoken lines, through whom the composer achieves an afterlife in which his work is renewed through interpretive acts of performance. In giving the musicians the stage in the final moments of the play, moreover, Friel suggests an equivalence between spoken word and sounded notes that are capable of conjuring a rich off-stage world that is part of a continuum of theatrical space. And, as Adrian Dunbar's 2013 production suggests, this is a continuum that includes the absent Kamila Stösslová, whose presence is suggested by the transformation of Masha Dakič into a figure not unlike the woman Janáček made his muse. It is by giving the musicians the last 'word' that Friel seems to suggest that it is above all for the performing artist that the making artist creates—the performer whose body is the means by which what was made can be remade, and through whose will immortality can either be granted or denied.

'Excellent testimony!'[59]

In the light of *Performances*, then, the Frielian onstage muse would appear to be not only an embodiment of inspiration but also a performing body through whose actions the desires of the inspired are brought to fruition. This is a productive lens for looking at other, earlier examples of what are often problematically gendered examples of the relationship between inspirer and inspired in Friel's work. An analysis of *Molly Sweeney* through the lens of musedom is a notable example of how such a lens might generate productive ways of reading gender in Friel's oeuvre beyond such dominant and reductive paradigms as the woman-as-Ireland trope. This, incidentally, is a metaphor that has refused to die ever since Seamus Heaney's not-unfounded reading of the silenced Sarah in *Translations* as a 'Cathleen Ni Houlihan [...] struck dumb by the shock of modernity'.[60] Other notable examples include Scott Boltwood's reading of the deceased Maire O'Donnell née Gallagher in *Philadelphia, Here I Come!* 'as if she were born the Free State's twin'[61] and, most significantly for this chapter, Karen M. Moloney's mapping of Molly Sweeney onto not one but several Irelands: 'the blind Molly acts as a symbol for Gaelic Ireland, the partially sighted Molly serves as a metaphor for the colonized country, and Molly hospitalized for madness represents the postcolonial state'.[62]

There are, of course, more nuanced readings of Friel's gender politics within existing criticism that do not rely so heavily on the woman-as-nation trope, or which at least take the next logical step and consider the ways in which Friel might be complicit in setting up his women characters as easy targets for symbolic abstraction. For instance, Anna McMullan points out that the Frielian subaltern's ability to destabilise 'the structures and individuals who subject and limit them' is in many ways dependent on their gender. Men get to be jokers, exposing the structures of authority by 'mocking or mimicking them'; women, on the other hand—much like Anezka—'may occasionally flout authority, but they rarely perform it'[63]:

> [Women's] bodies function increasingly in the later work as conduits to the unconscious or to repressed areas of individual or cultural history. These female performances may provide liberation from confining gender roles, but they often reproduce uncritically the gendered construction of women as the non-rational and corporeal "other" to both social and symbolic authority.

Consequently, for McMullan, *Molly Sweeney* is a play that 'directly stages the performance of male authority on the female body' without any significant troubling of gender: 'Molly's corporeal subjection and role as symbol, rather than agent or author, may have the performative force of naturalizing what it purports to critique'.[64] This is certainly borne out in Friel's notes for the character of Molly (then named Martha) in which she is portrayed as a woman who is '<u>all</u> feeling, <u>all</u> sensibility; between 2 indifferent disciplines'[65] (emphasis in original). Though the play is unmistakably critical of the two men who project their own ideas of (in)completeness onto a way of being that Molly herself 'didn't think of [...] as a deprived world' (Friel, *P2*, 466), it does so in ways that reinforce a particularly tired gendered construction—that of feeling woman versus thinking man.

What, then, can the lens of Friel's performing muse add to this discussion? I would suggest that, in seeing Molly in this light, we see how it is not only the female body that is made subject to male authority but also the actions of that body. In other words, part of the way in which Molly's body serves as an inspiration for both her surgeon and her husband is in their conception of how she will *use* it to navigate her relationship with reality afterwards, performing their desires in the 'doing' of sightedness. This is made evident throughout the play's overlapping monologues. Molly's recollection of her feelings on the night of the operation certainly show an explicit awareness of the fact that she is 'being used'; that '[n]one of this is my choosing' (Friel, *P2*, 473). Only slightly more subtly, her husband Frank expresses his sense that 'Molly was about to inherit a new world; and [...] I had a sense that maybe I was, too' (Friel, *P2*, 476). Certainly, his self-appointed role as Molly's teacher after her operation reveals a desire in him to see her put *his* learning into practice. For instance, when recounting Frank's 'lesson[s]' in which he'd ask her to identify pieces of fruit by sight, Molly betrays her frustration at the way he speaks about her recovery using a vocabulary that effectively positions her as the subject of a study in which he is engaged rather than the wife to whom he 'couldn't have been kinder':

> [He'd say, "]You already have your tactical engrams. We've got to build up a repertory of visual engrams to connect with them."
> And I'd say. "For God's sake stop showing off your posh new words, Frank. It's a banana." (Friel, *P2*, 491)

The echoes of Molly's father teaching her to recognise flowers by touch and by smell and indeed by rote are obvious on Frank's part, though with a stark new addition that is Molly's resistance to the process.

That Frank is far too 'concerned with teaching [Molly] practical things' to listen to her when she tries to explain 'how *terrifying* it all was' (Friel, *P2*, 492; italics in original) is symptomatic of the extent to which he is trying to make himself a new world through his latest learning obsession—a world that only Molly's actions can realise. It is, in Donoghue's terminology, a misguided attempt to be put in touch with the mysterious by managerial means—an attempt he makes over and over again. Frank's disastrous efforts to keep jet-lagged Iranian goats off the coast of Mayo, for instance, likewise constitute an attempt to bring the experience of sentient beings under his control until they behave in a way that will turn the dream in his head into reality. These 'extraordinary goats' with their fabled high milk yield and coveted pelts ('untrue as it turned out') are Frank's performing muses in this regard, simultaneously a source of inspiration and the means by which the outcome of that inspiration is achieved. Unfortunately for Frank, in an obvious metaphor for Molly's inability to adjust to partially sighted space, the goats 'never adjusted to Irish time' (Friel, *P2*, 461). This is due—or so Frank supposes—to '[s]ome imprint in the genes [that] remained indelible', which he characterises as a temporal 'engram' (Friel, *P2*, 462). As Molly's friend Rita puts it, this would indeed appear to be '[a]ll part of the same pattern' of quirky obsessions: 'bees—whales—Iranian goats—Molly Sweeney' (Friel, *P2*, 480).

The trouble here is, of course, that Molly is a woman, not a goat. Moreover, unlike the musicians of *Performances*, Molly's agency as a performing muse is limited: they can choose to play or not to play; Molly can choose only to do or not to do, which—or so the ending of the play implies—is tantamount to a decision to be or not to be. From the outset, Frank's privileging of Molly's blindness over Molly's personhood is uncomfortable, and is even more pronounced in Friel's notes. For instance, in an earlier version of a speech in which Frank decides to take Molly dancing, the troubling power dynamics that underpin Frank's consideration are unmistakable:

> You would have no responsibilities [...] You would be—literally—in my hands. [...] I would be your eyes, your ears [...]—leading, guiding, controlling. Surely that must be the ultimate relaxation, the supreme sensual experience?[66]

These are not the kinds of power dynamics that are to be entered into without express trust and, above all, consent. Moreover, as we later realise, the liberation Molly gains from dancing is rather one she gains from dancing alone, not so much out of control but out of others' control: 'Mad and wild and frenzied. But so adroit, so efficient. No timidity, no hesitations, no falterings. Not a glass overturned, not a shoulder brushed' (Friel, *P2*, 473). Again, however, and in a manner reminiscent of McMullan's critiques of the earlier *Dancing at Lughnasa* (1990), we are faced with a moment that 'reproduce[s] uncritically the gendered construction of women as the non-rational and corporeal "other"'[67] even in the midst of an assertion of selfhood. Similarly, in making Molly's blindness another example of Frank's attempts to reduce the mystery of experience to a problem to be solved, Friel again reinforces a gendered binary even as he appears to critique it.

The way in which Molly functions as performing muse to Mr Rice (the surgeon) is subtly different to the way she functions for Frank. This is due in part to the fact that Rice is in many ways a less cynical precursor of the Janáček Friel would conjure for *Performances*—an artist figure with some sense of the centrality of his destructive fantasy life to his creative process. Like the dead composer, Rice has some awareness of the extent to which he is being a user. This is in stark contrast to Frank Sweeney, who doesn't know himself well enough to grasp the implications of what he's doing and who never comes to the realisation that 'that courageous woman had everything, everything to lose' (Friel, *P2*, 481). Rice, on the other hand, is well aware that he has 'crossed the frontier into the fantasy life again' when imagining the consequences of a partially sighted world for Molly and is, what's more, 'ashamed' (Friel, *P2*, 469). Similarly, Rice is fully conscious of his having been inspired once again by Molly to think of himself not as a surgeon but as an artist and, as his treacherous former friend and fellow surgeon Roger Bloomstein used to put it, 'perform' (Friel, *P2*, 488). Indeed, the knowing vocabulary Rice uses to describe Molly's operation is in many ways reminiscent of Frank Hardy's 'performance[s]'[68] in *Faith Healer*. Like Frank Hardy's cures, Rice's operations are performances in which healing is an act that demands that the bodies of the healed bear witness to it in order for the performance to be real: 'if he cured a man, that man became for him a successful fiction'.[69] As Rice himself describes it, he has a mad impulse to let his former friends and colleagues know not only that his actions may be about to 'give [...] vision' to a patient but also that her actions and experiences will be a testament to his artistry: 'And for the first time in her life—how does Saint Mark put it in the gospel?—for the first time in her life she will "see men walking as if like trees"' (Friel, *P2*, 470). It is therefore extremely telling when Molly recounts Mr Rice saying that partial sight for her 'would be a total success for [him]'. She goes on: 'But I'm sure he meant it would be great for all of us' (Friel, *P2*, 483).

For Rice to be an artist, then, Molly must be a performing muse in the sense that her body is transformed from a source of inspiration to a work of art that bears witness to Rice's 'mastery' (Friel, *P2*, 490) through performing sightedness. It is a dream of transformation that begins on the morning of the operation itself, when Rice—claiming, ironically, to have experienced a sudden moment of 'utter selflessness' (Friel, *P2*, 480)—turns from Molly to the shades of his former surgeon colleagues as to the traditional Muses of antiquity, whispering to them 'to gather round me this morning and steady my unsteady hand and endow me with all their exquisite skills' (Friel, *P2*, 481). Rice's recollection of the operation itself, moreover, is one in which everything but his sense that 'all the gifts were mine again' (Friel, *P2*, 489) and that 'a restoration [...] was possible' (Friel, *P2*, 490) vanishes in the moment of performance, including Molly herself. By the time of Rice's final monologue, he no longer recognises the Molly who sparked 'the phantom desire, the insane fantasy that crossed my mind that day' when he first saw her. Rice's final words reveal the extent to which he sees Molly's fate as an extension of his own successes and failures. His feeling of having been momentarily restored as an artist during the operation offers him the hope that restoration is possible; similarly, he attenuates his sense of having 'failed' Molly by consoling himself with the fact that 'at least for a short time she did see men "walking as if like trees"' (Friel, *P2*, 506).

This idea of Molly performing Rice's successes and failures is accentuated by her relationship with one of the most persistent threads running through her surgeon's monologue. Early in the play, Rice admits that Molly '[r]eminded me instantly of my wife, Maria'. Though it is only a 'superficial resemblance' (Friel, *P2*, 458) on a physical level, I would suggest that the true resemblance between the two women lies in the idea of musedom. Indeed, his wife was, for him and his high-flying club of brilliant eye-surgeons, a muse-like figure in her own right: 'our Venus—no, our Galatea' (Friel, *P2*, 474). This latter correction is significant: Galatea was the sculpted creation of the misogynistic artist Pygmalion, brought to life through his molestations and prayers (to Venus's Greek counterpart Aphrodite, no less). More significantly still, she was the classical prototype for another of Irish theatre's most iconic heroines—the elocutionarily and economically disadvantaged Eliza Doolittle of Shaw's *Pygmalion* (1913). The ending of this play was famously a bone of contention with its author, who was firmly against the idea that the newly independent and well-spoken Eliza is really in love with Higgins and will return to their arrangement in the end. In one of the play's many endings, according to Shaw's correspondence with its leading lady, Henry Higgins was to call out after Eliza:

> When Eliza emancipates herself—when Galatea comes to life—she must not relapse. She must retain her pride and triumph to the end. [...] He will go out on the balcony to watch your departure; come back triumphantly into the room; exclaim 'Galatea!' (meaning that the statue has come to life at last); and—curtain. Thus he gets the last word; and you get it too.[70]

Though admirable in his insistence that Eliza remains emancipated (from Higgins at least), what Shaw also does here is to posit Eliza's transformation into the real thing, as it were, as being the fulfilment of *Higgins's* desires. (This is brought home with rather more force in Lerner and Loewe's musical adaptation of Shaw's play, *My Fair Lady*, in which Eliza is cut off before she can finish singing the line 'I can do bloody well without [you]' by Higgins, crowing 'By George, I really did it! [...] I said I'd make a woman and indeed I did!'.[71] This is also a version of the story in which Eliza comes crawling back to Higgins to fetch his slippers.) Thus the muse of Friel's hot-shot eye-surgeons is characterised first as a woman with the power to grant desires and then as the desired body made flesh—a figure found again by Rice in Molly. She is a Shavian Galatea, whose so-called emancipation is framed at least in part as the achievement of the artist, even if it is superficially a life lived independently of him. In other words, even if Molly were to be at home with a sighted experience of the world, it would not be her victory.

'Stupid, useless, quirky mind...'[72]

To read Molly as one of Friel's performing muses allows for a more nuanced view of the play's gender politics. Frank and Rice not only impose their fantasies on Molly's body but also on her actions, reconfiguring her relationship with the world as an active agent in terms of their own successes and failures and the realisation of their desires. She is both a source of inspiration and the medium through which the inspired are able to achieve their ends. Moreover, when she is neither willing nor able to perform the desires of the two men, retreating to a 'borderline country' (Friel, *P2*, 509) somewhere between the imagined and the real, her breakdown is romanticised by Rice in a moment of wishful thinking that gets him subtly off the hook insofar as it imagines some degree of newfound agency for Molly: 'My sense was that she was trying to *compose* another life' (Friel, *P2*, 501) (my italics). I am rather more of a mind with actor Catherine Byrne (who originated the role of Molly) than with Friel when it comes to Molly's fate. As Christopher Murray recounts, when Friel told Byrne 'that there is hope at the end', she was 'appalled'[73]: 'Hope? But she dies!'[74] Optimistically, Murray maintains that Molly ends the play on her own terms, comparing her acceptance of 'irresolvable contradiction'[75] with the state of 'active repose, [...] the triumph of art over time'[76] that closes plays like *Aristocrats*. There is certainly a case to be made that this is what Friel may have been aiming for, though I for one am not inclined to make it here. Personally, I am tired of having to use my critical abilities to argue that a woman being able to put a positive spin on her own death is radically empowering. For all its subtleties, *Molly Sweeney* ends with yet another dead, dying, or periodically institutionalised woman whose mental health issues are abstracted into metaphor. She joins the ranks of Grace Hardy, Cass McGuire, Bridget Connolly, Berna Martin, Rose Mundy, and any number of unnamed, absent mothers in the Frielian canon (including Molly's own).

I would like to end this chapter with another archival turn, considering the extent to which Molly's fate within the world of the play resonates with Friel's creative process. Specifically, I wish to focus briefly on Friel's sources for *Molly Sweeney*—which were many and various—and consider the 'how' of influence in the context of the manifestation of Friel's research in gendered bodies onstage. Of particular interest is the extent to which there may be an affinity between effervescent autodidact Frank Sweeney and Friel himself, whose intellectual eclecticism on enduring themes finds a parodic echo in Frank's ebullient research. It is true that Friel gives no indication in this case of his being explicitly aware of such an affinity between himself and a character he was implicitly critiquing—a possibility he *did* entertain when writing Lombard in *Making History*.[77] However, there are certainly resemblances between Frank and Friel's use of a deliberately gendered subject as a means of realising the outcome of a synthesis of research materials. Indeed, I would argue that Frank is in many ways an embodiment and mouthpiece of Friel's synthesis of sources, performing onstage the kind of process that Adele Tutter ascribes to the real Janáček: 'mapping her object representation and his relationship to her onto the various characterizations and narratives specified' by his research.[78]

Like *Performances*, *Molly Sweeney* is a play in which a major character has been effectively gender-swapped. One of the play's significant sources, as has been well documented, was Oliver Sacks's account of a blind male patient he refers to as Virgil, who regained his sight but whose subsequent 'behaviour [was] of one *mentally* blind, or agnosic—able to see but not to decipher what he was seeing'.[79] Virgil is remarkably similar in character to Molly in many key respects, though it is notable that his 'limited, but stable'[80] pre-surgery life is portrayed as an extension of his 'striking passivity'—a 'modest' way of living when compared to the 'adventurous and aggressively independent' nature of 'some blind people'. Molly's adult life—similar to Virgil's insofar as she too has 'a steady job and an identity'—is portrayed by Friel as a mark of her independence. There are other, more cosmetically gendered differences. For instance, Virgil's 'passion for sports' and 'listen[ing]to [baseball] games on the radio'[81] is predictably absent from Molly's list of interests (though perhaps for geographical reasons as much as gendered ones). Post-surgery, moreover, Molly develops a preoccupation with her appearance that, as her mental health deteriorates, culminates in her trying to fix her hair in front of a mirror in the dark; Virgil gains weight dramatically and, as his vision worsens, begins to abandon the functional task of shaving in a mirror in favour of doing so by feel.

The significance of Molly's gender in relation to Sacks's patient Virgil, however, is more subtle than a discrepancy between surface details. It is true that the plot of *Molly Sweeney* follows Sacks's essay so closely that it is indeed more productive in some cases to examine how it differs from its source than to register its many echoes. For instance, Molly's childhood is entirely different from that of Virgil, who lost his sight after a childhood illness but who *did* go to a blind school. Molly's background is rather classic Friel, complete with a judge father with his own ideas about education and a troubled, institutionalised mother. Molly's relationships with others are also different from Virgil's. His partner Amy is not a self-taught researcher with a dossier full of lost causes but a woman with a degree in botany who keeps a journal. Amy takes Virgil to see her own ophthalmologist, Dr. Scott Hamlin, who suspects that Virgil may not have retinitis pigmentosa after all and may benefit from a cataract operation before his wedding:

> There was nothing to lose—and there might be much to gain. Amy and Virgil would be getting married soon—wouldn't it be fantastic if he could

see? If, after nearly a lifetime of blindness, his first vision could be his bride, the wedding, the minister, the church![82]

Sacks's ventriloquism here is reminiscent of Frank's enthused tone. Molly, however, is already married to Frank when she has the operation: in terms of another play of which Friel would later make his own version, she is a Hedda Tesman rather than a Hedda Gabler. The ophthalmologist, meanwhile, barely features in Sacks's piece.

These discrepancies are useful insofar as they allow us to highlight certain details of Friel's own invention (Rice's emotional life, Frank's serial devotion to madcap schemes, Molly's childhood, etc.). However, I feel that the gender-swapping of the patient Virgil is most significant where Friel recontextualises some of the play's most blatant reproductions of Sacks. Certainly, much of the dialogue of the play is instantly recognisable as having been not so much recycled as cut-and-pasted. This is very much the case when it comes to Friel's appropriation of Sacks for Molly's fantasy life. Her wish for 'a brief excursion to the land of vision [...] [a]nd then to return home to my own world' (Friel, *P2*, 483) is an elided but nevertheless close paraphrase of Sacks's appraisal of Virgil's experience as a man who went from blindness to partial sightedness to blindness again:

> It was an adventure, an excursion into a new world, the like of which is given to few. But then came the problems, the conflicts, of seeing but not seeing, not being able to make a visual world, and at the same time being forced to give up his native competence—a torment from which no escape seemed possible. But then, paradoxically, a release was given, in the form of a second and now final blindness—a blindness he received as a gift. Now, at last, Virgil is allowed to not see, allowed to escape from the glaring, confusing world of sight and space, and to return to his own true being, the touch world that has been his home for almost fifty years.[83]

What Molly wishes for is, to an extent, what Virgil gets (albeit at great personal cost): the chance to visit another world and then to return home. Molly, however—using the same spatialised metaphors as Sacks—ends the play in exile from both the sighted world and the blind, inhabiting a 'borderline country' that only 'seems to be all right' (Friel, *P2*, 509) because she relinquishes the task of questioning its veracity. Unlike Friel's other monologue play protagonist Frank Hardy, whose suicide by wedding party is a conscious choice to free himself from the maddening questions he believes are a condition of his artistry, Molly relinquishes the choice to choose what to believe any more so that she can once again experience something like '[un]qualified [...] sensation' (Friel, *P2*, 466). And yet Friel presents *both* scenarios as melancholically pyrrhic victories tinged with unmistakable lyricism.

But why is Molly's fate—a subtle variation on that of the patient on whom she was based—a matter of gender? *Faith Healer* itself is a part of the answer, insofar as Friel's decision to make the blind patient a woman was influenced to some degree by his chosen form. Initially, the play was floated as a '"DUET" or "LOVE STORY" between "Neurologist/ophthalmologist" man or woman and woman or man patient',[84] flexible in all but its fundamental heterosexuality. Once he had decided on three characters rather than 'a sonata for 2 voices',[85] however, Friel consciously used *Faith Healer* as a model for determining the nature of their roles:

Frank	Grace	Teddy
Neurologist	Blind	Husband/Wife?
Woman—man?[86]	M or F.?	

It would appear, then, that it is no accident that *Molly Sweeney* reads partly as a version of *Faith Healer* in which Grace Hardy is the central figure. Friel's notes suggest that he was aware of this to the point of being wary of reproducing the power dynamics of his earlier play in their entirety, discounting the '[possibility] that the ophthalmologist is the centre of the play' with one of his characteristic questions: 'Too close to Faith Healer?'[87] There are fundamental similarities that remain: like Grace before her, Molly is a woman whose father is a judge, whose mother has mental health issues, and who is herself suffering from the aftermath of a traumatic experience. However, unlike Grace, Molly is married to the Teddy figure of the play (who is, confusingly, named Frank). Thus, instead of a portrait of a woman whose sense of self has been obliterated through subordination to *one* abusive egomaniac, *Molly Sweeney* is a portrait of a woman whose ability to distinguish between realities is weakened by the actions of the *two* men who enact their fantasies upon her.

This decision that the patient should be a woman had almost immediate consequences for the play. The archive is tantalising in this respect, in that it reveals a brief period—perhaps no more than a week—in which Friel seems to have decided to create his own *male* version of Virgil. In a note dated 29 July 1993, it is clear that, had the patient indeed been a man, Friel envisioned him as '[a] musician',[88] i.e. an artist/performer in his own right. Though the patient had, as far as I have been able to tell, more or less consistent she/her pronouns from around 10 August 1993 onwards, it is still significant that a woman patient was never meant to have a craft of her own: 'Man (musician) wife doctor mother vs woman husband doctor father/mother'.[89] Though she is portrayed in the finished play as confidently independent with a love of swimming and (like Sacks's Virgil) a steady job as a massage therapist, there is nothing vocational about what Molly does. This is in some ways unsurprising: women don't get to be tortured artists or even artist-figures in Friel's plays, though there are a few peripheral pianists (Claire in *Aristocrats*, and Daisy in *Give Me Your Answer, Do!*), a dead actor (the mother in *Aristocrats*), and a handful of carnival performers (in *Crystal and Fox*). Occasionally we hear about them singing 'Oft in the stilly night' in a child-like voice (Grace in *Faith Healer*, Rita in *Molly Sweeney*), and sometimes they get to dance disruptively, but we never get to hear a woman talking about what it means to be an artist herself. Nor do we get to see women making musical jokes like George in *Wonderful Tennessee* or John in *Performances* (though the genders and names of the string quartet players are often changed to reflect the composition of the real quartet hired to do the job). This is a particular shame in *Molly Sweeney* given that we are meant to feel better about Molly's nervous breakdown because of Rice's sense of her having 'compose[d]' (Friel, *P2*, 501) a new reality for herself. Had this been backed up by a Molly who was in any way engaged with the idea of herself as a person able to shape and mediate of her own experiences, this might ring less hollow. As it is, Molly is a woman Friel created as 'all feeling, all sensibility' caught 'between 2 indifferent disciplines'[90] (emphasis in original), whose relationship with the world is characterised by receptivity above all things. Indeed, Molly gains most pleasure from a mode of experience that works to reinforce gendered stereotypes: when she describes the delight she gets from swimming, it is the delight of 'offering yourself to the experience' in 'a world of pure sensation, of sensation alone'—not of being creatively engaged with the world but of being '[in] concordance with it' (Friel, *P2*, 466). That she ends the play renouncing not the generative, torturous workings of chance but the imperative to question her own reality is symptomatic of a desire to return to a highly gendered state of non-creative receptivity. Frank Hardy dies on his own terms; Molly Sweeney trails away in a state of dreamy resignation as the world washes over her.

It is clear, then, that Molly's gender and the role it plays in her characterisation are, to a significant extent, constitutive of a choice based on unexamined assumptions about gender binaries. Though Rice attempts to exonerate himself by painting a picture of a Molly who is creating an alternative reality for herself in an artist-like role, the reality of the play is more in accordance with Robert Graves: 'She is either Muse or she is nothing'.[91] Friel's choice to make Molly a woman, based on his engagement with Sacks and his earlier experiments with the monologue play, renders hers a deliberately gendered body. Her character development, moreover, is determined by Friel's own unexamined prejudices that are discernible throughout his oeuvre, in this case his tendency to overlook the possibility that women might be the creators of art as well as its performers; Molly is ill-equipped to be either. Whatever demonstrable sympathy Friel had for Molly as a character—and the play is undeniably on Molly's side—it is a sympathy that is conditioned by Friel's own observable gender politics. If *Molly Sweeney* was, as Murray, suggests, 'a riposte to the feminist critique of the *Field Day Anthology of Irish Writing*'[92]—which famously failed quite spectacularly to represent women's voices and experiences *as artists*—then it was somewhat wide of the mark.

If I have emphasised Friel's decision not to make his leading lady a musician (as he would most likely have done had she been a man), it is because this, to my mind, affects her ability as a character to make the creative connections that are necessary to survive in the sighted world as one of its 'master intelligencers'. The expectations placed upon her are those placed upon a performing muse, but this Molly apparently lacks the capacity to perform. This is clear from Friel's use of Molly's husband Frank as a kind of mouthpiece for his own research, enacting Friel's syntheses of his various source materials. Indeed, Friel's/Frank's synthesis of sources in many ways constitutes the constructed reality that Molly is expected to realise but which only an artist/performer can be expected to meet.

Friel's research for the play in addition to Sacks's essay was extensive, and a detailed enumeration of his liberal borrowings from the multiple texts he used would be a chapter in and of itself. As a task that would perhaps be better suited to a critical edition of *Molly Sweeney* than this monograph, I have therefore left it undone. I would, however, encourage any interested researchers within reasonable distance of the National Library of Ireland to consult MSs 37,128/1–2, in which Friel has helpfully marked out all the relevant passages in his own copies and photocopies of his source materials. In fact, the only real legwork necessary here is the mammoth task of digitisation for public use. Friel's research included engagements with R. L. Gregory's *Recovery from early blindness: a case study* (1963),[93] Marius von Senden's *Space and Sight* (1932),[94] Alberto Valvo's *Sight restoration after long-term blindness* (1971),[95] and Semir Zeki's *A Vision of the Brain* (1993),[96] in which Friel acknowledges (by underlining) but ultimately ignores Zeki's reluctance to conceptualise seeing and understanding as discrete categories: '*if there is a case for separating the two processes of 'seeing' and 'understanding', that case has not yet been made convincingly*'[97] (italics in original). Three of these sources make mention of the word 'engram'. Friel's blending of source materials as expounded by Frank here is a significant example of how the latter uses incomplete synthesis to set up a series of impossible expectations for Molly. Frank's definition of an engram is as follows:

> [F]rom the Greek word meaning something that is etched, inscribed, on something. [...] [I]t accounts for the mind's strange ability to recognize instantly somebody we haven't seen for maybe thirty years. Then he appears. The sight of him connects with the imprint, the engram. And bingo—instant recognition! (Friel, *P2*, 462)

The term 'engram' is one used briefly by Sacks in the context of Virgil having to relearn the correlation between objects and their appearances: 'for Virgil, with half a century of forgetting whatever visual engrams he had constructed, the [...] relearning [...] required hours of conscious and systematic exploration each day'.[98] It appears again in Valvo, in a form recognisable from the play itself: '[t]he newly sighted are [...] compelled to build up a repertory of visual engrams* and to establish their connection with tactile engrams' (asterisk in original).[99] At the bottom of the page, unadorned with any markings from Friel, is the definition of engrams that accompanies the asterisk: 'A modification that is assumed to occur somewhere in the nervous system as a result of learning and that therefore provides the physiological basis for memory in higher organisms'.[100] The definition Friel appears to have adopted for *Molly Sweeney*, however, would appear to come from one of the appendices to Marius von Senden's *Space and Sight*, namely 'Anatomy and Physiology' by J. Z. Young:

> We can give no picture of how the web of interlacing axons and dendrites of the cortex somehow carries an imprint that enables us to recognize a face not seen for thirty years. What is this print? In what code is the information carried and how is it registered in the brain during learning?[101]

In the margins, Friel wrote a word connecting the language of Young with the terminology of Valvo: 'Engrams?'.[102]

Friel's decision to privilege a definition of engrams as coded imprints is one that he bolsters with some distinctly suspect etymology. In the play, Frank claims that the word 'engram' is derived from a word meaning 'something that is etched, inscribed, on something' (Friel, *P2*, 462). This is not, etymologically speaking, strictly accurate: the noun Frank is looking for is not 'engramma'—a word which I have been told does not exist in Ancient Greek—but 'epigramma'. It is rather the more similar-sounding corresponding verb 'engrapho' which has 'make incisions into; mark in or on paint on; engrave, inscribe' among its meanings.[103] Whilst it is not inconceivable that Friel should have made an error here, I prefer to think of it as being in keeping with Frank's character to have stitched together his patchwork knowledge with an incomplete understanding of its roots. It is certainly in keeping with Frank's confusion of the word 'agnosic'—the condition of 'seeing but not knowing, not recognizing what it is they see'—with the word 'agnostic': 'I always thought that word had to do with believing or not believing' (Friel, *P2*, 464). It is also a way of understanding engrams in which Molly's consciousness is passively impressionable material in the sense of its having images inscribed upon it, which suits Frank's self-appointed role as a teacher in the aftermath of the operation.

Frank's patchy understanding of his own research is one that leads him to see the newly sighted Molly as a kind of tabula rasa awaiting new impressions that she will then be able to use to create a new world. He seems to think that if he waves enough pieces of fruit in front of her face for long enough, she will receive the visual information as an imprint that will facilitate the 'instant recognition' (Friel, *P2*, 462) of which he speaks once she has pieced everything together. What he fails to appreciate, however, is something von Senden points out in the (unmarked) continuation of a passage underlined by Friel—namely the importance of fantasy:

For this connection up of old images to new intuitions is properly an act of fantasy. The patient has first himself to fill the new visual impression with a content intelligible to him, and must therefore make creative exercise of his imagination.[104]

The necessity of Molly 'creat[ing] a whole new world of her own' by 'establishing connections between these new imprints and the tactile engrams she already possessed' (Friel, *P2*, 464) is something that requires creativity on the part of the subject. Though Frank certainly gets the gist of it, the way he describes it is less a leap of the imagination than a matter of organisation: 'We aren't given [a] world [...]. We make it ourselves—through our experience, by our memory, by making categories, by interconnections' (Friel, *P2*, 463–4). As we have already seen, however, Molly is characterised from the outset by her receptivity rather than by her creativity. Moreover, though Frank is aware of the necessity of making a world, both he and Molly—drawing on Sacks's metaphors—speak of the sighted and non-sighted worlds as pre-existing spaces; places to enter and inhabit rather than something that is produced by the way we respond to and process different stimuli. Frank in particular talks about 'external reality' (Friel, *P2*, 509) as though this is something objective and immutable, expecting her both to navigate a world he has created for her through his expectations and to create a world of her own.

This was brought to the fore considerably in the 2014 Lyric Theatre/Print Room touring production of *Molly Sweeney*.[105] Here, Signe Beckmann's set design was crucial to the realisation of the way in which Frank and Mr. Rice claim to expect Molly to be able to create a world of her own whilst in reality expecting her to perform within a world they have made for her and according to their own standards. As in the original 1994 production, the stage was divided into three '*special acting area[s]*': '*Mr Rice stage left, Molly Sweeney centre stage, Frank Sweeney stage right*' (Friel, *P2*, 455). In this production, however, the three acting areas were set against the backdrop of the side of a house with a roof that sloped downwards from the middle: for both Rice and Frank, the house was an inside wall; both had windows behind them looking outwards, the former sitting in an armchair whilst the latter half-perched, half-leaned on a series of packing crates. Molly's acting area, however, was set against the outside wall of the house, which was set slightly behind the two panels of inside wall on either side of it and which featured a window looking in. Also in Molly's acting area were a large tree coming up out of the floorboards, the roots of which appeared to crack the floor where it divided the stage into three spaces, and a swing—on which Molly sat—hanging from the ceiling.

The way in which, throughout the production, both Ruairi Conaghan as Frank and Frankie McCafferty as Rice failed to respect the boundaries of the acting area occupied by Dorothy Duffy as Molly was a simple but striking manifestation of the way in which their characters deny the integrity of Molly's subjective space. The stage was set up so as to imply three characters inhabiting their own spatio-temporal realities, and yet the ease with which Rice and Frank crossed over into Molly's space suggested that the so-called different worlds of the play were created by the actions of the characters within them. Apparently tender gestures from the two men took on a more controlling tone: when Molly climbed up into the tree to tell the story of how she danced on the night before the operation, she was carried back down to the swing in the arms of Mr Rice; Frank, meanwhile, would cross over into Molly's space to push the swing as she sat. Molly was not the creator and determining agent of her own space but rather an object within it to be manipulated by Rice and Frank.

The tree and the swing served a further function: as figures of speech invoked by Rice and Frank respectively, which Molly attempted to inhabit with only limited success. When Rice imagines telephoning his old professor to tell him that Molly will 'for the first time in her life [...] "see men walking as if like trees"' (Friel, *P2*, 470), he is in fact drawing on Sacks's article, where the simile is put into quite a different perspective:

> But could it be that simple? Was not *experience* necessary to see? Did one not have to learn to see? [...] (There is a hint of it even in the Bible, in Mark's description of the miracle at Bethsaida; for here, at first, the blind man saw 'men as trees, walking,' and only subsequently was his eyesight fully restored.)[106]

For Sacks, the idea of the blind man with newly restored sight seeing men as trees walking is not, as it is for Rice, one of wonder, but of the confusion of not understanding a new way of experiencing the world. This is further emphasised by von Senden, who observes that, whilst '[t]he sighted person would discover almost nothing in common between a man and a tree; for the blind man the resemblance lies in the fact that they have the same schema: a trunk without edges which can be wholly or partially embraced in the outstretched arms'.[107] Rice, then, is a character for whom the prospect of Molly's sightedness is something that he 'sees' as the necessity of learning to see but 'understands' as a miracle of his own doing. The presence of the tree onstage in the Lyric/Print Room production was testament to this: that the physical embodiment of Rice's figure of speech existed in Molly's acting area was an intrusion into Molly's reality. That she attempted quite literally to inhabit the simile, climbing up into the tree several times during the play, only to be taken down by Rice himself, was a means of conveying the way in which Molly's attempts to make the connections necessary to understand her new world—literally an 'external' reality—were undermined by Rice's fantasy of having created it.

The swing, too, was a set piece inhabited by Molly which Frank attempted to bring under his control. In the script, it is he after all who relates the metaphor of the swing as told to him by Molly's psychotherapist, Jean Wallace (possibly named after J. G. Wallace, who co-authored Gregory's monograph), by way of explaining Molly's changes of mood (Friel, *P2*, 493). That Frank then went on to push Molly on the swing rather than allowing her the agency of which she was capable was again indicative of his wish to control Molly's relationship with a sighted 'world'. Though Molly was an active agent in the play, moving the swing herself to indicate and perform her mood, the fact that it was Frank who voiced the analogy of mood swings as a literal swing rendered its presence in her space intrusive. Moreover, through being bodily present in her acting area—an area containing the objective reality of a figure of speech appropriated by him—Frank rendered Molly's space an extension of his own, capable of being transformed by his speech and actions. Indeed, the Print Room production brought home the extent to which, for the two men, to have Molly perform her own version of sightedness within a sighted 'world' is insufficient. Rather they require her to perform *their* version of a newly sighted woman in a sighted space dominated by the physical manifestations of their own figures of speech—elements of a space with which she is only permitted to interact on *their* terms.

In Tutter's reading of the real Janáček's relationship with the woman he made his muse, she notes the composer's ability to organise his emotions according to 'the narrative rubric of fantasy [...] patterned after the significant literary works he chose to set to music':

In other words, he used his muse as a substrate and shape the way a tailor builds a garment on a dressmaking form, mapping her object representation and his relationship to her onto the various characterizations and narratives specified by those texts.[108]

For Tutter, in fact, the real Janáček's late, Stösslová-inspired works were a case of art imitating life imitating art, with the composer's attitude to the woman he made his muse being influenced by the literary texts that informed his creative work. As models of influence go, it's a hall of mirrors. *Molly Sweeney* is a play in which, in an extension of Tutter's reading of the real Janáček, two men map their own emotional, intellectual, and textual landscapes not only onto the object representation of a woman (i.e. her body) but also onto her (inter)actions in and with the world. Frank in particular sets up a series of fantastical expectations for Molly that she cannot meet, partly because the playwright (for reasons that are latently gendered) has not endowed her with a creative personality, and partly because her efforts to make her newly sighted experience of the world her own are repeatedly stymied, as is suggested in the Print Room production. The extent to which this is deliberate on Friel's part remains unclear: I doubt very much that he would have seen the two men's impositions on Molly as particularly gendered. On the contrary, his notes suggest that the two men are also in some way on a journey into sightedness, turning Molly's disability into a reasonably tired metaphor as he had done with limping Manus and stammering Sarah in *Translations*. 'Each of the characters has been afforded an opportunity to see—each has been offered promise. Cautiously, almost reluctantly, each has met that promise—and been destroyed by it'.[109] (Italics in original.)

This is where the play becomes uncomfortably self-reflexive, insofar as there is a persistent suspicion that the mechanisms by which Molly is assigned the role of performing muse—a role she categorically did not choose—are also, in part, the mechanisms by which the play was created. Frank's research is Friel's research; both have created a Molly of their own; both inventions are mapped onto the body of the actor playing Molly. Indeed, as Stanton B. Garner Jr. points out, 'form[s] of bodily appropriation [have] been historically applied to both female character and female actor'[110] alike. And as recent post 'Me Too'/'Waking the Feminists' scandals in the Irish arts industry have revealed with appalling clarity, many female actors working in the very theatres in which Friel's plays were performed have been subject to inappropriate behaviours and abuses of power that directly affected the extent to which they felt that their personal and professional choices were their own. The entire first half of this chapter lies in the shadow of allegations made against Artistic Director of the Gate Theatre Michael Colgan, who first introduced Friel to Janáček's letters.[111] To be clear, my intent here is not to smear Friel by association. Rather I wish to stress that theatre does not happen in a vacuum: characters do not exist solely on the page but are performed by bodied persons; and the way we talk about women on stage—and indeed the *creation* of female roles for the stage—matters. If the way Frank, as a synthesis of Friel's research, finds inspiration in the idea of a blind woman learning to see again in ways that he hopes will fulfil his own intellectually eclectic fantasies makes us feel a little uncomfortable about the way Friel created his female protagonist, perhaps we shouldn't gaslight each other into believing that Molly ends the play empowered. Indeed, *Molly Sweeney* is a play that makes clear the extent to which gendered (and, in this case, ableist) power dynamics affect the agency of those to whom we assign the task of performing our desires. Janáček's musicians, in the text world of the play at least, are playful and empowered: they can choose to take on the role of performing muse and thus guarantee the composer's immortality, or they can simply play something else. Molly Sweeney is left without the capacity to tell what is real and what is not, abandoned by those who were inspired by her and who should have helped her once it became clear that she could and would not make their dreams her reality.

Notes

1. 14–16 and 19–23 February 2013, the Great Hall, University of Ulster, Magee Campus, Derry. Directed by Adrian Dunbar. Produced by the Millennium Forum, Derry. The performance under discussion took place on Friday 15 February 2013.
2. 6 February–8 March 2014, Lyric Theatre, Belfast. Directed by Andrew Flynn. This performance under discussion took place on 5 March 2014.
3. Brian Friel, *Performances* (London: Faber and Faber, 2005), p. 28. Further references in parentheses in the text as 'Friel, *Performances*'.
4. Adele Tutter, 'Text As Muse, Muse As Text: Janáček, Kamila, and the Role of Fantasy in Musical Creativity', *American Imago* 72, No. 4 (Winter 2015), pp. 407–450 (p. 408).

5. Paul Anthony Griffiths, 'Years of the Fox', *Times Literary Supplement*, 20 September 2002, p. 18. See also Dublin, National Library of Ireland (NLI), Brian Friel Papers Additional (BFPA), MS 49,254/2.
6. See NLI, BFPA, MS 49,254/2.
7. Mirka Zemanová, *Janáček: A Composer's Life* (Boston: Northeastern University Press, 2002), p. 3. Further references in parentheses in the text.
8. Griffiths, p. 18.
9. Friel, *Performances*, p. 9. See also Zemanová, p. 43.
10. Leoš Janáček, letter to Kamila Stösslová dated 8 June 1927, in *Hádanka života. (Dopisy Leoše Janáčka Kamile Stösslové)* [The Riddle of Life. (Letters of Leoš Janáček to Kamila Stösslová)], ed. by Svatava Přibáňová (Brno: Opus Musicum, 1990), p. 218. Cited in Zemanová, p. 224.
11. Leoš Janáček, letter to Zdenka Janáčková dated 15 June 1927, in Přibáňová, p. 218. Cited in Zemanová, p. 224.
12. NLI, BFPA, MS 49,254/3. Handwritten note towards *Performances* in a 200-page red hardbacked Lismore Feint Ruled Book.
13. Pavel Fischer (first violin), Jana Lukášová (second violin), Radim Sedmidubský (viola), and Peter Jarůšek (cello). Typed drafts in MS 49,253/3 suggest that Friel may have used the names of this iteration of the Škampa Quartet as placeholders for his own fictional musicians. At one point in the same MS, he replaced these names with 'Karel', 'Anna', Jan', and 'Josef' respectively; later, the names changed according to the genders of the players in the Alba Quartet, who originated the roles of Janáček's caregiving performers.
14. See NLI, BFPA, MS 49,254/2. Photocopied pages.
15. NLI, BFPA, MS 49,254/2. The (as of January 2022) broken url in question is given as < http://www.measure.demon.co.uk/docs/Janacek.html > on the left-hand side of the footer of the three-page document printed by Friel at 19:27 on 27 August 2002.
16. See NLI, BFPA, MS 49,254/3.
17. 'Briefly Noted', *The New Yorker*, 30 September 2002, p. 139; Francine Prose, *The Lives of the Muses* (New York: HarperCollins, 2002), p. 17. See also NLI, BFPA, MS 49,254/2.

18. 'Briefly Noted', p. 139.
19. Francine Prose, *The Lives of the Muses* (New York: HarperCollins, 2002), p. 2. Further references in parentheses in the text.
20. *The Selected Letters of Lewis Carroll*, ed. by Morton N. Cohen (London: Macmillan 1982), p. 140, cited in Prose, p. 94.
21. NLI, BFPA, MS 49, 254/3. Excerpts from a typewritten draft of *Performances*, numbered pp. 4–5.
22. Robert Graves, *The White Goddess: A Historical Grammar of Poetic Myth* (New York: Noonday Press/Farrar, Straus & Giroux, 1997), pp. 446–47 cited in Prose, p. 14.
23. Griffiths, p. 18, cited in NLI, BFPA, MS 49,254/2. Undated handwritten note towards *Performances*.
24. Brian Friel, *The Enemy Within* (Oldcastle: Gallery Press, 1992), p. 77.
25. See Zemanová, p. 313 (footnote no. 140 on p. 211).
26. NLI, BPFA, MS 49,254/2. Page from an undated typed draft of *Performances*. Emendations in black pen.
27. Though Friel's stage directions specify that the play ought to end with the third movement of the String Quartet, with a '*[b]lackout the moment the moderato ends*' (Friel, *Performances*, p. 34), in this production the players continued until the end of the piece.
28. NLI, BFPA, MS 49,254/2. Undated handwritten note towards *Performances*.
29. NLI, BPFA, MS 49,254/2. Page from an undated typed draft of *Performances*. Emendations in black pen.
30. Leoš Janáček, letter to Kamila Stösslová dated 14 [*recte* 13] December 1927, in John Tyrrell, ed. and trans., *Intimate Letters: Leoš Janáček to Kamila Stösslová* (London: Faber and Faber, 2005), p. 162.
31. Leoš Janáček, letter to Kamila Stösslová dated 19 December 1927, in Tyrrell, p. 170.
32. Leoš Janáček, letter to Kamila Stösslová dated 19 December 1927, in Tyrrell, p. 170.
33. Leoš Janáček, letter to Kamila Stösslová dated 14 [*recte* 13] December 1927, in Tyrrell, p. 162.
34. NLI, BFPA, MS 49,254/3. Handwritten note towards *Performances* in a 200-page red hardbacked Lismore Feint Ruled Book.
35. Prose, p. 31.

36. Christopher Murray, *The Theatre of Brian Friel: Tradition and Modernity* (London: Bloomsbury, 2014), p. 187. It is reassuring to find that I am not the only Friel scholar to have combed Tyrrell's translations for these so-called letters without success.
37. Friel, *Performances*, p. 12.
38. NLI, BFPA, MS 49,254/7. Printed bound draft of *Performances* (undated).
39. Lisa Fitzpatrick, '*Performances* by Brian Friel', *Irish Theatre Magazine*, 15 February 2013, < http://www.irishtheatremagazine.ie/Reviews/Current/Performances > [accessed 17 May 2015].
40. 'Up there, her feet completely off the ground she will be just as irrelevant to the practical decisions of running the world as she was in her bad old days'. Chinua Achebe, *Anthills of the Savannah* (Oxford: Heinemann, 1987), p. 98.
41. Christopher Murray, *The Theatre of Brian Friel: Tradition and Modernity* (London: Bloomsbury, 2014), p. 188.
42. Friel, *Performances*, p. 33.
43. Murray, p. 185.
44. Anthony Roche, *Brian Friel: Theatre and Politics* (Basingstoke: Palgrave Macmillan, 2011), p. 206.
45. George Steiner, *In Bluebeard's Castle: Some Notes Towards the Redefinition of Culture* (London: Faber and Faber, 1971), p. 88.
46. George Steiner, *Real Presences: Is There Anything in What We Say?* (London: Faber & Faber, 1989), p. 8.
47. Steiner, *Real Presences*, p. 9.
48. Steiner, *Real Presences*, p. 196. See also NLI, BFPA, MS 49,253/1.
49. George Steiner, 'Silence and the Poet', in *Language and Silence: Essays and Notes, 1958–1966* (London: Faber & Faber, 2010), pp. 53–81 (p. 64).
50. See NLI, BFPA, MS 49,253/1.
51. NLI, BFPA, MS 49,253/1. Handwritten letter from Brian Friel to Peggy Paterson dated 10 November 2002.
52. NLI, BFPA, MS 49,253/1. Typed letter from Brian Friel to Michael Colgan, 8 December 2002.
53. Listening to the Škampa Quartet recording, it is easy to see how their unapologetically, stubbornly stodgy, and slowly bombastic rendering of these opening notes suggested Ruth's interpretation.

54. George Steiner, 'Silence and the Poet', p. 64.
55. Leoš Janáček, letter to Kamila Stösslová dated 26 April 1928, at night, in Tyrrell, p. 260.
56. Friel, *Plays One* (London: Faber and Faber, 1996), p. 445.
57. See Steiner, *In Bluebeard's Castle*, p. 72.
58. Leoš Janáček, letter to Kamila Stösslová dated 1 February 1928, at night, in Tyrrell, p. 196.
59. Brian Friel, *Plays Two* (London: Faber, 1999), p. 457. Further references in parentheses in the text as 'Friel, *P2*'.
60. Seamus Heaney, '...English and Irish', *The Times Literary Supplement* no. 4047, 24 October 1980, p. 1199.
61. Scott Boltwood, *Brian Friel, Ireland, and the North* (Cambridge: Cambridge University Press, 2009), p. 57.
62. Karen M. Moloney, 'Molly Astray: Revisioning Ireland in Brian Friel's *Molly Sweeney*', *Twentieth Century Literature* 46, No. 3 (Autumn 2000), pp. 285–310 (p. 285).
63. Anna McMullan, 'Performativity, Unruly Bodies and Gender in Brian Friel's Drama', in *The Cambridge Companion to Brian Friel*, ed. by Anthony Roche (Cambridge: Cambridge University Press, 2006), pp. 142–53 (p. 143).
64. McMullan, p. 145.
65. NLI, BFP, MS 37,128/3. Note towards *Molly Sweeney* dated 29 November 1993.
66. NLI, BFP, MS 37,128/5. Undated note towards *Molly Sweeney*. Compare with Friel, *Plays Two*, p. 478.
67. McMullan, p. 145.
68. Friel, *Plays One*, p. 343.
69. Friel, *Plays One*, p. 345.
70. G. B. Shaw, Letter to Mrs Patrick Campbell, c. 5 February 1920, in Dan H. Lawrence, ed., *Selected Correspondence of Bernard Shaw: Theatrics* (Toronto: University of Toronto Press, 1995), p. 155.
71. See Alan Jay Lerner, *My Fair Lady: A Musical Play by Alan Jay Lerner* (New York: Coward-McCann, 1956).
72. Friel, *Plays Two*, p. 488.
73. Murray, p. 153.
74. Tony Coult, *About Friel: The Playwright and the Work* (London: Faber and Faber, 2003), p. 156, cited in Murray, p. 153.
75. Murray, p. 153.

76. Murray, p. 154.
77. See NLI, BFP, MS 37,100/1. Note towards *Making History* dated 1 October 1986.
78. Tutter, p. 409.
79. Oliver Sacks, 'A Neurologist's Notebook: To See and Not See', *The New Yorker*, 10 May 1993, pp. 59–73 (p. 62), cited in NLI, Brian Friel Papers, MS 37,128/1.
80. Sacks, p. 61.
81. Sacks, p. 60.
82. Sacks, p. 59.
83. Sacks, p. 73.
84. NLI, BFP, MS 37,128/3. Note towards *Molly Sweeney* dated 23 November 1993.
85. NLI, BFP, MS 37,128/3. Note towards *Molly Sweeney* dated 1 August 1993.
86. NLI, BFP, MS 37,128/3. Undated note towards *Molly Sweeney*.
87. NLI, BFP, MS 37,128/3. Note towards *Molly Sweeney* dated 18 November [1993].
88. NLI, BFP, MS 37,128/3. Note towards *Molly Sweeney* dated 29 July 1993.
89. NLI, BFP, MS 37,128/3. Note towards *Molly Sweeney* dated 29 July 1993.
90. NLI, BFP, MS 37,128/3. Note towards *Molly Sweeney* dated 29 November 1993.
91. Robert Graves, *The White Goddess: A Historical Grammar of Poetic Myth* (New York: Noonday Press/Farrar, Straus & Giroux, 1997), pp. 446–447 cited in Prose, p. 14.
92. Murray, p. 145.
93. Photocopied from Gregory's *Concepts and Mechanisms of Perception* (1974).
94. M. von Senden, *Space and Sight: The Perception of Space and Shape in the Congenitally Blind Before and After Operation*, trans. by Peter Heath, appendices by A. H. Riesen, G. J. Warnock, and J. Z. Young (London: Methuen, 1932), in NLI, Brian Friel Papers, MS 37/128/1.
95. Alberto Valvo, M. D., *Sight Restoration After Long-Term Blindness: The Problems and Behavior Patterns of Visual Rehabilitation*, ed. by Leslie L. Clark and Zofia Z. Jastrzembska (New York:

American Foundation for the Blind, 1971), in NLI, Brian Friel Papers, MS 37,128/1.
96. Semir Zeki, *A Vision of the Brain* (Oxford: Blackwell Scientific Publications, 1993), in NLI, Brian Friel Papers, MS 37,128/2.
97. Zeki, p. 319.
98. Sacks, p. 66.
99. Valvo, p. 19, in NLI, Brian Friel Papers, MS 37,128/1.
100. G. A. Miller, *Psychology* (Hammondsworth: Penguin Books, 1962), p. 372, cited in Valvo, p. 19, in NLI, Brian Friel Papers, MS 37/128/1.
101. J. Z. Young, 'Appendix II: Anatomy and Physiology', in von Senden, p. 319, in NLI, Brian Friel Papers, MS 37,128/1.
102. NLI, Brian Friel Papers, MS 37,128/1.
103. 'ἐγγράφω', in *LSJ: The Online Liddell-Scott-Jones Greek-English Lexicon*, http://stephanus.tlg.uci.edu/lsj/#eid=30926&context=lsj&action=from-search [accessed 20 December 2015]. I am grateful to Dr. Enrico Emmanuelle Prodi for his assistance in tracking down the etymology of this word.
104. von Senden, p. 202, in NLI, Brian Friel Papers, MS 37/128/1.
105. 8 February–21 March 2014. Directed by Abigail Graham. 8 February–8 March 2014, Lyric Theatre, Belfast. The production referenced here occurred on 6th March 2014 and was a surtitled performance. This was a Lyric Theatre/Print Room production of the 2013 Print Room production of the play.
106. Sacks, p. 59, in NLI, Brian Friel Papers, MS 37,128/1.
107. von Senden, p. 70, in NLI, Brian Friel Papers, MS 37/128/1.
108. Tutter, p. 409.
109. NLI, BFP, MS 37,128/3. Note towards *Molly Sweeney* dated 18 November [1993].
110. Stanton B. Garner, Jr., *Bodied Spaces: Phenomenology and Performance in Contemporary Drama* (Ithaca and London: Cornell University Press, 1994), p. 188.
111. Sean Nolan, 'Independent Review at Gate Theatre Finds Michael Colgan Has "Case to Answer" Over Allegations', *Irish Independent*, 9 February 2018, https://www.independent.ie/irish-news/news/independent-review-at-gate-theatre-finds-michael-colgan-has-case-to-answer-over-allegations-36586535.html [accessed 7 March 2022].

CHAPTER 6

'Don't Anticipate the Ending': Towards a Legacy of Artistic Practice

I began this book with a chapter that focused on Friel's influences at the level of artistic practice. I would like to finish it by extending this approach methodologically through practice-based research that privileges archival encounter from the point of view of archive users. I want to consider how Friel's own ways of working as revealed by his literary archives might inspire not only scholars of his work but also other artists, as well as how such models of influence might be seen to operate. Specifically, the backbone of this chapter will be my own creative collaboration with performance-maker and composer Robbie Blake (they/them) and dancer-choreographer Jessie Keenan (she/her) on a practice-based research project that came to be known as 'Don't Anticipate the Ending'—a quotation taken from Friel's notes towards *Dancing at Lughnasa* (1990). Funded by the Irish Research Council and Arts Council Ireland, and with additional support from a number of Irish cultural and academic institutions,[1] the project involved two creative leads (Keenan and Blake) in collaboration with me as research lead and dramaturge. Drawing on Friel's artistic practice as revealed by his notes for *Dancing at Lughnasa*, we created two original short film works: 'Running the Ending' (Blake) and 'So What Is Surfacing (Trio)' (Keenan, with music by Blake). These subsequently formed the basis of a digital exhibition I curated for the Museum of Literature Ireland (MoLI), showcasing the intersections between Friel's process and that of the two creative leads, using archive material from both the Brian Friel Papers and material generated over the course of the project itself. This exhibition, titled *Don't anticipate the ending: creative encounters with the Brian Friel Papers*, is available online in perpetuity and can be accessed via MoLI's website.[2] Taking the view that the Brian Friel Papers are the record not of a life's work but rather a life's work in progress, the project aims to extend Friel's legacy in terms of his creative practice. Crucially, the project holds that this legacy of artistic practice is one whose significance goes beyond the academy alone, insofar as it has a demonstrable potential to influence current and future practitioners in the arts. Acknowledging the extent to which Friel's career was devoted to creative explorations of how artists make art—including himself—the project asks how Friel's ways of working might influence and inspire contemporary artists working in different disciplines to generate new work of their own. In so doing, it extends the idea of Friel's models of influence to Friel as influencer.

Central to the project is the idea of the archive as a site of encounter and of practice: a space where the event of being brought face to face with an artefact—of being mutually present in a given 'now'—takes place. As Rebecca Schneider puts it in her book *Performing Remains* (2011), the archive is 'a house […] built for live encounter with privileged remains', and as such is a site for the 'live practices of access'[3] associated with it; a place, as Ann Cvetkovich notes succinctly, 'where we do things with objects'.[4] This encompasses an idea of liveness that resonates with Friel's own sense of creative encounter—which, as we have seen in Chapter 2, becomes particularly apparent when he writes of 'the chance of reading Bacon at this time'[5] whilst writing *Faith Healer* (1979). So too does it resonate with Bacon's privileging of the role of the accidental in his work, in that it acknowledges the extent to which archival research, far from being a rigorous and methodical process *at all times*, often feels highly subjective in practice and is as much about the informed 'manipulation'[6] of chance as it is about expertise: luck and instinct have their part to play. Consequently, one of the main focuses of the collaboration is the 'how' of archival presence, drawing particularly on the questioning elements of Friel's process to generate new material.

A further consideration that informs this collaboration is the extent to which the experience of these 'live practices of access'[7] is determined by a sense of agency and/or belonging. This stems in part from the degree to which archive users feel comfortable in an official space designed to hold and preserve material that has been selected according to official criteria from which they may feel excluded. As Helen Freshwater notes, 'the archive's very existence indicates an a priori value judgement concerning the worth of the documents or artifacts [*sic.*] it contains'.[8] As 'tangible evidence' that 'the work has value',[9] the archive must therefore be made to answer the question as to how and by what measure of authority this value is determined before it can be destabilised. This is certainly true of the National Library of Ireland, which is—as its Collection Development Policy 2009–2011 reminds us—'a national cultural institution charged with collecting for and on behalf of the State'[10] (and which is permitted by law to accept substantial donations of heritage material in return for tax credits). Indeed, the extent to which the NLI's values are representative of present-day Ireland is currently under scrutiny from within, as the remarks of its then Director Dr Sandra Collins in the introduction to its Diversity and Inclusion Policy 2018–2021 will avow:

> The national collections tell the story of Ireland. How we collect and how we share and interpret these collections tell a story also. [...] Irish society has changed and evolved. Social norms and the diversity of Irish society look very different now from 50 years ago.[11]

This is in contrast to the relative conservatism of the acquisitions criteria currently (as of 2022) available on the NLI's website, which includes an undated but indubitably outdated leaflet titled *Treasuring our Heritage*.[12] Whilst its definition of Irishness extends to emigration and diaspora in the category '[t]he Irish abroad', it is telling that there is no equivalent emphasis on immigration. It is also remarkably heteronormative in its emphasis on the nuclear family through the privileging of 'genealogical records'.[13] The heteronormative bias of the NLI's collections has since improved thanks to its activist-led acquisition of the Irish Queer Archive in 2009. However, the title of this collection is—by the admission of those involved in compiling it—aspirational rather than descriptive, insofar as unambiguously trans lives are relatively under represented.

These examples of implied social conservatism are in keeping with the RTÉ News coverage of the NLI's acquisition of the Brian Friel Papers from 8 February 2001, where there is a strong suggestion that Friel's archive was expected to preserve the construction of a very particular kind of Irishness. When interviewed for the report, for instance, then director of the NLI Brendan O'Donoghue remarked that they would be adding the papers to an existing collection of 'writers of previous generations [...] like Shaw, Yeats, Joyce, and so on'—in other words, to a well-established and overwhelmingly white male literary canon. Noel Pearson, meanwhile, who produced the film adaptation of *Dancing at Lughnasa* (1998), had this to say: 'What makes Friel powerful and great and wonderful is that he is true to himself, true to where he comes from, true to the parish he comes from, and true to the place he comes from'. The report also showed interview footage of Meryl Streep, who played Kate Mundy in the same film, calling Friel's storytelling 'lovely': 'very moving and [...] sad and sweet'.[14] Indeed, the overall impression from this report is that Friel's archive is both monumentally significant and fundamentally unthreatening to the status quo in its construction of a superficial and uncomplicated kind of Irishness, sitting comfortably within a pseudo-genealogical narrative of a line of defanged literary patriarchs sprung from Irish soil. This is a disservice both to what Friel's archive is and to its potential to be a useful resource for contemporary artists whose work is redefining what it means to be an Irish artist today. For instance, though the creative directors of 'Don't Anticipate the Ending' all benefit from white privilege, able-bodied privilege, a university education, and a middle-class background, there is much to do with issues of gender identity, queerness, cultural identity, and precarity that informed our collective engagements with Friel's archive and which caused us to question our relationship with it. The project therefore takes an intersectional approach to its connection with legacies of influence, considering how our different interlacing identities (with their greater or lesser degrees of privilege) affect our position within a narrative of cultural inheritance.

A final overarching consideration for the project was the relationship between archive and performance in the context of bodied engagements with the Brian Friel Papers. The foundations for this line of enquiry are to be found in Taylor's *The Archive and the Repertoire* (2003). To recap, Taylor makes a case for performance as another kind of archive, which she calls the 'repertoire'. This repertoire consists of what Taylor refers to as embodied practices that can transfer and transmit 'social knowledge, memory, and a sense of identity'[15] through repeated and repeatable behaviours. Examples include: 'performances, gestures, orality, movement, dance, singing—in short, all those acts usually thought of as ephemeral, nonreproducible knowledge'.[16] It is a fundamentally anticolonial approach insofar as, if we see the repertoire as enduring through performance rather than disappearing because it hasn't been written down, we begin to challenge the authority of the written archive, which grants 'only the literate and powerful [...] social memory and identity'.[17] Crucially, the acts that make up the repertoire can only be carried out with the presence and/or participation of living bodies. In this way, the body can be seen as a way of storing and passing on knowledge that doesn't automatically privilege the written word. In other words, the body is capable of participating in ways of doing that are also ways of knowing and enduring—an idea that is key to practice-based research itself. Indeed, it is Schneider's extension of Taylor that informs the project's approach to the liveness of archival access, wherein the *practice* of archival access is posited as part of Taylor's repertoire.

This performance studies-based approach is supplemented in places by a practice-based understanding of archival encounter that I subsequently found to be particularly resonant with queer archival methodologies as theorised by Cvetkovich and others. I include some of these resonances here, not because I want to claim retroactively that these were key to the project from the outset, but rather because they later emerged as a way in which I as a queer researcher working within a predominantly queer collaborative team found I could understand certain elements of our shared archival praxis. For instance, building on the work of scholars like Carolyn Dinshaw, Jack Halberstam, and Horacio Ramírez and Nan Boyd, Amy L. Stone and Jaime Cantrell emphasise the queer temporality of an affective experience of archival access that 'require[s] a deeply personal, embodied research':

> Engaging in archival research offers a profoundly queer temporal experience—and temporary existence. Research within the archive necessitates a dissociative shift in being and thought: scholars become lost in the present, enveloped in the past.[18]

I have found that this is particularly relevant both to my own experience of archival research and to the way in which encountering Friel's question-heavy way of working influenced Keenan (see below). Similarly, my own engagement with Blake's work whilst curating the project archive we had created for the MoLI exhibition was one in which I found myself 'shifting the presence of LGBT lives and histories within archival scholarship from margin to center'[19] in ways I had not anticipated. The budding of a now tentatively blooming critical interest in queer archival methodologies that grew out of my reflections on the project, therefore, is worth acknowledging.

In making a case study of the archive of a globally significant playwright whose place in the Irish canon is assured, I am well aware that this project does little to challenge the hierarchies of cultural significance that have long dictated the acquisitions policies of some of Ireland's cultural institutions. Nevertheless, it does lay some of the groundwork for future projects by engaging with literary archives in ways that set artistic legacies in motion rather than in stone. By developing a repertoire of practices of access that enable processes of understanding and transforming the archive through the body, the project has been a useful testing ground for engaging with archives in what I hope is both a more radical and a more accessible way—one that 'affirm[s] the importance of the archive as a site of practice'[20] above all else. Certainly, I am of a mind with Cvetkovich when she asserts that to see archives as 'places where we do things with objects'[21] may well be the key to their longevity. Indeed, it is through foregrounding archives as sites of practice rather than letting them remain 'static collections'[22] that we are able to pursue 'a model for scholarship that is theoretically informed, affectively engaged, and materially grounded', and which is capable of generating 'new methods of inquiry that will keep us returning to the archives for some time to come'.[23] It is in this spirit, then, that the project focuses on the cultural inheritance that is Friel's written archive as a record of ways of doing that can be transferred across artistic disciplines, exploring the extent to which an artistic legacy can be known and transmitted through the body.

Project Background

I had first contacted Blake and Keenan (with whom I had worked before as a performer via Blake's vocal ensemble Tonnta) during the funding application process for a Government of Ireland Postdoctoral Research Fellowship. The idea of adding a practice-based element to my research was an important part of my thinking around my own relationship with academia, which was (and still is, to an extent) characterised by mine and my peers' increasing disillusionment with a sector in which early career researchers in particular are treated as disposable labour. If I was going to attempt to devote my life and mind to a fundamentally unstable career path, it was not going to be so that I could abide by a definition of 'impact' that prioritised citations of my work by other academics. In other words, if there was to be any talk at all about my research, it would not be exclusively among ourselves: I wanted to expand archival access to the

Friel Papers in a way that had the potential to engage people living and working outside the academy. I was particularly keen to work with creative practitioners in a way that acknowledged Friel's archive as a record of the process of making art, making the Brian Friel Papers intelligible and accessible as the product of a way of working.

I had chosen to focus on Friel's composition process for *Dancing at Lughnasa*, as it seemed a logical choice to use material with which Keenan (a dancer-choreographer) and Blake (a performance-maker and composer) might find an easy affinity. At the time of our first workshop session at the UCD Humanities Institute on 22 January 2019, the only archive material Keenan and Blake had seen was a document I had compiled and sent on 5 November 2018, which contained selected material from Friel's notes towards *Dancing at Lughnasa* (1990) along with some relevant excerpts from my doctoral thesis. My own research on *Dancing at Lughnasa* up to this point had revealed the extent of Friel's thinking around music and dance, and some of our earliest conversations were based on teasing out its nuances. As Blake's notes will attest, we also discussed Taylor and Schneider, Denis Donoghue, and my ideas around the relationship between form and core, as well as Friel's tendency to think in musical terms. It was not until the three of us went to consult the Brian Friel Papers together in the National Library of Ireland on 5 February 2019, however, that the vital importance of the materiality of Friel's composition process became fully apparent in the context of establishing a collaborative process of our own.

INTO THE ARCHIVE

Our first trip to the Manuscripts Reading Room at the NLI as a collaborative team was to consult MS 37,104/1–7, pertaining to Friel's writing process for *Dancing at Lughnasa*. As a researcher, I had always benefitted from a sense of belonging in the archive. I had been working with the Brian Friel Papers since 2012, having drawn on them extensively for my doctoral research. I was familiar with the procedures, knew many of the archivists by sight if not by name, and had found security and library staff alike to be kind, helpful, and generally accommodating. Although I had initially been struck by a sense of being in the presence of 'privileged remains', my overwhelming sense of working with the Brian Friel Papers quickly gave way to the excitement of being in the presence of a mind and work (Friel's). Keenan's experience was fairly similar:

> There's a lot of rules and regulations [...] and I was slightly charmed by that [...] There was something in the ritual of it I think that I quite enjoyed. But then I think there was this really interesting contrast between this quite rigid ritual of using the space and then the material that you're actually looking at [...] [which] was really alive and in the middle of the process [...].[24]

Blake, on the other hand, found the experience initially unsettling, as they recalled in an interview at MoLI in 2021:

> I remember feeling quite at odds, I think, actually, with being in that space—feeling like it was a space for someone else. [...] But then I think the experience really twisted because I had been invited in: I had a guide [in Zosia] and a colleague in Jessie as another creative practitioner who was experiencing [it] in the same way as I was, and I felt like I could have a little bit more freedom than I initially felt.[25]

It was in this facilitatory, 'insider' capacity, then, that I entered the archive with Keenan and Blake to introduce them to Friel's way of working in the context of his writing process for *Dancing at Lughnasa*.

First performed in April 1990 at Dublin's Abbey Theatre, *Dancing at Lughnasa* is one of Friel's better-known plays thanks to its having won both an Olivier and three Tony Awards on its transfers to the West End and Broadway in 1991. It was also made into a slightly underwhelming film starring Meryl Streep in 1998, with a screenplay by Frank McGuinness. The play, as is widely known, is loosely based on the lives of Friel's mother's family in Glenties, the MacLoones. As Friel wrote on 28 May 1989 (referencing a diary entry for 18 May):

> I suppose the play is about the McLoone family, Fr. Barney—and my father. Family life—make-believe—remembering and remaking the past—betrayal—groping towards love. Really original stuff for me![26]

Friel's tongue appears to have been firmly in his cheek at this juncture.

The play was written within a relatively short space of time and draws largely on Friel's own family history by way of source materials. Indeed, there are two accounts of the life and death of Rev. Bernard MacLoone preserved in the Brian Friel Papers, one from the *The Derry Journal* on 10 July 1950 and the other from *The Ulster Herald* on 15 July 1950. Both refer to him as the 'Wee Donegal Priest' and take an uncritical view of what the *Derry Journal* calls his 'great missionary career'.[27] Other major sources for the play are not readily apparent, with the possible exception of travel writer Joseph Hone's *Duck Soup in the Black Sea* (1988), cited by Friel on 13 May 1989. Significantly, it is not so much Hone's writings on his travels in Africa that are reminiscent of *Lughnasa* as his final chapter in which he returns to his childhood home in Ireland: 'But Irish landscapes are so often deceptive. [...] Beyond the most placid or secure vision, there is always a feeling of impending decay, surprise, disruption, even violence'.[28] It is the continuation of this passage that appears in Friel's notes:

> There's a strong aura in Ireland—in the landscape and the people—of much that will always be ungoverned, untutored, where any imposed order has the air of a mere holding operation, a temporary clearing or civilisation won from a ragged and voracious nature.[29]

The unseen spectre of the burned boy in the hills where the Lughnasa fires are lit comes forcibly to mind here. So too does Hone's prose evoke the contrast between the nostalgia of Michael's 'placid' narration and the 'impending decay, surprise, disruption, even violence' that animates the Mundy household.

Friel does not quote from Hone beyond the above. Nevertheless, there are further resonances in the finished play if not necessarily in its composition process. For instance, Hone's recollection of the first time he became aware of 'a larger world beyond' was at the age of seven, when 'someone, listening to the wireless, shrieked out of a window, "The allies have taken Rome!"',[30] drawing his attention to the fact that there was a global conflict in progress. As in *Lughnasa*, the radio is a mouthpiece for a global interconnectedness; as in *Lughnasa*, there is a disruption of a child's sense of reality by 'shrieking strangers'.[31] There is also, I think, the possibility of a case to be made for this particular chapter of *Duck Soup* as a kind of informing mood for *Lughnasa*. Indeed, Friel's portrait of the dreamily haunted Michael is remarkably similar to Hone's own sense of time being out of joint:

> When I return to the house I have the eerie feeling of compassing a giant span of time [...] Quite suddenly, in one of the rooms or attics, I can find myself back in my own past or in one even more distant.[32]

More tellingly still, Hone writes of memory as fundamentally transformative. 'The past', he writes, 'is so much more than mere sentiment: it can become reincarnate, encrusted with marvels'.[33] Compounding this, he cites Ariel's haunting song from Act 1 Scene 2 of *The Tempest*, in which he tells the young prince Ferdinand that his father has drowned and been transfigured: 'Those are pearls that were his eyes:/ Nothing of him that doth fade,/ But doth suffer a sea-change/ Into something rich and strange'.[34] And indeed, Michael's memories of that summer of 1936 are characterised by a rich strangeness, with all the many things he could not understand as a boy remembered now through movement: 'All of this is observed and only obliquely understood by the boy. And he sees it all in terms of dance. All the significant emotion of the story is expressed through dances and is therefore more open to personal interpretation'.[35] Unlike Hone, however, Michael is unable to navigate by his memories, instead becoming lost in them. Hone ends *Duck Soup* by observing that '[m]emory lane needn't be a cul-de-sac, but a road to an undiscovered country, suggesting exits, not ends':

> Our own history—that even weightier, largely unopened ragbag we lug about with us—offers lodestars among the sawdust and tinsel. And that ragbag, for me, has always been the traveller's real luggage, his map and compass, sustenance and ticket. In opening it, and rummaging about suitably, we may draw our real co-ordinates, plot where we are now and so travel on with more accuracy and assurance.[36]

Michael, on the other hand, is never enough of a presence in his own memories to be able to plot a course between now and then—between the unanchored narrator and the absent boy who speaks a child's words with the voice of a man.

When it comes to the experiences of the play's returned missionary, however, it is not to the travel writer that Friel looked for inspiration. There is evidence that Friel did some basic research on Uganda—possibly from an encyclopaedia, given the kind of information contained in booklet 'B' in MS 37,104/1. For instance, Friel makes a note of Uganda's major cities, lakes, ethnic groups, languages, and a short timeline of its colonial history.[37] Rather more controversially, there is also evidence to suggest that Friel's idea of Ugandan culture and its rituals in the 1930s owes a great deal to Chinua Achebe's *Things Fall Apart* (1958), which depicts Igbo culture in pre-colonial Nigeria in the 1890s. For instance,

Friel refers himself to Achebe's depiction of the Feast of the New Yam in honour of the earth goddess Ani, who is 'the ultimate judge of morality and conduct [...] in close communion with the departed fathers of the clan whose bodies had been committed to earth'.[38] Hence Fr. Jack's description of a festival of the same name to honour the similar-sounding but apparently made-up[39] 'Obi, our Great Goddess of the Earth, so that the crops will flourish' or else 'to get in touch with our departed fathers' (Friel, *P2*, 73). MS 37,104/1 also contains a substantial citation from *Things Fall Apart* in which Ezeani, priest of the earth goddess Ani, chides the book's protagonist Okonkwo for beating his wife during the Week of Peace: '[O]ur forefathers ordained that before we plant any crops in the earth we should observe a week in which a man does not say a harsh word to his neighbour [...] to honour our great goddess of the earth without whose blessing our crops will not grow'. Ezeani, as noted by Friel, then goes on to demand that Okonkwo make amends by bringing 'one she-goat, one hen, a length of cloth and a hundred cowries'[40] to Ani's shrine. This would appear to be the source of Fr. Jack's tales of appeasing spirits with 'a rooster or a young goat' (Friel, *P2*, 61). Indeed, it would seem that the Ugandan deities and rituals of *Lughnasa* are largely based on a fictionalised portrayal of a completely different part of pre-colonial Africa some twenty years before the arrival of Fr. Jack in Uganda (around forty years before his return to Donegal). The authenticity of Friel's depiction of Ugandan cultural traditions through Fr. Jack is therefore highly questionable. (It is also a source of considerable regret that I did not discover this in time for it to factor into our creative engagements with the archive.)

As an alternative title for a play in which '[m]ere anarchy is loosed upon the world' in the brief moments during which five women are '[t]urning and turning in the widening gyre',[41] *Things Fall Apart* is not a bad choice. In the play, the five Mundy sisters (Kate, Maggie, Agnes, Rose, and Christina) are scraping a subsistence in Friel's ubiquitous imaginary Donegal town of Ballybeg. It is the summer of 1936, when their priest brother, Fr. Jack—based on Friel's uncle Bernard MacLoone, 'The Wee Donegal Priest'—returns home from missionary work in a leper colony in Uganda. This is ostensibly because he has malaria, though in truth, as per Friel's notes, he has been 'dabbling in joyous paganism'.[42] At the same time, Gerry, the father of Christina's son Michael and who 'dances divinely',[43] comes to visit twice and throws the household dynamics into further disarray. A further catalyst for change is the sisters' newly acquired radio, which connects the house to the wider modern world at a time of year when the old world reasserts its hold on the local in the form of the Festival of Lughnasa, which honours the Celtic God of the Harvest, Lugh. The radio is also the catalyst for one of the most famous and viscerally moving moments in the play, when the sisters, witnessed by the absent boy, break into a defiant, frantic, slightly grotesque, frustration-venting, taboo-breaking dance, in which 'there is a sense of order being consciously subverted' (Friel, *P2*, 37). By the end of the play, the household is at breaking point: two of the sisters will go to England and die there in abject poverty; Fr. Jack will die within the year; Gerry will go to fight Franco in Spain and an injury will put an end to his dancing days. The play is narrated by Christina's grownup son Michael, who also speaks the lines of his childhood self, who never physically appears onstage.

Friel's notes towards *Lughnasa* reveal the extent to which his thinking around dance and its function in the play had implications for its form. Unsurprisingly for a playwright who was often writing with the indigence of language in mind, Friel was exploring what he called 'this nagging idea of Dance'[44] as a way of giving form to the linguistically inexpressible. Indeed, writing on 30 May 1989, Friel suggests that the core of *Lughnasa* might be 'the notion of something forbidden, or at least something not publicly blessed, being expressed + celebrated in dance'.[45] However, as Friel's earlier note of 17 May suggests, this was only one of a number of ways in which Friel was thinking about dance and its function. Moreover, this function has a direct relationship with the way reality itself is constructed in the play:

> Of course the play can be written and adequately, maybe fully, realised in a naturalistic style. But this nagging idea of Dance (naturalistic dance, dance as metaphor, dance as essential theatre, dance as complete self-expression*) persists. And that distances the play from naturalistic/realistic expression.[46] (Asterisk in original)

On 7 June, Friel added an asterisk and expanded that definition of dance further: '*Dance as memory—dance as dream-memory, dance as substitute for language, dance as worship'[47] (emphasis in original).

Here, we can see that, for Friel, dance is the key to realising the play as one that has more than one layer of reality. The play might well have been written perfectly adequately as an Irish cottage play, in which the young boy Michael is a physical presence (as in Frank McGuinness's film adaptation of *Lughnasa*). In order for dance to function on these different levels, however, a narrator in a different reality had to be introduced. These were terms in which Friel was demonstrably thinking around 28 May 1989:

> If there is no narrator there can be no highly polished dream dances—and Fr. Jack can't parade in his splendid white officer's uniform. There can be other—simpler—spontaneous dances.
>
> But:—
> Has the play its <u>own</u> reality?
> OR has it existence only in the head of the narrator?

In other words, it is left open to interpretation whether the action of the play is the actual past (played out on the stage as though it were the present) or whether it exists only as memory. If the play has its own reality, then dance functions as what Friel calls 'complete self-expression'[48]—a way for the sisters to convey something they are unable to articulate; if the play has existence only in the head of the narrator, then dance functions as what Friel calls 'dream-memory'[49]—a way for the narrator to access memories that cannot be articulated or which could not be understood and processed at the time. This was something I had found particularly intriguing during my doctoral research, and which I had told Blake I was keen to explore as early as November 2016. If the reality of the sisters' world could be questioned, could one also question the reality of the narrator? Indeed, something I had suggested in the extract of my doctoral thesis that I had somewhat optimistically included in my workshop materials was that the adult narrator might function as a projection of the sisters' desire to have their stories told. The opening line of the play is highly suggestive in this respect: 'When are we going to get a decent mirror to see ourselves in?' (Friel, *P2*, 9).

ROBBIE BLAKE: 'RUNNING THE ENDING'

It was only through the physicality of the archive, however, that some of these ideas about dance began to find a new form for Blake, who drew inspiration from Friel's holographic notes in MS 37,104/1 to create a graphic score[50] for a work in progress that came to be known as 'Running the Ending'. As Blake's own notes will attest, we had already discussed the prevalence of a musical idiom in Friel's thinking. In his published interviews and essays, it is not uncommon to see Friel talk about a play in musical terms. In 'Seven Notes for a Festival Programme' (1999), for instance, Friel talks about words as being 'scored' and of 'keys' and 'tempi'.[51] In the same piece, he goes on to refer to actors as 'wonderful singers of the written line'.[52] As the archive reveals, this tendency of Friel's to draw on a musical vocabulary extends to the composition process itself. For instance, it is far more common to see Friel talking about a duet than it is to see him talking about a duologue. He also frequently thought about plays in terms of being for voices: Friel's typed diary towards *Wonderful Tennessee* suggests '[m]onologues, trios, duets, quartets'[53] as possible forms. In the *Lughnasa* manuscripts, too, Friel had made a note of the definitions of the musical terms 'recitative' and 'oratorio'.[54]

What resonated with Blake's practice, however, were certain material features of Friel's composition process. For instance, Friel's early notes were almost always on loose sheets of paper collated into booklets, hole-punched, and treasury-tagged in the top left-hand corner. Often these booklets would be labelled 'A', 'B', 'C', or with the name of a character, or with a feature of Friel's background research. Moreover, though with some exceptions, Friel was generally reliable when it came to dating his notes. Indeed, Friel had a habit of referring himself to a previous or subsequent note by date, the practical upshot of which was that knew where to look when cross-referencing his own notes. Some of these habits were subsequently adopted by Blake, partly by way of entering into the spirit of things, but also because they turned out to be useful: 'not to [...] hold it in one's head only, but to actually write these things down and to allow them to evolve on the page—that's really influenced me, and I've been able to incorporate that in[to] my own practice going forward'.

On a deeper level of influence, it was Friel's editing habits that led directly to Blake's idea for a graphic score. There are, to my mind, three distinct ways in which Friel would make use of a strikethrough in his notes (as opposed to his drafts). The first is a straightforward scribbling-out of a misspelled word or a word put down in error, usually in the same pen or pencil in which the rest of the note is written. The second is a clear strikethrough added later in pencil, which goes through a specific line of text. The third is either a series of strikes or a large, loose scribble across either the whole page or a larger chunk of text. These latter two examples are occasionally ambiguous, in that there are times when they appear to be *discarding* a larger idea and other times when they appear to be marking a particular line of thought as having been *dealt-with*. The visual effect, for Blake, was one of having been 'immediately struck by [...] graphic information'. Indeed, the first thing Blake did when looking at a draft of one of the Narrator's speeches from 19 May 1989 was to transcribe Friel's markings divorced from the text (see Fig. 6.1):

> Brian Friel would have this way of essentially engraving his own notes so as to show different stages of the process of his composition. [...] And I just found that really interesting as a graphic means to develop the work, and that immediately inspired the process for making 'Running the Ending', where I've been using graphic notation or graphic score-making as part of my practice.

Blake's initial idea was to produce a noise piece for radio using the markings as a score. This developed, however, into a way of notating a performance piece called 'Running the Ending' that 'built from an ongoing conversation with Zosia and Jessie about dance, and what dance was for Brian Friel as part of *Dancing at Lughnasa*'. Over a fixed period of five minutes, it 'used just three main physical states: running; resetting or shaking out the body; and then dancing or just completely free movement'.[55] Blake's initial score for 'Running the Ending' (see Fig. 6.2) was developed during a workshop/studio day at the UCD Humanities Institute on 20 February 2019 with three performers in mind (namely the three of us) performing in unison. Blake then had a chance to develop this as part of a short Dance Ireland residency with Keenan in May 2019.[56] The earlier score was adapted and workshopped to create a single set of instructions over five pages that could potentially be performed simultaneously by live and recorded performers (see Fig. 6.3). During the performance, the score would be taped to a surface visible to the performer (a music stand or, in the case of studio rehearsals, a wall), using a timer displayed on a screen (for instance, a mobile phone).

On 12 May 2019, Blake, Keenan, and I used mobile phones to record partial and/or complete performances of 'Running the Ending' in and around the UCD Humanities Institute for the purposes of compiling a trailer for an illustrated talk at the Belfast Book Festival the following month.[57] In the event, the footage and sound were used as part of the talk, with Blake performing 'Running the Ending' live alongside a projection of Keenan's recorded version with sound taken from different recordings. At this point, we had planned for the collaboration to

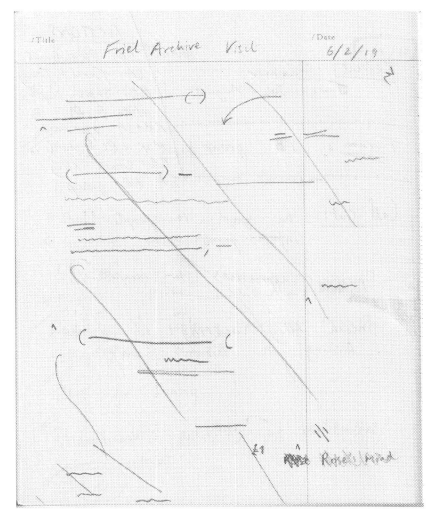

Fig. 6.1 Robbie Blake's transcription of Friel's markings on a draft from MS 37,104/1 dated 19 May 1989

6 'DON'T ANTICIPATE THE ENDING': TOWARDS A LEGACY ...   207

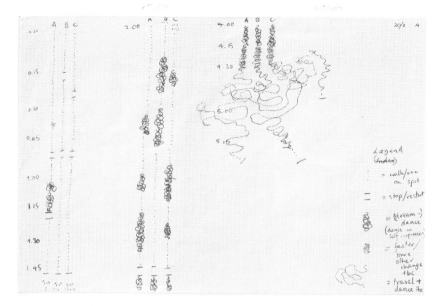

Fig. 6.2 Robbie Blake's first attempt at producing a graphic score inspired by Friel's creative process

Fig. 6.3 Performers Michelle O'Rourke, Marion Cronin, Sarah Ryan, Lucia Kickham, and Bláthnaid Conroy Murphy workshop 'Running the Ending' by Robbie Blake, using copies of their final five-page score taped to the studio walls (Dance House, 14 August 2020)

culminate in a live performance, and so we were keen to use multimedia elements to explore Friel's ideas around an event having 'its own reality'.[58] Consequently, as Blake's notes will attest, we had discussed 'layers of multiple versions: video; audio; live running'.[59] Following a second version of the talk at the UCD Humanities Institute in February 2020, however, our plans for live performance were derailed by the continuing COVID-19 pandemic and were subsequently abandoned in favour of film (see below).

Blake's use of free movement came partly from their sense of Friel's conception of 'dance as something that can be truer than any other form of communication' in the context of his notes towards *Lughnasa*. Though Blake's first draft of the piece conflated dance as dream-memory and dance as complete self-expression (see Fig. 6.2), the workshopping process seemed to clarify the function of dance in 'Running the Ending' as 'a means of expressing something that I hadn't been able to express, or expressing something that needed to be expressed for me around [...] frustration and exhaustion'.[60] This was in keeping not only with a thematic trend Blake was observing in their own work at the time but also with our discussions around different interpretations of the famous kitchen dance in *Lughnasa*. A frequent point of early discussion was a 2015 Lyric Theatre production of *Lughnasa* directed by Annabelle Comyn[61] (the first woman ever to have taken on a revival of the play in Ireland), with choreography by Liz Roche. Acknowledged by reviewers as something of a riposte to a growing tradition of 'lyrical or flowery' productions that have 'a tendency to get dewy-eyed [and] wrap it in sepia',[62] Comyn's interpretation of the play was altogether bleaker—though still not bleak enough for some, as Katy Hayes writes of its transfer to the Gaiety for the *Irish Independent*. With a dark set reflected in a mirror-surface backdrop that heightened 'the pull between the women's reality and the processing of their lives through the prism of Michael's memory'—which Hayes identifies as 'one of the tensions in the text, and challenges of staging it'[63]—the setting was a far cry from the original Abbey Theatre production in 1990. As Sara Keating writes in relation to a 2010 production at Dublin's Helix Theatre that also aimed to buck the rose-tinted trend: 'Ireland was on the cusp of transformation, from a modern into a globalised economy, and Joe Vanek's epic set—an endless field of corn and poppies—helped *Dancing at Lughnasa* become one of Ireland's key cultural exports at this crucial time'.[64] As Patrick Lonergan notes, there is an extent to which 'the canonical status of the play within Ireland was earned not through its reception before Irish audiences, but instead through those audiences' knowledge and appreciation of its success in America'.[65]

My own enduring memory of Comyn's production—tinged though it may be by my own profound sense of exhaustion at a time when I was struggling to complete my doctoral thesis—is of being moved to tears by the kitchen dance, because it was very clear to me that, despite the temporary release it afforded them, these women were (for want of a better word) not OK. In this way, our discussions around some of the backlash against overly-nostalgic productions of the play were a contributing factor in Blake's use of the three principal physical states of 'Running the Ending'. As a piece which requires performers to run on the spot for extended periods of time over and over again, with small pauses for resetting or shaking out the body, it has the potential to generate a build-up of both exhaustion and frustration that is increasingly released by periods in which dance is used as a means of complete self-expression:

> [I]t's constant movement, constant pushing through, and running on the spot, which in a way acts as a sort of Dynamo where there's this energy that's built up that needs releasing or expressing, or allowing it to topple over [...] [and] I was able to arc that into this moment of just moving in any way that feels good at the time, [by] means of dancing, and that allowed that piece to take shape.[66]

Though central to the creation of the piece, however, it was not exhaustion and frustration that came to represent the 'core' of the piece—a term we adopted from Friel over the course of the collaboration. Interviewed after the final filmed version of 'Running the Ending', Blake explained how a rediscovered note from Friel's archive completed the piece for them. In a note dated 30 May [1989], Friel wrote:

> People suddenly find the opportunity and the means to escape from imperial colonialism (of religion, politics, domesticity, convention etc.)
>
> So [the] play should <u>grow</u> in joyousness.[67]

The latter part of this note essentially became a performance note for Blake's piece in a modified form: '[T]he performance note [for "Running the Ending"] is "the piece grows in joyousness", and this was [from] a statement that Friel had used [in his notes] for *Dancing at Lughnasa*'. Blake continues:

> There was something about that that I really loved, and I realized that it was kind of the golden piece that was missing from the graphic score that I had made [...] and I realized that this was the thing that I could ask the performers [...] to hold as an intention. And so I asked them to think about the piece growing in joyousness as a way to evolve past the piece being just about frustration and just about exhaustion and just about my experience of 2019.[68]

In a sense, Blake had come full circle. Having engaged with the materiality of Friel's process to create a graphic score, Blake had gone on to engage with Friel's thinking around dance in addition to debates around the staging of dance in *Lughnasa*; now, they had returned again to Friel's creative practice as a means of animating the piece.

The trajectory of the core of 'Running the Ending' has, as I have come to believe, a great deal to do with the working conditions in which we found ourselves as we attempted to make art during a pandemic. In many ways, we were incredibly fortunate, insofar as we had Arts Council funding and flexible project partners. As Keenan put it in a succinctly understated manner: 'The people were amazing; the situation was challenging'.[69] This meant that, unlike many freelance artists in Ireland, we were able to continue to work in one form or another. Indeed, Blake found that one of the greatest rewards of the project was 'being in a position (albeit masked [and] cleaning surfaces three times a day) [...] to be in the studio with other artists'.[70] Nevertheless, the first year of the COVID-19 pandemic created an atmosphere of profound uncertainty that had a tangible impact on the mental health of everyone involved in the project. Certainly, my own reflections on the process during an interview at MoLI made me realise the extent to which the experience of trying to make art in a pandemic had made me rethink the 'Necessary Uncertainty' of *Give Me Your Answer, Do!* (1997): 'being able to say you can live with uncertainty indefinitely comes from quite a place of privilege, and I don't think that really living with uncertainty for that long is something anyone should be asked to do'.[71] In a similar vein, Blake found that one of the greatest difficulties presented by the pandemic was the necessity of 'continually reinventing the wheel'.[72]

It is for these reasons that I have come to think that Blake's determination to have their performers 'SEEK THE JOY' and 'endeavour to AVOID the rest'[73] must be considered in relation to the intersection between Friel's and Blake's artistic practices rather than rosier interpretations of the *Lughnasa* dance. Blake describes their process as 'a mixture of embodied processes and compositional processes'. Originally a student of music and philosophy, Blake's practice evolved from a classical choral tradition to encompass ideas around 'the body as a conduit and as a medium for performance and for art'. What struck them about Friel's creative process was 'this really amazing sense of a person really giving their all', and they found a great deal of 'positive role modeling' when witnessing 'Brian Friel kind of being his own coach'[74] as an artist. Blake found 'the space that [Friel] would give himself and the way in which he would interrogate certain aspects of the work' to be highly influential, and their project notes are, I think, a reflection of this. Friel's process for writing *Lughnasa* was, in many ways, an exercise in resisting tragedy— something that can be observed in the composition of many of his plays. We have already seen how Friel warned himself against 'the huge, jokeless, joyless allegory'[75] when writing *Faith Healer*. Similarly, when writing *Aristocrats*, Friel gave himself the following talking-to:

> Absorb all the frustrations + disillusions + panics + despairs into yourself. Make them the mute bedrock.
>
> Then write a frothy play.[76]

Most significantly for the collaboration, Friel's notes for *Lughnasa* contain a note to self that informed the entire project in ways we had not expected:

> Don't think in elegaic [*sic*.] tones.
>
> All these people are spirited—even fiery—full of fight.
>
> Don't anticipate the ending.[77]

This note appears again almost word for word in a note dated 24 May 1989. This was adopted as the title and increasingly ironic mantra of a project that began in the spirit of embracing the moment of encounter and of doing, but which ended with a highly stressful ongoing inability to anticipate the end point of the project. Hence, Blake's rediscovery of Friel's note about the play growing in joyousness—and their note to self to seek joy above all else—is in many ways a means of using Friel's process as a way of navigating the uncertainty and frustration of making art in a pandemic. The animating spirit behind 'Running the Ending', therefore, is in many ways the spirit of the project: 'Stay present and stay alive to what's happening and don't predetermine or grip or get too fixed in what you expect or hope for'.[78] In other words, it is through the process of '[f]inding the what in the doing'[79] (emphasis in original) that 'there might be some experience of journeying from somewhere around frustration into somewhere around joyousness'.[80]

This was very much in evidence in the filmed version of 'Running the Ending', which was shot on location at MoLI in April 2021 and which is available online as part of the digital exhibition I curated for the museum.[81] The nature of film allowed Blake to edit together an iteration of the piece in which there was a clear transformative aspect to the movement. In a nod to the five Mundy sisters of *Lughnasa*, the film used the five female performers with whom we had been developing material over the course of the project (see below): three dancers (Marion Cronin, Lucia Kickham, and Sarah Ryan) and two vocalists with performance backgrounds (Bláthnaid Conroy Murphy and Michelle O'Rourke). Each was filmed in two different states, performing 'Running the Ending' whilst responding live to Blake's graphic score. In the first state, the performer would be dressed in blacks and greys, whilst wearing neutral make-up, with hair 'off the face, but by the end loose strands are natural/expected'. This first state was filmed with a locked shot, with performers beginning in a position where they were visible from above the knee and becoming increasingly uncontained by the frame as they moved around in the free movement sections; natural lighting was used. In the second state, Blake wanted 'Glitter!': 'think sequins [...] embrace your camp', with performers '[a]dd[ing] in Favourite bright coloured lip stick or eye-shadow'.[82] Now, performers were shot with coloured lighting that changed between blues, pinks, and purples, and sparkled off the body glitter on their faces. Unlike in the first state, they were shot from a variety of different angles, incorporating close-ups of different parts of the body.

Effecting a transformation of each performer from one state to another over the course of the film entailed finding a balance between the liveness of the performance and the potential of film to work with different temporalities, as Blake's editorial notes will attest:

1. Can the film have an arc, like the score? So the step-by-step, blow-by-blow feel of the score can translate.
2. Introduce each character; show pivotal/transformational moments, capture this personality.[83]

Blake chose to open the film with their own voice setting up the recording, with shots of each performer preparing for a take (in the 'first state'). After a shot in which Ryan clapped to begin her take, the screen then divided into five, with each performer in her own frame (see Fig. 6.4). As the score progressed, and as more and more energy was generated, individual frames would cut to fragments from the 'second state' played in slow motion, before returning to the 'first state' run. These switches to the second state became more and more frequent, until by the end multiple frames at a time were in the 'second state'. By the end of the piece, all five performers were permanently transformed into the 'second state', no longer moving but visibly elated and out of breath. From the outside in, each square then turned black, until there was only a black screen and the sound of the performers' panting. The sounds generated by the performance of the piece in the 'first state'—including not only the performers' feet but also their breathing and vocalisations—were present throughout.

This use of the two 'states' enabled by the filming process has, to my mind, achieved a version of Blake's archival engagement that acknowledges some of its queerness, even perhaps beyond Blake's own intentions. This is not just because of the camp-embracing elements of the second state, nor the *Wizard of Oz* style transformation into colour. For me, this comes back to the idea of joy and of the piece growing in joyousness. Whilst it is still true to say that Blake's Friel-inspired performance note is partly a response to the frustration of making art at a time of unprecedentedly global uncertainty, I find that I also respond to the finished film both as a queer researcher invested in 'shifting the presence of LGBT lives [...] from margin to center'[84] and as a member of a queer community for whom joy will always be in some way radical. This is not an uncomplicated claim: at the time of writing, calls for media representation that acknowledge queer joy (instead of indulging in such tired tropes as 'bury your gays') are matched only by equally fervent calls—generally from the same people—for an end to the corporatisation of queer culture whereby queer joy is rendered mainstream and unthreatening ('Pride was a protest!'). To

Fig. 6.4 Screenshots from 'Running the Ending' by Robbie Blake (Performers left to right: Bláthnaid Conroy Murphy, Lucia Kickham, Marion Cronin, Michelle O'Rourke, and Sarah Ryan)

me, Blake's piece finds a relationship with dance and with joy that productions of *Lughnasa* can only ever aspire to, insofar as it acknowledges that dance as complete self-expression is a transformation of energy from one state to another—a conscious redirection of effort from the exhaustion of the daily grind towards an experience of joy that does not negate that exhaustion. It is not an escape but rather a hard-fought change. We see the glitter and the sweat; we hear the shouts of joy and the gasping for air. In the presence of it, in the decision to exist 'in the doing', in the fleeting moments of transformation that give way to the long catching of the breath, 'Running the Ending' evokes a relationship with the self in the moment that is fundamentally queer: 'We stand defiant and grasp our recognition of rules [...] by the writhing roots and refashion them into a single ringing statement: in this moment, I am this, yes, I am this'.[85]

Jessie Keenan: 'So What Is Surfacing'

Ideas around presence were also crucial to the making of Jessie Keenan's film piece, 'So What Is Surfacing (Trio)'. When Keenan came to the archive, the thing that resonated most with her own creative practice was the extent to which Friel's practice was driven by questions and indeed by talking to himself more generally. A dancer-choreographer with an interest in interdisciplinary work, her practice frequently involves a blending of art forms: 'I've worked with science, or architecture, and now archives with this project, so I'm really excited by that, because I feel like it opens up a whole new space to work into'. Though her practice has, by her own admission, changed in ways she is as yet unable to process over the course of the pandemic, she has a strong sense of what her practice has been historically:

> [G]enerally in the past I would tend to do a lot of research first and then gather a lot of materials, and then once I've got that with me, I'll bring that into the studio and I'll work with those materials and images to make tasks for myself to generate material. And then what I like to do if I can is to bring in other people to work with these tasks on and see where it goes from there. But I do start from a place of research, [...] and gathering materials, so I feel like with this project there was a nice tie-in there with the archive and with Zosia being a researcher.

When we first visited the archive to consult MS 37,104, she found that Friel's questioning processes felt familiar to her own way of working, in addition to bringing the archival encounter into a palpably present moment:

> I think the thing that struck me when I was looking through the materials was all of these little questions that [Friel] asked himself, or just little sentences checking in that he was going along the right path, or never allowing himself to get content with it. [...] And those little things when I saw them brought me really into the present, because they were just like a question that anyone would ask themselves. [...] these are things that I do myself in my own notes. I feel like it really connected that thing that came from the past into the present for me, so that was something that I took to then develop on a little bit further with this project.[86]

As Keenan's experience in the archive will attest, questions have their own peculiar temporality. In this light, Friel's questioning tendencies effectively open up a whole new dimension to the archive in terms of its relationship with time. Even more so than the experience of a 'dissociative shift' whereby 'scholars become lost in the present, enveloped in the past',[87] Friel's creative practice allows for an event that 'leaves the temporal frames of [...] inheritance'[88] behind and replaces them with the disruptive, revenant 'now' of encounter. Indeed, a creative practice fuelled by questions is capable of connecting the 'now' of the composition process with both the 'now' of encountering the question and the 'now' of responding to it. In much the same way as, for Thornton Wilder, '[o]n the stage it is always *now*',[89] a question is always 'now' in the moment of its asking. To engage with and respond to Friel's archives, then, is to bring these questions into the present moment and imbue them with new significance.

This was a key element of Keenan's process in the early stages of the project. Following our archival visit in February 2019, Keenan transcribed a list of questions and question-like fragments from MS 37,104/1, initially with a view to choreographing gestures for each of them:

1. What is the 'Core'?
2. What is the right form to express this core?
3. Is the play about this?
4. Now is it coming together?

5. Don't anticipate the ending.
6. So what is surfacing?[90]

Appropriately enough for a project concerning a playwright whose idea of truth extends to 'something I *thought* I experienced'[91] (my italics), the first two questions on Keenan's list were not Friel's words but rather my own, which she had noted down during a workshop session during which I had talked about my ideas around form and core in Friel. 'Don't anticipate the ending' and 'So what is surfacing' were not questions either, strictly speaking. The former, as has been made clear, became the name for the overall project. In the case of the latter, however, Keenan added an implied question mark to a phrase she had found peculiarly evocative.

When Keenan came to work with this material as part of a Dance Ireland residency in April 2019, she used these questions and questioning statements as the basis of a series of generative tasks. Bringing them emphatically into the present, Keenan asked herself the questions she had selected (or responded to statements) and recorded herself doing so *in relation to her own practice*. (To this day, I have not heard this audio. Indeed, part of our discussions throughout the project involved observing the relationship between public and private.) She then played her answers back through a set of earphones and filmed herself improvising a series of movements to those answers, adding an additional layer of archival response to the process.[92]

Ordinarily, Keenan would have used these improvisations as raw material, harvesting them for gestures or phrases that would form the backbone of set dance pieces. However, due to a combination of ongoing conversations about different layers of liveness and the fact that we were given the opportunity to present some work in progress at the Belfast Book Festival as part of an illustrated talk, Keenan found her practice taking a new turn with regard to improvisation:

> I think through doing this and through this project I did end up finding a new way to perform and generate material. […] And that's really exciting, because one of the things that we did in the illustrated talk […] was […] sharing some of the research that we did, and as part of that, […] I was listening to a recording of myself answering a question [from Friel's archive] and then I was performing it live in an improvised way. And that actually was a very new process for me, to do live improvisation. So it's something that I've then taken further and [am] beginning to use in other work as well now as we go on[.][93]

In this way—and this may need reading more than once—Keenan's improvisations were a live response (dance) to an encounter with an archived response (recorded answer) to a record (transcribed questions) of a live archival encounter (accessing the Friel Papers) with material that is the record of a live process of composition (Friel's notes). Moreover, in an additional temporal layer of the archival and the live, as part of Keenan's improvisations at the Belfast Book Festival, video recordings of her original improvisations to the same questions were projected on a screen behind her at the same time. Some of these were then overlayed with a soundscape of processed radio static produced by Blake. Keenan would later improvise live once more to her recording of her response 'So what is surfacing' in a shorter version of the talk at the UCD Humanities Institute in February 2020.

Following Keenan's successful bid for a Dance Project Award from Arts Council Ireland, the next stage of the process would have been to begin workshopping material with the three dancers she had recruited for the project: Lucia Kickham, Marion Cronin, and Sarah Ryan. Blake, meanwhile, had enlisted Bláthnaid Conroy Murphy and Michelle O'Rourke as vocal performers. However, before we were able to get into the studio together, Ireland went into its first nationwide lockdown of the COVID-19 pandemic. At a time of strict social distancing and in the absence of a clear roadmap for the easing of restrictions, we decided to use the time to work with what we had with the tools that we had available—including the then novel but subsequently ubiquitous video conferencing platform 'Zoom'.

The remote workshops we held in April 2020 were a time of learning. Remaining very much in the spirit of a project we had called 'Don't anticipate the ending', Keenan, Blake, and I had made a conscious decision to work with our new conditions rather than against them and to factor in this new way of being present into our ways of working. To this end, we created a series of tasks designed to explore ways of making and responding to archive materials. These were based not only on our experiences of archival access/encounter so far, but also on conversations we'd had following my introduction of Taylor/Schneider into our earlier workshops on the one hand, and the function of dance in *Lughnasa* as it relates to language and memory on the other. Some of these tasks were geared towards finding ways to be live and present together whilst in different buildings. For instance, one task was a twenty-minute synchronised improvisation in real time, which was—as Blake's notes will confirm—'long!'. Others were overtly archival in nature, including one task in which all participants (including the three project leads) were asked to archive their day and then curate it in whatever form seemed appropriate. Crucially, as Blake noted in their workbook in the lead-up to these online rehearsals, these tasks were to be performed with a '[f]ocus on creative practice' and a '[l]ight touch'.[94] This is reflected in the instructions for some of the tasks: 'Try to be present in the doing of the task. Try not to anticipate what comes next. Allow the sounds to lead you: consciously, imaginatively, aurally'.[95]

It was also during this time that progress was made in developing what Keenan came to think of as the 'capsule'[96] of 'So what is surfacing'. On 14 April 2020, the three project leads and all five performers recorded themselves answering the question '"So what is surfacing?" (…in you now…)'.[97] The dancers recorded themselves using sound only; the singers used a camera; both sets of performers then created improvised responses in their own art form—the dancers to the audio of their responses and the musicians to the muted visuals.[98] Over the next few days, the performers created multiple layers of responses, describing and improvising on the basis of direct engagement with recordings or as a memory response. Inspired by both the title of the project and a related piece of dialogue I had introduced from *The Enemy Within* (1962), Blake and Keenan advised the performers: 'Try "to begin again"[99] each time. Be present in the doing of the task. Try not to anticipate what comes next'. Each performer now had four responses to work with, after which a new layer to the task was introduced:

> Choose the recording of the response that felt the best to do. Watch (dancers) / listen (vocalists) back to this recording and create 3 different 'scores'.
> 1. Record your spoken description of what you see in real time whilst watching/listening back.
> 2. Write what you see in real time whilst watching/listening back.
> 3. Create a graphic score—using whatever means fits best for you—draw, use diagrams, directions, words, images, etc. You can take more time with this, it does not have to be completed in real time.[100]

What we were asking of our participants (and indeed ourselves) was, in effect, to both create and respond to their own archive, based on an initial encounter with material from the Brian Friel Papers. In this way, both Friel's creative practice and our experiences of archival access became ways of generating material.

It was not until August 2020 that we were able to work with the performers in a studio. By this time, restrictions in Ireland had eased slightly, and so we were able—albeit with strict safety measures in place—to build on the material we had gathered during our online sessions in April 2020. Rehearsals began on Monday 10 August 2020 with an exercise that began a more in-depth exploration of the relationship between dance, language, and truthful communication. Friel's archive had revealed the extent to which Friel saw dance in the play as 'release and entrance to suppressed + almost forgotten truths'. This was, however, only one aspect of Friel's thinking around dance as a means of expressing inarticulable taboos, or else as a means of being 'put in touch with deeper, truer wells of authenticity'.[101] Some days earlier, Friel had asked himself another probing question: 'If dancing is the alternative to language, has language been inadequate for these people? Has language failed these people? Has language betrayed these people?'[102] Now, with a week of in-person rehearsals ahead of us and a further week in September, Keenan, Blake, and I were able to generate tasks that might allow the performers to examine these questions, with the opportunity for ongoing feedback as the weeks progressed. For instance, to generate our own archive of thinking around dance, music, and language, we used automatic writing—a technique favoured by Blake in particular, wherein participants transcribe a stream of consciousness for a fixed period of time—to generate continuations of the following prompts: 'dance is…', 'music is…', and 'language is…'. On 1 September, Keenan also worked consciously with memory and ways of communicating memory, with each dancer telling a story through words and movement about a favourite performance/piece of art she had seen or experienced. Sometimes, Keenan would ask them to begin with the story, begin moving, and then allow words to become less and movement more; sometimes Keenan would ask them to begin with movement and allow the voice to come in as required.

Although I was only physically present for one day of each rehearsal block to minimise contact during a time when social distancing was still in operation, I found I was able to be involved through daily feedback sessions where I would suggest extensions of tasks or link the day's work back to the archive:

Zosia gave us research, and then we [...] reacted to it through our own processes, and then Zosia through looking and watching that process then fed back again into what we were doing, so that I think that feedback loop is something that helped a lot of the work[.][103]

I had also provided additional materials at Keenan and Blake's request. These included Michael's opening and closing speeches from the play, to be used in a series of listening exercises. Being an Anglo-Polish woman in her early thirties at the time, this was obviously far from ideal casting, but it did at least seem emblematic in some way that Friel's dialogue should be voiced by a researcher rather than an actor in the context of this project.

After instructing Cronin, Kickham, and Ryan to listen to my recording of Michael's opening monologue through individual sets of earphones, Keenan then asked them to respond live multiple times with different focuses. These included free response, focus on the rhythm of the words, focus on words and imagery, and a response that aimed to communicate information. This was later developed during September studio rehearsals at Dance House (see Fig. 6.5), with Keenan choosing the point at which each dancer would begin their live improvisation, creating a staggered effect. Dancers would respond freely, choosing between different focuses, and allowing themselves to suspend movements or to repeat gestures. In this way, they moved in and out of states of listening and liveness, at times paying attention to the recording and responding in the moment, at times becoming absorbed by or lost in the gestures of the response itself. Had the project culminated in a live performance, this would most likely have been further developed. Nevertheless, I found this particular engagement with Friel's creative process to be illuminating. Keenan had created a task that required performers to listen and respond whilst carving out a space to explore their own movements, whilst at the same time being attentive to the choices being made as to the communicative intentionality of the response. In doing so, Keenan had effectively combined the live improvisational practices she had begun exploring whilst responding to archive material in the 'now' with questions around the relationship between dance as a form of communication that was, for Friel, 'a substitute for language'.[104]

What I also found, observing a performance of Michael's first monologue on 3 September 2020, accompanied live by a thoroughly disconcerting improvised soundscape from Conroy Murphy and O'Rourke,[105] was that what was being conveyed had far less to do with the content

Fig. 6.5 Double-exposure of Marion Cronin, Sarah Ryan, and Lucia Kickham performing live improvisations to a recording of Michael's opening monologue from *Dancing at Lughnasa* (Dance House, 3 September 2020)

of the monologue than the dancers' encounters with sounded speech, which were, or so it seemed, tinged by their experience of making art during a pandemic. Certainly, one of the most powerful rehearsal images I was able to capture was of Cronin frozen in a silent scream—a response, as I worked out, to the line 'shrieking strangers' (Friel, *P2*, 8)—that we all instantly connected with our feelings around the current situation (see Fig. 6.6). It seemed that the dancers had managed to translate the dreaminess of the monologue into an unsettling blend of dance and tableau-vivant, in which the dancers were able to explore elements of their own responses in their own time, both within and working against the narrative time imposed by the monologue.

In privileging our own responses to what was effectively our own evolving archive, moreover, the project was becoming increasingly meta-archival. This deepening of archival layers was particularly evident in the creation of Keenan's short dance film, 'So What is Surfacing (trio)'. On 11 August 2020, Keenan began teaching Cronin, Kickham, and Ryan a phrase she had learned from a film recording of her rehearsal performance of an improvised response to her answer to the question 'So what is surfacing?' at the UCD Humanities Institute on 25 February 2020.

Fig. 6.6 Marion Cronin and Sarah Ryan performing in a live improvisation to a recording of Michael's opening monologue from *Dancing at Lughnasa* (Dance House, 3 September 2020)

> It felt important to have a physical language to share with the dancers when they came into the space in the middle of all this uncertainty with the project and everything else; it was like this very solid thing that we could all do together and that became a bit of an anchor for a phrase called 'So what is surfacing' which then has been used in the film.[106]

Again, Keenan worked with different intentions and different timings, partly as a means of adding an element of liveness and/or presence to the performance of it. In her notes, she had wondered aloud: 'To set—what that does to improvised material—is that good or bad or just a decision[?]'. Answering her own question, she mused:

> So in the body in live response in improv + then when you set it it feels static + surface again but when you repeat & refine it enters the body again in a different way but the play of it comes back again.[107]

Eventually, the phrase was performed with one dancer (Ryan) being an anchor for the phrase, performing it from beginning to end; Cronin and Kickham were then free to repeat or explore certain movements before catching up with Ryan and returning to synchronised movement.

The August and September workshops also gave Keenan the chance to develop the dancers' responses to the 'So what is surfacing' prompt: 'I wanted to pass this technique of listening and responding over to the bodies of the three performers that were in the project and then to see what responses would come out of their bodies'.[108] On Wednesday 12 August, Keenan planned the following:

> Dancers listen to voice recording from April's rehearsals of them describing their movement response to 'so what is surfacing' while watching it back on video. Use this as starting point to create solo material. Interested in seeing them and their movement, energy, rhythm and choreographic choices.[109]

Each dancer accordingly created her own solo from this material, which was then set—something Keenan felt would not necessarily have been done in a less uncertain situation: 'We had just two weeks of live work together with the performers and our goal in those two weeks was just [to] generate material [...] and then [we'd] have all of these things to play with if we [got] into the studio again sometime'.[110]

At this point in the process, there was still a vague possibility that we were making a live dance show. However, as time passed and multiple lockdowns became the 'new normal', it eventually became necessary to let go of this idea. For Keenan, this involved nothing less than a rethink of the core of her work:

> It's strange because the work changed so much over the time, it's like it had several different cores at different points in time. And then [...] we had to work from a different place to make the film, because we had to go back and work with the material that we already had. We kind of embraced the archive and [...] our *own* archive, and used this as material to bring forward. So in a way the core is probably the project itself, and the film is something that grew from that.[111]

Keenan's notes certainly reflect this:

> Looking back to move forward—never more so than now in this moment—can looking back to my own archives help to move forward creatively with this new work. The creative cycle is the idea for the new work embedded in the old—dig back to move forward more clearly—mine, excavate, expose.[112]

Accordingly, when it came to creating a film of 'So What Is Surfacing', Keenan decided to work with the medium rather than against it, with the capture of moving images as a starting point rather than an end point. Indeed, creating good quality footage of the anchoring phrase and the dance solos was never intended to be a substitute for live performance. Instead, these were recorded with a view to using them as archive material that could then be processed and edited together with elements of the project's existing sound archive to create something new.

The film also required original sound. During our August and September workshops, Blake had worked with Conroy Murphy and O'Rourke at Dance House and Smock Alley Theatre with a view to creating a series of improvised soundscapes that would be performed live. For instance, when rehearsing Michael's monologue, the singers had workshopped ways of improvising sound to the same recording being used by the dancers, including mouthing along with the words to create an uncannily percussive state or vocalising whilst following the rhythm of the speech. Blake had also experimented with using redacted text from online privacy policies as an accompaniment to Keenan's phrase, having been inspired by our discussions around the voyeurism of the archive[113] and by my own haphazard summaries of Friel's interpretation of Steiner's ideas around the public and private nature of language.[114] Blake had been particularly inspired by some of the material I had introduced early on from Donoghue's *Ferocious Alphabets* (1981), which had also inspired Friel whilst writing *The Communication Cord* (1982). At one point, the two of us had even tried performing a graphic score[115] based on Donoghue's ideas around communion (see Chapter 4). It was also Friel's composition process for *The Communication Cord* that furnished Blake with material from which to develop the intent behind a piece called 'Talk is...', which was recorded in the same session as music used for Keenan's film, but which was itself never used. Indeed, on 27 April 2021, Blake made a note of Friel's citation of the man I had mistakenly informed Blake was the twentieth-century painter Francis Bacon rather than his early modern predecessor: 'Talk is but a tinkling cymbal where there is no love'. This gave rise to a piece that experimented with live improvisation arising from creating a space that sustained a sense of connection, with the two singers facing each other (and on one occasion using the word 'love' to produce a vowel on which to sing). The music that ended up in the film emerged not from Friel's archive specifically but rather from the workshopping process during the August/September rehearsals at Dance

House and Smock Alley in 2020. Known among ourselves as 'The Drone' and 'The Groove',[116] the two pieces used as part of the film's soundscape surfaced in parallel with Keenan's workshopping of the phrase. Keenan had particularly enjoyed the rhythm of 'The Groove', and so Blake had found a way to link the two pieces together for a recording session on 30 April 2021, five days after the filming of 'So What is Surfacing (trio)'.

The visual material for 'So What is Surfacing (trio)' was filmed on location at the Museum of Literature Ireland, which is housed in UCD Newman House—a pair of Georgian townhouses that had been home to the Catholic University of Ireland. Working with film-maker Steve O'Connor, lighting designer Matt Burke, and a production team,[117] Keenan directed Cronin, Kickham, and Ryan in both the phrase and their individual dance solos. Wearing light blouses tucked into high-waisted trousers in a nod to the time period of *Lughnasa*, the three dancers were dressed in a palette of light ochre, pale pink, and olive green. The phrase was performed in a large, yellow-wallpapered room, with large, ornate windows. Kickham's solo was performed along a large stone staircase; Ryan's was performed in an exhibition room with orange, pink, and blue tinted windows; Cronin's was performed in a light blue painted room with a large wooden door behind her, an ornate blue sofa to the left of the screen and a red velvet curtain to the right; her solo was later filmed again outside the building in bright sunshine.

The editing process was collaborative, and in many ways entailed all involved asking themselves 'so what is surfacing' all over again. Keenan worked with O'Connor to produce a version of the film, and then Blake and I were given the chance to offer feedback and suggestions before producing a final version, which can be accessed freely via MoLI's digital exhibition. Keenan had chosen to build from a sparse opening, beginning with a black screen overlaid with the original, phone-recorded audio from which Kickham had built her dance solo, describing a previous danced improvisation to her spoken response to the question '"So what is surfacing?" (…in you now…)': 'Busying myself, chin, shoulders, spreading out, hesitant…opening, surrounding…limbs moving, balance'. This was followed by the first visual of the piece—an overhead shot of Kickham standing on the stone staircase at MoLI, her left arm raised, holding a position, accompanied by the hiss of the audio recording. This was followed by another black screen, again overlaid with Kickham's phone recording: 'Resetting…shaking it off, resetting, restabilising…becoming still…to flop, to shake…reaching energy through the fingers'.

This was followed by a shot of Cronin through the door of the indoor location for her dance solo, holding a kneeling position with her arms stretched down by her sides and her fingers pointing inwards to her legs, again with white noise from Kickham's recording. Another black screen followed with more of Kickham's spoken recording. The next static shot was of Ryan standing in the middle (pink) window of the room with the tinted glass, subtly balanced on one foot, again holding the position. This time, Kickham's spoken audio continued over the visual: 'Moments of pause, but not for very long'. Almost immediately afterwards, an extract from the original audio from which Cronin had built her solo was introduced into the soundscape, as Ryan began to move her hands. From this point on, the visuals alternated slowly between the three solos, using audio from all three dancers' spoken material, gradually introducing more movement, both in the dancers' bodies and in the camera. After a while, the audio began to overlap and the cuts between the dancers became more frequent, with many of the gestures evoking moments of settling or resetting that never quite evolved into fluid movement. At times, the words were undistinguishable from one another, whilst at others, the words were given space: Ryan's voice is heard 'reaching out to gather in'; Cronin's voice corrects itself, 'touching the heart...collapsing the heart...(*inhale*) no! opening'.[118]

The next phase of sonic development was the layering in of a low, unsettling 'loaded drone' with a 'whistly tone, buzzy-whistle'[119] feel sung by Conroy Murphy and O'Rourke, from a sound palette developed with Blake and recorded at MoLI in April 2021. Meanwhile, the overlapping audio from the dancers' spoken recordings continued, until the first solo fragments portion of the film ended with Kickham's audio—'pause held'—and another black screen, overlaid with a repeated phrase from Kickham's audio from earlier in the film: 'sudden but small little movements'.[120] The next portion of the solo section gradually phased out the dancers' spoken audio, continuing the drone whilst featuring more cuts between the same dancer's solo instead of alternating, making more use of close-up shots that only showed parts of the moving body. As the drone became a higher-pitched major third full of harmonic overtones, the second extended solo section ended with each dancer performing a settling gesture.

After another black screen, a static shot of the three dancers together followed, with the dancers performing the phrase in unison. The camera then began to cut between different moving shots, as another sonic phase began: a piece developed by Blake with Conroy Murphy and O'Rourke known as 'The Groove'. In this piece, the two vocalists sang a tone apart, each repeating their own rhythmic phrase for a set period of time before hitting one of a sequence of chord progressions. As in rehearsals, Ryan was the anchor for the phrase, whilst Cronin and Kickham were free to hold or repeat gestures before catching up. As the phrase ended and the camera continued to move, 'The Groove' reached a point where it consisted solely of held interval progressions. After another, brief black screen, the film cut to Cronin, rising from the ground on location outside the building, squinting slightly in the blazing April sunshine. Bending upwards from the waist, with arms outstretched and visibly tensed, she raised and held her palms outwards, holding tension in her hands to the point where they vibrated (see Fig. 6.7). As 'The Groove' ended with several blasts of strident, bare open fifths that seemed to articulate the movement in Cronin's hands and arms, the film ended with a quick cut to black as the music ended and Cronin began to leap out of position, letting go.

What I found particularly striking about the film was that there was a palpable but subtly articulated contrast between the halting, fragmented, frustrated individuality of the solo sections and the continually

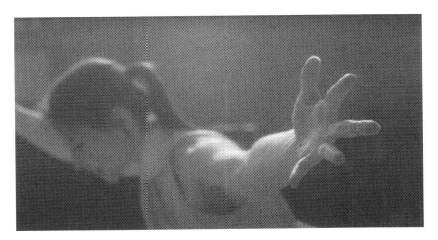

Fig. 6.7 Screenshot from 'So What Is Surfacing (Trio)' with Marion Cronin

reasserted flow of the phrase, which—whilst allowing for a human experience of time in its arrested or extended moments—ultimately mimicked the chronology of Keenan's original improvisation. Moreover, that we had only had time to film one of the outdoor shoots (Cronin's) ended up providing the film with what was, appropriately enough, an unanticipated ending. Personally, I like to think of the sudden translation from the museum building into the outside world—though in truth merely the gardens of the same museum—as particularly appropriate for a project that aims to expand the reach of the archive beyond the confines of the 'house built for live encounter with privileged remains'.[121] It is not a moment of unambiguous liberation: Cronin appears a little blinded by the sun; the tendons in her arms are taut with whatever is surfacing in her at that moment, as though trying to open a stiffly invisible sash window. It is beautiful, but there is effort; as with the project, there is the holding on that comes before the letting go. And as with the project there is the mining of archive material, the going back to move forwards, the constant settling and resettling and beginning again that comes before being able to move in a way that can be appreciated only in the doing—that which cannot be replicated or represented and so can only be gestured towards before it occurs behind a blank screen.

Don't anticipate the ending

Our project began with a view to live performance; the pandemic forced us to engage with new ways of being present and of engaging with layered temporalities through film. From our experiences of presence in the archive—of encountering a mind at work among the privileged remains—we had found ways of working that challenged our ideas about what it means to make art from archives. Blake had begun with a graphic score inspired by the materiality of Friel's process and ended with a piece that evoked queer presences, seeking joy through exhaustion. Keenan, meanwhile, had begun with the peculiar temporality of Friel's questioning notes to self as experienced live in the archive, and ended with a piece that grew out of a newly-developed element to her artistic practice, generating work from multiple layers of live improvisation. Along the way, both had gained inspiration from Friel's ways of working—from his constant dialogue with himself throughout the making process and his efforts to keep that process in motion. The studio walls are testament to the touchstone presence of Friel's archives and their reminders to find the work 'in the doing'. Three extracts from Friel's notes towards *Lughnasa* stand out among the paper slips of transcribed archive material:

1. '[This has all become very formal and inhibiting. Allow the play to breathe. Let it drift as it wishes. A line on a page isn't a solemn commitment.]'[122] (Square brackets in original.)
2. 'Once more: allow the play to ramble; don't corset it with preconceived ideas of form'.[123]
3. 'At least it is a starting point. And all starting points are arbitrary—and then become an essence'.[124]

Or, as a sticky note pasted in Blake's notes (next to the word 'MOTTO') would have it:

Throw shit-at-the-wall week!
If it feels good, Go with it![125]

Indeed, Keenan found that, through a combination of working through uncertain times and using Friel's ways of working as a guideline, she was finding the studio process more freeing than usual:

[I]t was actually a really nice thing and I think I'll probably take that with me, because I think sometimes it can get a bit heady in the studio space, wanting to form stuff before it's ready, so it was this idea of trying not to get it into form, just kind of getting it out there.[126]

It was not only Friel's process as revealed by the archive that proved to be influential for Keenan and Blake, but also the experience of archival access itself in the context of a project that attempted to blend different forms of research. Blake, for instance, found they were no longer 'seeing academic research and creative practice research as two separate spaces, but seeing them as something that can be a little bit more intertwined, or indeed that [...] could really benefit from being a little bit more entwined'. They also found their thinking around archives had changed 'mostly in terms of the idea of access, or the idea of them being outside of one's reach':

"Archive" is kind of a scary word, but it shouldn't be, you know, because 'archive' is kind of anything, you know, it's like a collection—it's another way of saying a group of things that someone thought about and brought together.[127]

Keenan, meanwhile, found that she had discovered a way of thinking about something that had been integral to her practice all along:

I suppose I don't really think I thought a whole pile about [archives], and now I'm thinking about them constantly, so it's quite a big jump! In my own practice before this, I've also been really interested in working with memory, and so in some ways I've been looking into archives without even giving it a name. And as part of this project I started to even think about my own archive, so I think there's this new and interesting space that now has a name that I would actually really love to delve into further.[128]

Through the project, both Keenan and Blake had also found creative avenues to explore in their future work. For instance, in addition to potentially exploring some of the unrealised ideas from the studio sessions, Keenan found that the 'So what is surfacing' capsule had generated a genuinely productive way of working that she began to play with after the completion of the films. On 7 July 2021, as part of the Dancer from the Dance Festival from Irish Modern Dance Theatre, a new piece choreographed and performed by Keenan was screened during a live-streamed performance programme. Titled 'So What Is Surfacing (a study)', it was essentially a continuation of the techniques Keenan had developed during our collaboration. As Keenan wrote as part of the promotional material for the event:

I am interested in questions around personal archive, live response and creative practice as investigation. I return again to this original study to reconnect with the liveness of the task. Going back to go forward.[129]

In this short piece, Keenan was filmed improvising live outdoors to a recording of herself describing a home video of herself giving a dance performance as a child. At the time of writing, Keenan is working on a new project, 'The Picture Palace', which further develops techniques from 'Don't Anticipate the Ending' and makes use of archival material relating to Cavan's Townhall. (I am involved in the project in a research/creative capacity.) Blake, meanwhile, had found in Donoghue's ideas something to consider for their future composition practice.

The fruits of our collaboration, then, seemed to bear witness to the fact that a significant aspect of the legacy of the Brian Friel Papers was Friel's way of working and the potential for his artistic practice to provide inspiration for artists who were in the process of developing a practice of their own. Moreover, the evolution of the project over the course of the pandemic had caused me to think more deeply about 'Don't anticipate the ending' as a means of expanding archival access. We had been in talks with MoLI for some time about the possibility of some onsite pop-up performances alongside a small onsite exhibition to accompany a live performance at the Dublin Fringe Festival. When this became a logistical improbability, MoLI instead agreed to offer us a filming location, sound recording equipment, and in-kind support to produce film pieces that would form part of a digital exhibition about the project, exploring the relationship between Friel's creative practice and our own. Curating this, I found I had the opportunity to work with MoLI's digital curator to create what was essentially an interactive mind-map of different elements of the project and the ways in which they interconnected.[130] For all three of us, this represented an opportunity to present the Brian Friel Papers in a way that gave members of the public a choice of access points to the archive material and the freedom to explore the connections between different elements of the projects. As Keenan put it:

> I think what we're trying to do in some ways is find a different access point into archives, and I'm hoping that it will maybe open up a little bit of space or a little excitement or curiosity for people.[131]

As for me, the project had opened up a practical way of looking at Friel's archive as a record of a way of making art, as well as providing me with a repertoire of practices of archival access. Working with the archive in a facilitatory role, I found that the archive was not a space in which the pre-determined answers to a given set of questions were to be finalised, but rather a resonant space within which the liveness and presence of encounter generate new ways of thinking about the process of making art. The Brian Friel Papers are certainly a rich scholarly resource; what remains to be appreciated is their potential to make a rich and temporally intricate creative practice accessible to contemporary practitioners beyond the reading room, making a life's work a work in progress. The archive, in fact, is in the doing.

Notes

1. Dance Ireland, Smock Alley Theatre, Museum of Literature Ireland, UCD Humanities Institute, Cavan Arts, Cavan County Council, Dublin City Council, Tonnta, and the National Library of Ireland.
2. *Don't Anticipate the Ending: Creative Encounters with the Brian Friel Papers*, Museum of Literature Ireland, https://exhibitions.moli.ie/brian-friel [accessed 27 November 2022].
3. Rebecca Schneider, *Performing Remains: Art and War in Times of Theatrical Reenactment* (Abingdon: Routledge, 2011), p. 108.
4. Ann Cvetkovich, 'Foreword', in *Out of the Closet, Into the Archives*, ed. by Amy L. Stone and Jaime Cantrell (Albany: SUNY Press, 2015), pp. xv–xviii (p. xviii).
5. Dublin, National Library of Ireland (NLI), Brian Friel Papers (BFP), MS 37,075/1. Note towards *Faith Healer* dated 21 May [1975].
6. David Sylvester, *Interviews with Francis Bacon* (London: Thames and Hudson, 1975), p. 52.
7. Schneider, p. 108.
8. Helen Freshwater, 'The Allure of the Archive', *Poetics Today* 24, No. 4 (2003), pp. 729–258 (p. 740).
9. Brian Friel, *Give Me Your Answer, Do!* (London: Penguin Books, 1997), p. 79.
10. 'National Library of Ireland Collection Development Policy, 2009–2011' (Dublin: National Library of Ireland), p. 4, https://www.nli.ie/en/udlist/reports-and-policy-documents.aspx [accessed 26 April 2022].
11. 'National Library of Ireland Diversity and Inclusion Policy 2018–2021' (Dublin: National Library of Ireland, 2018), p. 1, https://www.nli.ie/en/Policy.aspx [accessed 10 March 2020].
12. The undated leaflet is branded with a logo that was no longer in use by the time of the NLI's Financial Statement for 2010. It also makes no reference to the NLI's Twitter account founded in 2009 (the same year the NLI acquired the Irish Queer Archive).

It does, however, mention having acquired the Brian Friel Papers (2001) and 'strong Government support' (up to 2007), so can be safely dated to around the mid-2000s.
13. National Library of Ireland, *Treasuring Our Heritage: Donation of Materials to the National Library of Ireland*, p. 3, https://www.nli.ie/GetAttachment.aspx?id=41a1a39f-86bb-498f-9519-efd20c0d3df6 [accessed 26 April 2022] in 'How We Acquire', www.nli.ie/how-we-acquire-our-collections.aspx [accessed 26 April 2022].
14. 'National Library Receives Friel Papers 2001', *RTÉ Archives*, First broadcast 8 February 2001, https://www.rte.ie/archives/2016/0205/765690-brian-friel-papers/ [accessed 25 June 2022].
15. Diana Taylor, *The Archive and the Repertoire: Performing Cultural Memory in the Americas* (Durham and London: Duke University Press, 2003), p. 2.
16. Taylor, p. 20.
17. Taylor, p. xvii.
18. Amy L. Stone and Jaime Cantrell, 'Introduction: Something Queer at the Archive', in *Out of the Closet, Into the Archives*, ed. by Amy L. Stone and Jaime Cantrell (Albany: SUNY Press, 2015), pp. 1–22 (p. 11).
19. Stone and Cantrell, p. 3.
20. Cvetkovich, p. xvii.
21. Cvetkovich, p. xviii.
22. Cvetkovich, p. xvii.
23. Cvetkovich, p. xviii.
24. Interview with Jessie Keenan, Museum of Literature Ireland, 26 July 2021. See 'Mixed Interview, Extract 3', *Don't Anticipate the Ending: Creative Encounters with the Brian Friel Papers*, Museum of Literature Ireland, https://exhibitions.moli.ie/brian-friel/m/mixed-interview-extract-3 [accessed 27 November 2022].
25. Interview with Robbie Blake, Museum of Literature Ireland, 26 July 2021. See 'Mixed Interview, Extract 3', *Don't Anticipate the Ending: Creative Encounters with the Brian Friel Papers*, Museum of Literature Ireland, https://exhibitions.moli.ie/brian-friel/m/mixed-interview-extract-3 [accessed 27 November 2022].
26. NLI, BFP, MS 37,104/1. Note towards *Dancing at Lughnasa* dated 29 May 1989.

27. 'The "Wee Donegal Priest" Passes Away: Twenty Years Among the Lepers', *The Derry Journal*, 10 July 1950, p. 4.
28. Joseph Hone, *Duck Soup in the Black Sea: Further Collected Travels* (London: Hamish Hamilton, 1988), p. 236.
29. Hone, p. 236, cited in NLI, BFP, MS 37,104/1. Note towards *Dancing at Lughnasa*, dated 13 May 1989.
30. Hone, p. 237.
31. Brian Friel, *Plays Two* (London: Faber and Faber, 1999), p. 8. Further references in parentheses in the text as 'Friel, *P2*'.
32. Hone, p. 238.
33. Hone, p. 240.
34. William Shakespeare, *The Tempest*, in *The Complete Works of William Shakespeare*, ed. by W.J. Craig (London: Oxford University Press, 1963), pp. 1–22 (p. 6).
35. NLI, BFP, MS 37,104/1. Note towards *Dancing at Lughnasa* dated 30 May 1989.
36. Hone, p. 240.
37. See NLI, BFP, MS 37,104/1. Note towards *Dancing at Lughnasa* dated 21 May 1989. Second page of booklet 'B'. Note begins: '"You are my KABAKA" (King)'.
38. Chinua Achebe, *Things Fall Apart* (London: Penguin Modern Classics, 2001), p. 27. See also NLI, BFP, MS 37,104/1. Undated note towards *Dancing at Lughnasa*. (Small, torn sheet of paper, written in pencil. Begins with the word 'OGENE'.)
39. Should it become apparent that my working assumption that 'Obi' is a made-up goddess is indicative of my own ignorance rather than Friel's, I offer my unreserved apologies. However, the evidence does seem to point to Friel having simply chosen a similar-sounding name to Achebe's Ani (a dialectical variant of the Igbo earth goddess Ala) for a generically African-sounding, harvest-festival-adjacent equivalent to the Irish Lugh. Interestingly, and almost certainly coincidentally, 'Obi' is actually an alternative spelling for 'Obeah', which is not the name of a goddess but rather an African-Caribbean system of beliefs and practices developed among enslaved people in the West Indies—a process of which Haitian Vodou is perhaps the most well-known example.
40. Achebe, p. 23. See also NLI, BFP, MS 37,104/1. Undated note towards *Dancing at Lughnasa*.

41. W.B. Yeats, 'The Second Coming', in *W.B. Yeats: The Major Works*, ed. by Edward Larrissy (Oxford: Oxford University Press, 2001), p. 91.
42. NLI, BFP, MS 37,104/1. Note towards *Dancing at Lughnasa* dated 29 May 1989.
43. NLI, BFP, MS 37,104/1. Note towards *Dancing at Lughnasa* dated 20 May 1989.
44. NLI, BFP, MS 37,104/1. Note towards *Dancing at Lughnasa* dated 17 May 1989.
45. NLI, BFP, MS 37,104/1. Note towards *Dancing at Lughnasa* dated 30 May [1989].
46. NLI, BFP, MS 37,104/1. Note towards *Dancing at Lughnasa* dated 17 May 1989.
47. NLI, BFP, MS 37,104/1. Note towards *Dancing at Lughnasa* dated 7 June [1989]. Emphasis and date in red ink.
48. NLI, BFP, MS 37,104/1. Note towards *Dancing at Lughnasa* dated 17 May 1989.
49. NLI, BFP, MS 37,104/1. Note towards *Dancing at Lughnasa* dated 7 June [1989].
50. Whereas a traditional Western musical score has certain unchanging elements (a stave, a clef, a time signature, standard music notation, etc.), a graphic score is under no obligation to do so. Instead, it uses graphic symbols to denote sound or rather the production of sound by various means.
51. Brian Friel, 'Seven Notes for a Festival Programme (1999)', in *Brian Friel: Essays, Diaries, Interviews: 1964–1999*, ed. by Christopher Murray (London: Faber and Faber, 1999), pp. 173–180 (p. 173).
52. Friel, 'Seven Notes for a Festival Programme, p. 174.
53. NLI, BPF, MS 37,123/2. Typed diary towards *Wonderful Tennessee* dated 12 July 1990.
54. NLI, BFP, MS 37,104/1. Undated note towards *Dancing at Lughnasa*.
55. Interview with Robbie Blake, Museum of Literature Ireland, 26 July 2021. See 'Robbie Blake Interview, Extract 1', *Don't Anticipate the Ending: Creative Encounters with the Brian Friel Papers*, Museum of Literature Ireland, https://exhibitions.moli.ie/brian-friel/m/robbie-blake-interview-extract-01 [accessed 27 November 2022].

56. 'Running the Ending (Work in Progress)', *Don't Anticipate the Ending: Creative Encounters with the Brian Friel Papers*, Museum of Literature Ireland, https://exhibitions.moli.ie/brian-friel/m/running-the-ending-may-2019 [accessed 27 November 2022].
57. 'Belfast Book Festival Trailer', *Don't Anticipate the Ending: Creative Encounters with the Brian Friel Papers*, Museum of Literature Ireland, https://exhibitions.moli.ie/brian-friel/m/belfast-book-festival-trailer [accessed 27 November 2022].
58. NLI, BFP, MS 37,104/1. Note towards *Dancing at Lughnasa* dated 29 May 1989.
59. Robbie Blake, notes towards 'Running the Ending', 24 April 2019.
60. Interview with Robbie Blake, Museum of Literature Ireland, 26 July 2021. See 'Robbie Blake Interview, Extract 1', *Don't Anticipate the Ending: Creative Encounters with the Brian Friel Papers*, Museum of Literature Ireland, https://exhibitions.moli.ie/brian-friel/m/robbie-blake-interview-extract-01 [accessed 27 November 2022].
61. Lyric Theatre, Belfast. 26 August–27 September 2015. Directed by Annabelle Comyn. My own point of reference was a performance on 27 August 2015.
62. Jimmy Fay (executive producer of Belfast's Lyric Theatre), quoted in Fionola Meredith, 'The Dark Heart of Dancing at Lughnasa', *Irish Times*, 1 September 2015, https://www.irishtimes.com/culture/stage/the-dark-heart-of-dancing-at-lughnasa-1.2332117 [accessed 3 May 2022].
63. Katy Hayes, 'Dancing at Lughnasa, Gaiety Theatre review: Not Quite Bleak Enough, but Still Utterly Brilliant', *Irish Independent*, 8 October 2015, https://www.independent.ie/entertainment/theatre-arts/dancing-at-lughnasa-gaiety-theatre-review-not-quite-bleak-enough-but-still-utterly-brilliant-31592450.html [accessed 3 May 2022].
64. Sara Keating, 'Dancing at Lughnasa', *Irish Times*, 5 November 2010, https://www.irishtimes.com/culture/music/2.749/dancing-at-lughnasa-1.672898 [accessed 3 May 2022].
65. Patrick Lonergan, '"Dancing on a One-Way Street": Irish Reactions to *Dancing at Lughnasa* in New York', in *Irish Theater in America: Essays on Irish Theatrical Diaspora*, ed. by John P. Harrington (New York: Syracuse University Press, 2009), pp. 147–162 (p. 148).

66. Interview with Robbie Blake, Museum of Literature Ireland, 26 July 2021. See 'Robbie Blake Interview, Extract 1', *Don't Anticipate the Ending: Creative Encounters with the Brian Friel Papers*, Museum of Literature Ireland, https://exhibitions.moli.ie/brian-friel/m/robbie-blake-interview-extract-01 [accessed 27 November 2022].
67. NLI, BPF, MS 37,104/1. Note towards *Dancing at Lughnasa* dated 30 May [1989]. Friel added an arrow pointing to the word 'grow' in red ink.
68. Interview with Robbie Blake, Museum of Literature Ireland, 26 July 2021. See 'Robbie Blake Interview, Extract 1', *Don't Anticipate the Ending: Creative Encounters with the Brian Friel Papers*, Museum of Literature Ireland, https://exhibitions.moli.ie/brian-friel/m/robbie-blake-interview-extract-01 [accessed 27 November 2022]. See also 'Robbie Blake's Blue Notebook, 1', *Don't Anticipate the Ending: Creative Encounters with the Brian Friel Papers*, Museum of Literature Ireland, https://exhibitions.moli.ie/brian-friel/m/robbie-blakes-blue-notebook-no-1 [accessed 27 November 2022].
69. Interview with Jessie Keenan, Museum of Literature Ireland, 26 July 2021. See 'Mixed Interview, Extract 6', *Don't Anticipate the ending: Creative Encounters with the Brian Friel Papers*, Museum of Literature Ireland, https://exhibitions.moli.ie/brian-friel/m/mixed-interview-extract-6 [accessed 27 November 2022].
70. Interview with Robbie Blake, Museum of Literature Ireland, 26 July 2021.
71. Interview with Zosia Kuczyńska, Museum of Literature Ireland, 26 July 2021.
72. Interview with Robbie Blake, Museum of Literature Ireland, 26 July 2021.
73. Robbie Blake, undated note towards 'Running the Ending', c. March 2020.
74. Interview with Robbie Blake, Museum of Literature Ireland, 26 July 2021. See 'Mixed Interview, Extract 2', *Don't Anticipate the Ending: Creative Encounters with the Brian Friel Papers*, Museum of Literature Ireland, https://exhibitions.moli.ie/brian-friel/m/mixed-interview-extract-2 [accessed 27 November 2022].
75. See Dublin, National Library of Ireland (NLI), Brian Friel Papers (BFP), MS 37,075/1. Notes dated 11, 12, and 25 June [1975].

See also Howard Brenton, 'Petrol Bombs Through the Proscenium Arch', *Theatre Quarterly* 5, No. 17 (1975), pp. 4–20 (p. 6).
76. NLI, BFP, MS 37,081/2. Note towards *Aristocrats* dated 17 May 1977, bracketed in red ink.
77. NLI, BFP, MS 37,104/1. Undated note towards *Dancing at Lughnasa*. An almost identical note appears marked 'N.B.' with red ink at the top of a page dated 24 May 1989.
78. Interview with Robbie Blake, Museum of Literature Ireland, 26 July 2021. See 'Mixed Interview, Extract 1', *Don't Anticipate the Ending: Creative Encounters with the Brian Friel Papers*, Museum of Literature Ireland, https://exhibitions.moli.ie/brian-friel/m/mixed-interview-extract-1 [accessed 27 November 2022].
79. Robbie Blake, undated note towards 'Running the Ending', c. July 2020.
80. Interview with Robbie Blake, Museum of Literature Ireland, 26 July 2021. See 'Robbie Blake Interview, Extract 1', *Don't Anticipate the Ending: Creative Encounters with the Brian Friel Papers*, Museum of Literature Ireland, https://exhibitions.moli.ie/brian-friel/m/robbie-blake-interview-extract-01 [accessed 27 November 2022].
81. 'Running the Ending', *Don't Anticipate the Ending: Creative Encounters with the Brian Friel Papers*, Museum of Literature Ireland, https://exhibitions.moli.ie/brian-friel/m/running-the-ending [accessed 27 November 2022].
82. Robbie Blake, undated note towards 'Running the Ending', c. April 2021.
83. Robbie Blake, note dated 26 May 2021.
84. Stone and Cantrell, p. 3.
85. Laurel Lynn Leake, 'Defining Drag: A Vymifesto', *Velour: The Drag Magazine*, Collected Issues 1–3 (House of Velour, 2018), pp. 54–55.
86. Interview with Jessie Keenan, Museum of Literature Ireland, 26 July 2021. See 'Mixed Interview, Extract 2', *Don't Anticipate the Ending: Creative Encounters with the Brian Friel Papers*, Museum of Literature Ireland, https://exhibitions.moli.ie/brian-friel/m/mixed-interview-extract-2 [accessed 27 November 2022].
87. Stone and Cantrell, p. 11.

88. J. Jack Halberstam, *In a Queer Time and Place: Transgender Bodies, Subcultural Lives* (New York and London: NYU Press, 2005), p. 6.
89. Thornton Wilder and Richard H. Goldstone, 'Thornton Wilder, The Art of Fiction No. 16', *The Paris Review* 15 (Winter 1956), https://www.theparisreview.org/interviews/4887/the-art-of-fiction-no-16-thornton-wilder [accessed 27 November 2022].
90. 'Jessie Keenan's questions', *Don't Anticipate the Ending: Creative Encounters with the Brian Friel Papers*, Museum of Literature Ireland, https://exhibitions.moli.ie/brian-friel/m/jessie-keenan-s-questions [accessed 27 November 2022].
91. Brian Friel, 'Self-Portrait (1972)', in Murray, ed., pp. 37–46 (p. 38).
92. 'So What Is Surfacing, Original Improvisation', *Don't Anticipate the Ending: Creative Encounters with the Brian Friel Papers*, Museum of Literature Ireland, https://exhibitions.moli.ie/brian-friel/m/so-what-is-surfacing-original-improvisation [accessed 27 November 2022].
93. Interview with Jessie Keenan, Museum of Literature Ireland, 26 July 2021. See 'Mixed Interview, Extract 2', *Don't Anticipate the Ending: Creative Encounters with the Brian Friel Papers*, Museum of Literature Ireland, https://exhibitions.moli.ie/brian-friel/m/mixed-interview-extract-2 [accessed 27 November 2022].
94. Robbie Blake, 'Robbie Blake's Blue Notebook, 5', *Don't Anticipate the Ending: Creative Encounters with the Brian Friel Papers*, Museum of Literature Ireland, https://exhibitions.moli.ie/brian-friel/m/robbie-blake-blue-notebook-05 [accessed 27 November 2022].
95. 'Task Sheet 2', Thursday 16th April 2020.
96. Interview with Jessie Keenan, Museum of Literature Ireland, 26 July 2021. See 'Jessie Keenan Interview, Extract 2', *Don't Anticipate the Ending: Creative Encounters with the Brian Friel Papers*, Museum of Literature Ireland, https://exhibitions.moli.ie/brian-friel/m/jessie-keenan-interview-extract-02 [accessed 27 November 2022].
97. Robbie Blake, 'Robbie Blake's Blue Notebook, 5', *Don't Anticipate the Ending: Creative Encounters with the Brian Friel Papers*, Museum of Literature Ireland, https://exhibitions.moli.ie/brian-friel/m/robbie-blake-blue-notebook-05 [accessed 27 November 2022].

98. 'Task Sheet, 14 April 2020', *Don't Anticipate the Ending: Creative Encounters with the Brian Friel Papers*, Museum of Literature Ireland, https://exhibitions.moli.ie/brian-friel/m/task-sheet-14-april-2020 [accessed 27 November 2022].
99. Brian Friel, *The Enemy Within* (Oldcastle: Gallery Press, 1992), p. 77.
100. 'Task Sheet 2', Thursday 16th April 2020.
101. NLI, BFP, MS 37,104/1. Note towards *Dancing at Lughnasa*, dated 30 May 1989.
102. NLI, BFP, MS 37,104/1. Note towards *Dancing at Lughnasa*, dated 25 May 1989.
103. Interview with Jessie Keenan, Museum of Literature Ireland, 26 July 2021. See 'Mixed Interview, Extract 5', *Don't Anticipate the Ending: Creative Encounters with the Brian Friel Papers*, Museum of Literature Ireland, https://exhibitions.moli.ie/brian-friel/m/mixed-interview-extract-5 [accessed 27 November 2022].
104. NLI, BFP, MS 37,104/1. Note towards *Dancing at Lughnasa*, dated 18 May 1989.
105. 'Dance House, 3 September 2020', *Don't Anticipate the Ending: Creative Encounters with the Brian Friel Papers*, Museum of Literature Ireland, https://exhibitions.moli.ie/brian-friel/m/dance-house-3-september-2020 [accessed 27 November 2022].
106. Interview with Jessie Keenan, Museum of Literature Ireland, 26 July 2021. See 'Jessie Keenan Interview, Extract 1', *Don't Anticipate the Ending: Creative Encounters with the Brian Friel Papers*, Museum of Literature Ireland, https://exhibitions.moli.ie/brian-friel/m/jessie-keenan-interview-extract-01 [accessed 27 November 2022].
107. Jessie Keenan, 'Jessie Keenan Notes, 3', *Don't Anticipate the Ending: Creative Encounters with the Brian Friel Papers*, Museum of Literature Ireland, https://exhibitions.moli.ie/brian-friel/m/jk-notes-03 [accessed 27 November 2022].
108. Interview with Jessie Keenan, Museum of Literature Ireland, 26 July 2021.
109. 'Wednesday Plan', Jessie Keenan, 12 August 2020.
110. Interview with Jessie Keenan, Museum of Literature Ireland, 26 July 2021. See 'Jessie Keenan Interview, Extract 2', *Don't Anticipate the Ending: Creative Encounters with the Brian Friel*

Papers, Museum of Literature Ireland, https://exhibitions.moli.ie/brian-friel/m/jessie-keenan-interview-extract-02 [accessed 27 November 2022].
111. Interview with Jessie Keenan, Museum of Literature Ireland, 26 July 2021. See 'Jessie Keenan Interview, Extract 1', *Don't Anticipate the Ending: Creative Encounters with the Brian Friel Papers*, Museum of Literature Ireland, https://exhibitions.moli.ie/brian-friel/m/jessie-keenan-interview-extract-01 [accessed 27 November 2022].
112. Jessie Keenan, 'Jessie Keenan Notes, 5', *Don't Anticipate the Ending: Creative Encounters with the Brian Friel Papers*, Museum of Literature Ireland, https://exhibitions.moli.ie/brian-friel/m/jk-notes-05 [accessed 27 November 2022].
113. 'Robbie Blake, Denis Donoghue-Inspired Score', *Don't Anticipate the Ending: Creative Encounters with the Brian Friel Papers*, Museum of Literature Ireland, https://exhibitions.moli.ie/brian-friel/m/robbie-blake-denis-donoghue-inspired-score [accessed 27 November 2022].
114. Robbie Blake, note towards *Don't Anticipate the Ending*, 6 March 2020.
115. Robbie Blake, 'Robbie Blake's Blue Notebook, 6', *Don't Anticipate the Ending: Creative Encounters with the Brian Friel Papers*, Museum of Literature Ireland, https://exhibitions.moli.ie/brian-friel/m/robbie-blake-blue-notebook-06 [accessed 27 November 2022].
116. 'The Groove', *Don't Anticipate the Ending: Creative Encounters with the Brian Friel Papers*, Museum of Literature Ireland, https://exhibitions.moli.ie/brian-friel/m/the-groove [accessed 27 November 2022].
117. Seán Mac Erlaine (Sound Mix and Master Engineer), Benedict Schlepper-Connolly (Vocal Recording Engineer), Eoin Kilkenny (Production Manager), Sophie Coote (Producer, 2021), Natalie Hands (Producer, 2020), Michelle Cahill (Production Support), LaurA Fajardo Castro (Costume Assistant).
118. 'So What Is Surfacing', *Don't Anticipate the Ending: Creative Encounters with the Brian Friel Papers*, Museum of Literature Ireland, https://exhibitions.moli.ie/brian-friel/m/so-what-is-surfacing [accessed 27 November 2022].

119. Robbie Blake, undated note towards 'So What Is Surfacing', c. April 2021.
120. 'So What Is Surfacing', *Don't Anticipate the Ending: Creative Encounters with the Brian Friel Papers*, Museum of Literature Ireland, https://exhibitions.moli.ie/brian-friel/m/so-what-is-surfacing [accessed 27 November 2022].
121. Schneider, p. 108.
122. NLI, BFP, note towards *Dancing at Lughnasa* dated 26 May 1989.
123. NLI, BFP, note towards *Dancing at Lughnasa* dated 26 May [1989].
124. NLI, BFP, note towards *Dancing at Lughnasa* dated 18 May 1989. Crossed through in red pen.
125. Robbie Blake, 'Robbie Blake's Blue Notebook, 8', *Don't Anticipate the Ending: Creative Encounters with the Brian Friel Papers*, Museum of Literature Ireland, https://exhibitions.moli.ie/brian-friel/m/robbie-blake-blue-notebook-08 [accessed 27 November 2022].
126. Interview with Jessie Keenan, Museum of Literature Ireland, 26 July 2021. See 'Jessie Keenan Interview, Extract 2', *Don't Anticipate the Ending: Creative Encounters with the Brian Friel Papers*, Museum of Literature Ireland, https://exhibitions.moli.ie/brian-friel/m/jessie-keenan-interview-extract-02 [accessed 27 November 2022].
127. Interview with Robbie Blake, Museum of Literature Ireland, 26 July 2021. See 'Mixed Interview, Extract 3', *Don't Anticipate the Ending: Creative Encounters with the Brian Friel Papers*, Museum of Literature Ireland, https://exhibitions.moli.ie/brian-friel/m/mixed-interview-extract-3 [accessed 27 November 2022].
128. Interview with Jessie Keenan, Museum of Literature Ireland, 26 July 2021. See 'Mixed Interview, Extract 3', *Don't Anticipate the Ending: Creative Encounters with the Brian Friel Papers*, Museum of Literature Ireland, https://exhibitions.moli.ie/brian-friel/m/mixed-interview-extract-3 [accessed 27 November 2022].
129. Jessie Keenan, 'So What Is Surfacing (A Study)', *Dancer from the Dance 2021: Wednesday 7 July—Schedule of Events*, https://www.irishmoderndancetheatre.com/july72021 [accessed 25 June 2022].

130. 'Exhibition Map, 31 August 2021', *Don't Anticipate the Ending: Creative Encounters with the Brian Friel Papers*, Museum of Literature Ireland, https://exhibitions.moli.ie/brian-friel/m/exhibition-map-31-august-2021 [accessed 27 November 2022].
131. Interview with Jessie Keenan, Museum of Literature Ireland, 26 July 2021. See 'Mixed Interview, Extract 6', *Don't Anticipate the Ending: Creative Encounters with the Brian Friel Papers*, Museum of Literature Ireland, https://exhibitions.moli.ie/brian-friel/m/mixed-interview-extract-6 [accessed 27 November 2022].

CHAPTER 7

Conclusion: So What Is Surfacing (?)

In transforming this statement from Friel's archive into a question that evoked his own self-reflexive, recurrently interrogative creative process, Jessie Keenan discovered a means of responding to the Brian Friel Papers in a moment that performs the 'now' of archival access. Here and now, in the final pages of a monograph representing almost a decade spent with Friel's notes and manuscripts, I find myself compelled to respond to the same question on two separate counts. In the first instance (A), I want to gesture towards some of the implications 'arising', as it were, from the work presented in this book, which takes an approach to Friel's archive rooted in the 'how' of creative practice. Following on from this (B), I want to look ahead briefly to some of the challenges 'coming up' for future scholars of this and other literary archives in terms of access ('being able to get to the resource') and accessibility ('being able to use it').[1] Each response is, in many respects, a call to action—one to which I hope that scholars, creative practitioners, archive users, archivists, cultural institutions, and indeed the policy-makers responsible for their funding will likewise feel some sense of invitation to respond.

(A)

To approach a literary archive in the spirit of encounter—which is to say as both a record and a site of 'live practices of access'[2]—is to open up a legacy of creative practice that can be engaged with both within and outside the academy. In the case of the Brian Friel Papers, a focus on the 'how' of influence reveals a history of intellectual eclecticism and subtle formal experimentation underpinning a globally significant oeuvre that is still a tangible presence in Ireland's cultural landscape. Friel's plays are accessible enough to be a safe bet for an unchallenging Abbey Theatre revival, but they are also in dialogue with Steiner and Donoghue, Bacon and Sinyavsky, Paz and Landes, Dowling and Prose, Janáček and Proust, and untold articles from the *Times Literary Supplement*. Their foundations are built on spaces that reverberate with the desire to communicate; their forms are mirrored in the layouts of the walls of art galleries; their songs are attestations in a managerial world; their ghosts are impossible artworks out of time.

As these models of influence come to light, it becomes possible to enrich a critical discourse—and indeed a production history—that has historically privileged the immediate cultural and socio-political environment in which his plays were written and produced as a contextual lens. To resituate Friel's oeuvre within a history of often chance encounters with other works that also impacted on his ways of working is to generate new lines of enquiry both within Friel studies and beyond it. How do we begin to write about a poetics of the manipulation of chance? How do we talk about dramatic influence on a structural level? How do borrowed words function in theatrical space, as live performance? What are the implications of seeing a modern classic as the product of a detoxification of highbrow white supremacist lines of thought? What does it mean to assess a body of work in the light of a relationship between 'form' and 'core'? How do we engage productively and responsibly with the gender politics of an artist whose process throws his own biases into sharp relief? And what happens when interdisciplinary practices intersect within a given creative process? These are just some of the questions raised by the fragment of archival research I have been able to develop in the writing of this monograph. I hope that future Friel scholars might find and engage with more of them, either in this book or through their own research.

At the same time, what is surfacing is the richness of the literary archive as a resource for contemporary practitioners in the arts. In being attentive to live, bodily practices of access, archival engagement can become a generative process in which—in the case of the Brian Friel Papers—different artistic practices can be put into dialogue. My own collaborations with Keenan and Blake have shown how an artistic legacy can inspire innovation in the arts in a very real way, generating both new work and new ways of working. Crucially, this is a model of influence in which the importance of the literary archive lies not in who the writer is but rather in what the writer does—a model in which the preservation of archival records is, above all, for future *use*. In the case of the Brian Friel Papers, media coverage around the time of their acquisition more than hints at their having been collected in a spirit of relative conservatism, adding to the store of material pertaining to writers of previous generations. For me, and I hope for readers of this book, the collaborative process for 'Don't Anticipate the Ending' has underlined the importance of actively facilitating archival encounters that allow us not necessarily to reverence but to interrogate privileged remains as part of a repertoire of live practices of access. In the event, Keenan's film was developed by disrupting the temporality of Friel's oeuvre, recontextualising Friel in the 'now' of the temporality of access; Blake's film reappropriated Friel's words as an argument for queer joy. In finding such fresh perspectives on Friel through bringing the time of creation into dialogue with the time of encounter, we find what is missing from the story we want to be told by '[naming] its absence[s]'.[3] In other words, by foregrounding the liveness of a creative process and bringing it into dialogue with the liveness of access, archive users can play an active role in shaping the significance of inherited culture.

(B)

This imperative to interrogate the archive and its artefacts makes questions of access and accessibility vital: it is only through processes of archival encounter that we can ask a given archive, so to speak, what it is doing here. There is, however, a lot more work to be done. I have engaged with some of these issues in the fairly limited context of making something relatively hermetic available through alternative channels of engagement, working to demystify the idea of the archive itself through artistic and curatorial projects. Nevertheless, there are practical questions of access and accessibility that still need to be addressed by those with the power to effect structural change, many of which are concerned with digitisation as both an enabling solution and a can of worms that can perpetuate some of the injustices to which it would appear to be the cure (of which more presently). Whilst acknowledging the sheer amount of labour and resources committed to the Brian Friel Papers by the NLI and its archivists in order to make physical access possible—labour without which this monograph could not exist—the fact that the vast majority of this particular archive remains undigitised has undeniable drawbacks. Despite major steps taken by the 'Friel Reimagined' project at Queen's University Belfast,[4] which has, at the time of writing, digitised archival holdings for *Philadelphia, Here I Come!*, *The Freedom of the City*, *Faith Healer*, *Translations*, and *Dancing at Lughnasa*, most of the manuscripts in the Brian Friel Papers still need to be physically accessed in order to be consulted. Such consultations are time-consuming and expensive, even with permission to make photographic copies of archive material for later perusal. The latter is a process, moreover, that profoundly alters the affective experience of archival access, even if it reduces research costs by shortening a trip to what is, at the time of writing, one of the most expensive cities to visit in Europe.[5] Indeed, it only heightens what Maryanne Dever identifies as the 'narrow understanding of textual evidence'[6] characteristic of a culture in which 'researchers are trained and encouraged to transcribe the words we find in documents and then to let the possibilities of the page itself fall from view while we subject the words alone to our interpretive gaze'.[7] In this way, the prohibitive cost of accessing the material archive is already producing as a side-effect one of the most widely-lamented consequences of digitisation.

Further to the ways in which the undigitised archive is a barrier to access for low-income archive users, the unique material object is also something of a barrier to large-scale collaborative research such as that which might be required for community outreach, or indeed anything beyond the personal research project. Unlike the 'multiple and parallel access' afforded by the digitised archive, the physical archive is unable to accommodate multiple archive users accessing the same record. Although, as my own collaborative efforts have shown, a degree of shared access is possible, the physical archive is still unable to accommodate more people at a time than can crowd around a piece of paper on a desk. The undigitised archive is also geared decidedly in favour of the able-bodied and neurotypical. If an archive has not been transcribed, it cannot be made usable through reading software; nor can it be consulted without complying with a series of rules designed for the preservation of fragile objects that must be physically handled in a certain way. There are also many would-be archive users who have more reason to feel as though they might not belong in an official, semi-sanctified space than two relatively privileged artists and one relatively privileged researcher. Indeed, that Keenan, Blake, and I have been able to pursue our careers in our chosen fields at all in the context of a gig economy that screens out anyone without access to additional financial support is due in no small part to the operation of a system that is fundamentally sexist, classist, racist, and ableist. A radical democratisation of archive material is sorely needed in this respect, and digitisation is in many ways the bare minimum requirement for making a documentary archive accessible, insofar as it at least makes it usable on a textual level.

At the same time, digitisation presents its own set of challenges, with which future users of the now partially-digitised Brian Friel Papers will inevitably have to grapple to some degree. As Lina Bountouri points out, digitisation is neither a quick-fix solution to ensuring preservation nor a guarantor of expanded access:

> [Digitization] does not protect the object, and neither can it guarantee its authenticity and integrity. In order to ensure that a digitized object can be long-term preserved, digital preservation policies and methods have to be put in place.

It need hardly be pointed out that the 'human, financial, and technical resources' required of archival institutions in order to do so, at a time when 'the budget of cultural heritage institutions is decreasing',[8] are significant. To discuss in full the policies and methods required in order to ensure that a digitised archive fulfils its function is somewhat beyond the scope of this monograph. However, it is worth noting that some of the solutions being practised by archival institutions in the absence of adequate funding present their own set of issues. As noted by Benoit and Eveleigh, many have attempted to alleviate the prohibitive costs of digitisation by embracing a 'brave new participatory world'[9] of 'social tagging and commenting, crowdsourced transcription and crowdfunding models',[10] in which 'users [...] could be reconceptualised as active participants in the co-production of historical understanding'.[11] This amounts in practice to a substantial amount of 'volunteer labour', with an attendant blurring of 'the boundaries between archives and archivists and the communities they serve'.[12] In other words, there are vast theoretical and practical implications for the kind of democratisation afforded by digitisation, some of which are as radical in their welcome disruption of archival authority as they are exploitative in their reliance on free labour. Indeed, this is a solution that reproduces many of the dynamics of the very volunteer/gig economy that is currently pricing out would-be scholars of the physical archive.

The digitised archive also has implications for the ways in which future users of the Brian Friel Papers—those accessing them through 'Friel Reimagined', for instance—might engage with live practices of access and encounter. Indeed, the spatio-temporal and affective idiosyncrasies of the digitised object accessed via an interface demand an expansion of the repertoire of such practices. As Dorothy Kim points out, building on the scholarship of Karen Barad and Johanna Drucker, '[d]igital reading will be located in an ever-changing ecosystem where reader and text will constitute multiple points of "intra-action"'.[13] Future users of a digitised (or even partly-digitised) archive will therefore need to be attentive to the ways in which their navigation of that ecosystem contours their experience of encountering Friel's creative process. For instance, where 'Don't Anticipate the Ending' was concerned in part with questions of agency and belonging in the context of the physical archive, future projects that make use of a digitised archive will have to consider the ways in which the 'mediating structure' of the interface 'also disciplines, constrains, and determines what can be done in any digital environment'.[14] As Drucker notes:

> Interface [....] is an artifact of complex processes and protocols, a zone in which our behaviours and actions take place, but it is also a symbolic space in which we constitute ourselves through the experience of its particular structures and features. Interface *is what we read and how we read* combined through engagement [.][15] (Italics in original)

In other words, future users of a digitised Brian Friel Papers who are interested in doing so in the spirit of encounter will have to be as concerned with the live practices of access associated with the digital interface as they are to those of the physical reading room. Indeed, if this monograph as the latest intervention in its field has made a case for engaging with the

Brian Friel Papers at the level of creative practice, then it will be the task of those who go on to approach Friel's archive in this manner to do so with an awareness of the theoretical, practical, affective, and indeed sociopolitical implications of the expanded live practices of access that are even now becoming available to them.

Over the past ten years, I have been privileged to be able to spend time with a mind at work on paper and with minds at work in practice. I have uncovered much of the 'what' and the 'how' of Brian Friel's models of influence, taking delight in the ritual transformations of a writing process that produced plays that were almost always greater than the sum of their parts. I have experienced for the first time the joys and the challenges of collaborative research, having watched new work and new ways of working emerge from the archival encounters I have been able to facilitate. Above all, I have found that the archive can be a place of immediacy and vitality—a place where those *for whom* physical and digital artefacts are preserved exercise their right to interrogate what has been designated as their heritage. In the case of the Brian Friel Papers, this amounts to the mobilisation, problematisation, and reappropriation of a major artistic legacy opened up through a blend of scholarly, artistic, affective, and embodied encounters. So what is surfacing—I hope for readers of this monograph as well as for myself—is that the archive, far from being an '[embalming] in pieties'[16] or shrine to the dead, is above all else a resource for the living that 'we must never cease renewing'.[17]

NOTES

1. Stephen Brown, 'Access Is Not A Text Alternative', *The Journal of Museum Education* 34.3 (2009), 223–234, p. 232.
2. Rebecca Schneider, *Performing Remains: Art and War in Times of Theatrical Reenactment* (Abingdon: Routledge, 2011), p. 108.
3. Padraig Regan, 'Some Interpretation: Padraig Regan', *The Carcanet Blog*, 12 January 2022, https://carcanetblog.blogspot.com/2022/01/some-interpretation-padraig-regan.html [accessed 27 November 2022].
4. See 'Friel Reimagined', https://www.qub.ac.uk/sites/friel-reimagined/#friel-reimagined-project-team-1231019-1 [accessed 27 November 2022].
5. James Andrews, 'The ultimate city break', *Money.co.uk*, 12 April 2022, https://www.money.co.uk/travel/city-break-index

[accessed 28 June 2022].
6. Maryanne Dever, 'Papered Over, or Some Observations on Materiality and Archival Method', in *Out of the Closet, Into the Archives*, ed. by Amy L. Stone and Jaime Cantrell (Albany: SUNY Press, 2015), pp. 65–95 (p. 67).
7. Dever, p. 66.
8. Lina Bountouri, *Archives in the Digital Age: Standards, Policies and Tools* (Cambridge, MA; Kidlington: Chandos Publishing, 2017), p. 30.
9. Edward Benoit III and Alexandra Eveleigh, 'Defining and Framing Participatory Archives In Archival Science', in *Participatory Archives: Theory and Practice*, ed. by Edward Benoit III and Alexandra Eveleigh (Cambridge: Cambridge University Press, 2019), pp. 1–12 (p. 2).
10. Benoit and Eveleigh, p. 1.
11. Benoit and Eveleigh, p. 2.
12. Benoit and Eveleigh, p. 3.
13. Dorothy Kim, 'Building Pleasure and the Digital Archive', in *Bodies of Information: Intersectional Feminism and the Digital Humanities*, ed. by Elizabeth Losh and Jacqueline Wernimont (Minneapolis: University of Minnesota Press, 2018) pp. 230–260 (p. 235).
14. Johanna Drucker, *Graphesis: Visual Forms of Knowledge Production* (Cambridge, MA: Harvard University Press, 2014), pp. 138–9.
15. Drucker, p. 145.
16. Brian Friel, *Plays Two* (London: Faber and Faber, 1999), p. 330.
17. Brian Friel, *Plays One* (London: Faber and Faber, 1996), p. 445.

Appendix: Friel's Sources

This appendix includes a brief overview of the sources I have found for Friel's plays to date. Some are already given in the collection lists at the NLI; others are not. It begins with *The Loves of Cass McGuire* (1966) and ends with *The Home Place* (2005). I have only included plays where I have found significant evidence for new source material. I have not included his translated plays or plays after. I have no doubt that it is far from exhaustive. References are to be found in full in the Bibliography. I hope you will find it useful.

The Loves of Cass McGuire (1966)

This is a play in which Friel is demonstrably 'praying to Pirandello',[1] as he wrote in a draft letter to director Hilton Edwards. A further source for the play is a newspaper clipping featuring an extract from Graham Greene's introduction to Margaret Lane's *Edgar Wallace: The Biography of a Phenomenon* (1964): 'No one [. . .] is responsible for his own character: he can make only small modifications for good or ill'.[2]

Lovers: Winners and Losers (1967)

In his notes for *Winners*, Friel makes reference to 'The Eavesdropper'. This was a single-panel series in the *New Yorker* by Alex S. Graham, in which a man overhears a conversation and a thought bubble shows his related or unrelated thoughts.

Crystal and Fox (1968)

One partial source for the play, as a note dated 2 December 1967 reveals, is Oscar Wilde's 'The Ballad of Reading Gaol'. Friel's notes also make reference to a so-called maxim of Marcel Proust taken from Vol. II of his *Le Temps retrouvé*.

The Gentle Island (1969)

There are multiple references in MS 37,063/1 to Gola—an island off the coast of Donegal which was evacuated in the late 1960s but which has since been repopulated. Friel also makes reference to Tory island off the coast of Donegal where, according to legend, a man named Duggan was made King of the island by St. Columba. (The last King of Tory—Patsy Dan Rogers—died in 2018.)

The Freedom of the City (1973)

A copy of an undated four-page illustrated 'Derry Supplement' published by the *Irish Independent* and headlined 'Derry's Bloody Sunday' can be found in MS 37,066/3; a copy of the Widgery Report can be found in MS 37,067/1. The interpolations of the sociologist, Dr. Dodds, are heavily based on Oscar Lewis's *La Vida: A Puerto Rican Family in the Culture of Poverty—San Juan and New York* (1965) to the extent that Warren Brown of Curtis Brown wrote to Friel on 20 December 1972 advising him to paraphrase the eight instances of direct quotation for copyright reasons (see MS 37,067/1). Lily Doherty's speech in which she recalls the moment of her death draws on the same Proustian maxim Friel referenced during the composition process for *Crystal and Fox*.

Volunteers (1975)

One source Friel used for this play was P.V. Glob's *The Bog People* (1965) which was first translated into English in 1969 and which was also used as a source of inspiration by Seamus Heaney when writing the four bog body poems that appeared in *North* (1975) and the poem 'Tollund Man' from his previous collection *Wintering Out* (1972).

Living Quarters (1977)

For this play, Friel considered several options for a chorus, including a narrator in the same mould as the Joe Brennan of Friel's short story 'Foundry House' (i.e. a child who grew up in the gate-lodge of a Big

House). Friel drew on Northrop Frye's *Anatomy of Criticism* (most likely via the *Reader's Encyclopedia of World Drama*) in his exploration of the potential function of a chorus in the play, culminating in the creation of Sir (echoes of whom are to be found in Friel's earlier Pirandellian experiments during the composition processes for *The Loves of Cass McGuire* and *Lovers*). Friel also quotes from Nietzsche's *The Birth of Tragedy*.

MS 37,072/1 also contains three newspaper cuttings relating to the Irish military.[3] The first is titled 'Director of Army Medical Corps retired' and gives a brief account of the career of Colonel Tom Elliott. The second is an obituary for Commandant Michael Costello. The third, dated 10 January 1976, tells of 'Commandant J. J. Flynn, who was presented with his DSM by the Minister for Defence at McKee Barracks in Dublin yesterday afternoon'. Friel has underlined the following: 'Irish UNTSO'; 'UN Emergency Force'; a quotation from the Minister commending Flynn's 'exceptional devotion to duty'; 'Irish Defence forces in UN peace-keeping missions'; 'chief-of-staff of UNTSO, the other as deputy commander of the U.N. Emergency Force'.

Aristocrats (1979)

The play, as is well documented, is closely related to Friel's short story 'Foundry House'. There are frequent references to Chekhov—particularly *Three Sisters*—in these MSs. Friel also references *Small Change* (1976), a play by Welsh playwright Peter Gill. A further source for the play is a poem in loosely rhyming tercets by Alastair Reid titled 'My Father, Dying', which appeared in the 15 November 1976 issue of *The New Yorker*. It begins: 'At summer's succulent end,/ the house is green-stained./ I reach for my father's hand'. In the fourth stanza, 'In the other rooms of the house,/ the furniture stands mumchance', whilst in the seventh and eighth 'I do not call it waiting, but I wait,// anxious in the dark, to see if/ the butterfly of his breath/ has fluttered clear of death'; in the twelfth, 'The whole house is pending'.[4]

Faith Healer (1979)

Sources for the play include George Steiner—presumably *After Babel*, given that his ideas about language are referred to in passing—and David Sylvester's *Interviews with Francis Bacon*, both of which were first published in 1975. A further source is an interview in the *TLS* with Soviet dissident Andrei Sinyavsky (better known by his pseudonym Abram Tertz). Sinyavsky was sentenced to seven years in the Gulag after an unprecedented show-trial in which he and fellow writer Yuli Daniel were convicted for anti-Soviet agitation and propaganda solely on the basis of their literary work. A further source is an interview with playwright Howard Brenton in *Theatre Quarterly* 5.17 (1975) titled 'Petrol Bombs Through the Proscenium Arch', featuring a subheading in bold that ran 'A Jokeless Joyless Allegory' and an observation that 'the only thing that binds us together today is profound unease, and laughter is the language of that unease'; Friel apparently used the former as a kind of mantra to avoid descending into utter humourlessness.

Translations (1980)

Friel's sources include J.H. Andrews's *A Paper Landscape* (1975), Brian Bonner's *Our Inis Eoghain Heritage: The Parishes of Culdaff and Cloncha* (1972), Thomas Colby's *Memoir of the City and North Western Liberties of Londonderry* (1837), Patrick John Dowling's *The Hedge Schools of Ireland* (1935), George Steiner's *After Babel: Aspects of language and translation* (1975), George Steiner's *In Bluebeard's Castle: Some Notes Towards the Re-definition of Culture* (1971), and the letters of John O'Donovan, which are to be found in MS 37,085/6.

The Communication Cord (1982)

Friel's influences included Denis Donoghue's *Ferocious Alphabets* (1981), Peter Shaffer's *Black Comedy* (1965), and *The Reader's Encyclopedia of World Drama* (1969) edited by John Gassner and Edward Quinn. Friel also made use of four reviews from the *Times Literary Supplement*: Roy Harris's review of Erving Goffman's *Forms of Talk*, a review of George A. Miller's *Language and Speech* by Stuart Sutherland, Harold Hobson's review of John McGrath's *A Good Night Out: Popular Theatre: Audience, Class and Form* (1981), and Peter Kemp's review of Michael Frayn's *Noises off* (1982). Friel's notes also contain a copy of David Mamet's essay 'A National Dream Life'.

Making History (1988)

This is a play of many sources. In addition to a copy of Thomas Kilroy's *The O'Neill* (1969), Friel's notes contain a typewritten booklet titled 'QUOTATIONS FROM CONTEMPORARY SOURCES' and a series of handwritten notes possibly taken from Constantia Maxwell's *Irish History from Contemporary Sources: 1509–1610* (1923), of which he had made a note. He also made notes from Seán O'Faoláin's *The Great O'Neill*

(1942) and Cyril Falls's *Elizabeth's Irish Wars* (1950). The *TLS* features strongly once again: Denis Donoghue's review of Seamus Deane's *Celtic Revivals* (1985) and W.J. McCormack's *Ascendancy and Tradition in Anglo-Irish Literary History from 1789 to 1939* (1985); Hayden White's review of Paul Veyne's *Writing History* (1984), C. Behan McCullagh's *Justifying Historical Descriptions* (1984), José Ortega y Gasset's *Historical Reason* (1984), and Dominick LaCapra's *History and Criticism* (1985); and Peter Burke's review of Hayden White's *The Content of the Form* (1987) and LaCapra's *History and Criticism*. Friel was also sent a photocopy of poems by William Forbes Marshall, 'The Bard of Tyrone', including a poem called 'Tullymore' that mentions O'Neill. The sender, an unspecified 'Desmond', also sent Friel an extract from William Doherty's *Derry Columbkille* (1985). Given that the latter came with a 'Columban Fathers' letterhead, this may have been his brother-in-law, Fr. Desmond Morrison.

MS 37,100/1 is notable for a reference to Dylan Thomas's *Under Milk Wood* (1953). This is not the only reference in the Brian Friel Papers to Thomas's play for voices set in the fictional Welsh village of Llareggub ('bugger all' spelled backwards). It also appears in Friel's notes for *Dancing at Lughnasa* (1990) as a possible formal template (see MS 37,104/1, note dated 17 May 1989). When considering the appropriate form for *Wonderful Tennessee*, Friel suggested Thomas again: 'This becomes Under Milkwood. [T]he characters all seated in a semi-circle of chairs. A verbal cantata. Very possible. Perhaps a try-out on radio?' (See NLI, BFP, MS 37,123/2, note dated 13 July 1990.) Although there are no references to *Under Milk Wood* in Friel's own notes prior to 1985, it is entirely possible that his earlier plays may owe the occasional debt to Thomas, if only for their simultaneous portrayal of the interior and exterior lives of small-town people. *Lovers* in particular springs to mind in its use of Ardnageeha, the hill overlooking the town in *Winners*, which is reminiscent of the vantage point of Llaggerub Hill. There is even a possibility, albeit an unsubstantiated one, that Frank's litany of dying Welsh villages is an echo of the morning poetry of Reverend Eli Jenkins. This was something at least one early critic of Friel's work noticed. Writing for the *Hudson Review* in 1966, John Simon notes that Friel 'often manages to bring Ballybeg remarkably close to Llareggub' through the 'not consistently fresh and poetic language' of *Philadelphia, Here I Come!*, in one of the many news clipping saved by Friel. (See MS 37,048/5)

Dancing at Lughnasa (1990)

Though largely autobiographical, Friel drew on Chinua Achebe's *Things Fall Apart* (1958) for his descriptions of Ugandan culture. This is not unproblematic (see Chapter 6). His notes also reference Joseph Hone's *Duck Soup in the Black Sea* (1988). There are also two newspaper obituaries of Friel's uncle, Rev. Bernard MacLoone: one from *The Derry Journal* on 10 July 1950 and the other from *The Ulster Herald* on 15 July 1950. Friel may also have consulted an unspecified encyclopaedia regarding the history and demography of Uganda. Friel's notes for *Lughnasa* also reference Dylan Thomas's *Under Milk Wood* (1953).

Wonderful Tennessee (1993)

Sources include: David S. Landes's *Revolution in Time: Clocks and the Making of the Modern World* (1983); Denis Donoghue's *The Arts Without Mystery* (1983), comprising his 1982 Reith Lectures for the BBC with additional notes and extended commentaries; and Octavio Paz's *The Labyrinth of Solitude* (1985). Again, Friel references *Under Milk Wood*, alongside Chaucer's *Canterbury Tales*. The archive also contains a souvenir booklet from Doon Well (a holy well in Donegal) and a review for an unspecified publication by Deasún Breatnach of two books on Celtic mythology: Miranda Green's *Symbol and Image in Celtic Religious Art* (1989) and Peter Berresford Ellis's *The Celtic Empire* (1990).

Molly Sweeney (1994)

In addition to Oliver Sacks's *New Yorker* article 'A Neurologist's Notebook: To See and Not See' (10 May 1993), Friel's research included: R. L. Gregory's *Recovery from early blindness: a case study* (1963),[5] Marius von Senden's *Space and Sight* (1932), Alberto Valvo's *Sight restoration after long-term blindness* (1971), and Semir Zeki's *A Vision of the Brain* (1993).

Give Me Your Answer, Do! (1997)

In addition to the intertexts detailed by Friel in the text of the play (which I have not reproduced here), Friel's sources include Eamon Duffy's *The Stripping of the Altars: Traditional Religion in England 1400–1580* (1992), unspecified works by Wittgenstein, and Douglas Johnson's *TLS* review Alain Peyrefitte's *C'était de Gaulle* (1994) in the 28 July 1995 issue. Friel also references a *Guardian* article by Barry Hugill, 'Sex and

Sexuality'—a somewhat tongue-in-cheek report on reactionary arguments against critical theory.

Performances (2003)

Sources include: *Intimate Letters: Leoš Janáček to Kamila Stösslová* (1994), ed. by John Tyrrell; Mirka Zemanová's *Janáček: a composer's life* (2002); Paul Anthony Griffiths's review of Zemanová in the *TLS* from 20 September 2002; Francine Prose's *The Lives of the Muses* (2002); a review of Prose in the *New Yorker* from 30 September 2002; the Škampa Quartet's 2001 studio recording of Janáček's String Quartets on the Czech record label Supraphon; and an article on Janáček from the now defunct 'www.measure.demon.co.uk'.

The Home Place (2005)

A detailed list of Friel's research materials for this play can be found in the NLI's Collection List No. 180: Brian Friel Papers (Additional), which is freely available online; it makes little sense to reproduce it here. Moreover, several items are of uncertain origin (a booklet titled *Thomas Moore: Minstrel of Ireland* is a case in point). Where publication details are available and/or apparent, they are included in the bibliography. These include: Maureen Wall's *Glenswilly* (1973), Kissane's *The Irish Face* (1986), a newspaper article by Richard Girling (2003), Charles R. Browne's photographs at Trinity College Dublin, two articles by A. C. Haddon, Lawrence J. Taylor, John Beddoe, K. H. Connell, and Gearóid Ó Crualaoich. Otherwise, I strongly encourage researchers to consult the catalogue.

NOTES

1. MS 37,052/1 contains a draft of a letter to director Hilton Edwards dated 7 April 1965 in which Friel describes himself has having been 'praying to Pirandello' at the play's inception.
2. See Graham Greene, 'Edgar Wallace', in *Collected Essays* (London: The Bodley Head, 1969), pp. 226–231.
3. Two are undated; all three are missing publication data.
4. Alastair Reid, 'My Father, Dying', in *The New Yorker*, 15 November 1976, p. 50.
5. Photocopied from Gregory's *Concepts and mechanisms of perception* (1974).

Bibliography

Published Works

Achebe, Chinua, *Things Fall Apart* (London: Penguin Modern Classics, 2001)
Alkalay-Gut, Karen, 'The Thing He Loves: Murder as Aesthetic Experience in "The Ballad of Reading Gaol"', *Victorian Poetry* 35.3 (1997), 349–366
Andrews, J. H., *A Paper Landscape: The Ordnance Survey in Nineteenth-Century Ireland* (Dublin: Four Courts Press, 2006)
———, 'Notes for a Future Edition of Brian Friel's "Translations"', *The Irish Review (Cork)* 13, Autobiography as Criticism (Winter 1992/1993), 93–106
Augustine, Saint, *Confessions*, trans. by Henry Chadwick (Oxford: Oxford University Press, 2008)
Bacon, Francis, 'Of Friendship', in *The Essays of Francis Bacon*, ed. with intr. and notes by Mary Augusta Scott (New York: Charles Scribner's Sons, 1908), pp. 117–129
Barthes, Roland, *A Lover's Discourse: Fragments*, trans. by Richard Howard (New York: Hill and Wang, 2001)
Beddoe, John, 'The Kelts of Ireland', *The Journal of Anthropology* 1.2 (1870): 117–31
———, *The Races of Britain: A Contribution to the Anthropology of Western Europe* (Bristol: Arrowsmith, 1885)
Benoit III, Edward and Alexandra Eveleigh, eds., *Participatory Archives: Theory and Practice* (Cambridge: Cambridge University Press, 2019)
Berger, John, *Portraits: John Berger on Artists*, ed. by Tom Overton (London: Verso, 2017)

Boltwood, Scott, *Brian Friel, Ireland, and The North* (Cambridge: Cambridge University Press, 2009)
Bonner, Brian, *Our Inis Eoghain Heritage: The Parishes of Culdaff and Cloncha* (Baile Átha Cliath: Foilseacháin Náisiúnta Teoranta, 1972)
Bountouri, Lina, *Archives in the Digital Age: Standards, Policies and Tools* (Cambridge, MA; Kidlington: Chandos Publishing, 2017)
Brazeau, Robert, '"A Theatre Which Events do not Exceed": Brian Friel's *The Freedom of the City*', *Journal of Urban History*, 29.1 (2002), 39–61
Brenton, Howard, 'Petrol Bombs Through the Proscenium Arch', *Theatre Quarterly* 5.17 (1975), 4–20
'Briefly Noted', *The New Yorker*, 30 September 2002, p. 139
Brown, Stephen, 'Access Is Not A Text Alternative', *The Journal of Museum Education* 34.3 (2009), 223–234
Burke, Peter, 'Rethinking the historian's craft', *TLS*, 6 November 1987, p. 1218
Colby, Thomas, *Memoir of the City and North Western Liberties of Londonderry: Parish of Templemore* (Dublin: Hodges and Smith, 1837)
Cole M. Crittenden, 'The Dramatics of Time' *KronoScope* 5.2 (2005), 193–212
Connell, K. H., 'Ether- Drinking in Ulster', in *Irish Peasant Society: Four Historical Essays* (Oxford: Clarendon Press, 1968), 87–111
Davie, Donald, 'The clans and their world-pictures', *TLS*, 31 January 1975, 98–100
Dinshaw, Carolyn, *How Soon is Now? Medieval Texts, Amateur Readers, and the Queerness of Time* (Durham, NC: Duke University Press, 2012).
Doherty, William, *Derry Columbkille: Souvenir of the centenary celebrations, in honour of St. Columba; in the Long Tower Church, Derry, 1897–99* (Dublin: Brown & Nolan, 1899)
Donoghue, Denis, 'A myth and its unmasking', *TLS*, 1 November 1985, p. 1239
———, *The Arts Without Mystery* (London: British Broadcasting Corporation, 1983)
———, *Ferocious Alphabets* (London: Faber and Faber, 1981)
Dowling, Patrick J., *The Hedge Schools of Ireland* (Dublin: Talbot Press, 1935)
Drucker, Johanna, *Graphesis: Visual Forms of Knowledge Production* (Cambridge, MA: Harvard University Press, 2014)
Duffy, Eamon, *The Stripping of the Altars: Traditional Religion in England 1400–1580* (London, New Haven: Yale University Press, 1992)
Edelman, Lee, *No Future: Queer Theory and the Death Drive* (Durham and London: Duke University Press, 2004)
Falls, Cyril, *Elizabeth's Irish Wars* (London: Methuen, 1950)
Fitzpatrick, Lisa, '*Performances* by Brian Friel', *Irish Theatre Magazine*, 15 February 2013, http://www.irishtheatremagazine.ie/Reviews/Current/Performances [accessed 15 May 2015]

Foster, Roy, 'View from the Monument', *Times Literary Supplement*, 6 February 1976, p. 8
Frege, Gottlob, 'The Thought: A Logical Inquiry', *Mind* 65.259 (1956): 289–311
Freshwater, Helen, 'The Allure of the Archive', *Poetics Today* 24.4 (2003), 729–258
Friel, Brian, *Collected Plays: Volume One* (London: Faber and Faber, 2016)
———, *The Communication Cord* (Oldcastle: The Gallery Press, 1999)
———, *Crystal and Fox* (Oldcastle: The Gallery Press, 1984)
———, *The Gentle Island* (Oldcastle: The Gallery Press, 1993)
———, *Give me your answer, do!* (London: Penguin Books, 1997)
———, *The Home Place* (London: Faber and Faber, 2005)
———, *Lovers: Winners and Losers* (Oldcastle: The Gallery Press, 2002)
———, *The Loves of Cass McGuire* (New York: Farrar, Straus and Giroux, 1967)
———, *The Mundy Scheme* (New York: Farrar, Straus and Giroux, 1970)
———, *Performances* (London: Faber and Faber, 2005)
———, *Plays One* (London: Faber and Faber, 1996)
———, *Plays Two* (London: Faber and Faber, 1999)
———, *Volunteers* (Oldcastle: The Gallery Press, 2002)
Friel, Brian, John Andrews, and Kevin Barry, 'Translations and A Paper Landscape: Between Fiction and History', *The Crane Bag* 7.2 (1983), 118–24 (p. 122)
Frye, Northrop, *Anatomy of Criticism: Four Essays* (Princeton: Princeton University Press, 1957)
Garner, Stanton B, Jr., *Bodied Spaces: Phenomenology and Performance in Contemporary Drama* (Ithaca and London: Cornell University Press, 1994)
Gassner, John, and Edward Quinn, eds., *The Reader's Encyclopedia of World Drama* (New York: Dover Publications, 2002).
Gill, Peter, *Plays One* (London: Faber and Faber, 2014)
Girling, Richard, 'Facing the Past', *Sunday Times*, 21 September 2003
Glenny, Michael, trans., 'Sinyavsky: Fiction and Reality', *Times Literary Supplement*, 23 May 1975, p. 560
Glob, P. V., *The Bog People: Iron Age Man Preserved* (London: Faber and Faber, 1969)
Goffman, Erving, 'Response Cries', *Language* 54.4 (1978), 787–815
Greene, Graham, 'Edgar Wallace', in *Collected Essays* (London: The Bodley Head, 1969), 226–231
Gregory, R. L., *Concepts and Mechanisms of Perception* (London: Duckworth, 1974)
Grene, Nicholas, 'Friel and Transparency', *Irish University Review*, 29.1, Special Issue: Brian Friel (1999), 136–144

Griffiths, Paul Anthony, 'Years of the fox', *Times Literary Supplement*, 20 September 2002, p. 18

Haddon, A. C., 'Studies in Irish Craniology: The Aran Islands, Co. Galway', *Proceedings of the Royal Irish Academy (1889–1901)* 2 (1891): 759–67

Haddon, A. C., and C. R. Browne, 'The Ethnography of the Aran Islands, County Galway', *Proceedings of the Royal Irish Academy (1889–1901)* 2 (1891): 768–830

Harris, Roy, 'Performing in words', *TLS*, 19 December 1981, 1455–6

Harrington, John P., ed., *Irish Theater in America: Essays on Irish Theatrical Diaspora* (New York: Syracuse University Press, 2009)

Heaney, Seamus, '…English and Irish', *The Times Literary Supplement* no. 4047, 24 October 1980, p. 1199

Herman, Vimala, 'Deixis and Space in Drama', *Social Semiotics*, 7.3 (1997), 269–283

Hobson, Harold, 'Drama for workers' *TLS*, 1 January 1982, p. 18

Hone, Joseph, *Duck Soup in the Black Sea: Further Collected Travels* (London: Hamish Hamilton, 1988)

Hugill, Barry, 'Sex and Sexuality', *The Guardian*, 6 August 1995, https://www.theguardian.com/books/1995/aug/06/janeausten.fiction [accessed 15 January 2021]

Johnson, Douglas, 'Getting to know the General', *TLS*, 28 July 1995, p. 30

Kemp, Peter, 'Mixing mockery and homage', *TLS*, 5 March 1982, p. 252.

Kilroy, Thomas, *The O'Neill* (Oldcastle: Gallery Press, 1995)

Kim, Dorothy, 'Building Pleasure and the Digital Archive', in *Bodies of Information: Intersectional Feminism and the Digital Humanities*, ed. by Elizabeth Losh and Jacqueline Wernimont (Minneapolis: University of Minnesota Press, 2018) pp. 230–260

Kissane, Noel, *The Irish face* (Dublin: National Library of Ireland, 1986)

Kuczyńska, Zosia, '"[A] disoriented vision of…fact": Brian Friel, Francis Bacon, and *Faith Healer*', *Irish University Review* 50.2 (November 2020): 319–336.

Landes, David S., *Revolution in Time: Clocks and the Making of the Modern World* (Cambridge, Massachusetts; London, England: The Belknap Press of Harvard University Press, 1983)

Langer, Susanne K., *Feeling and Form* (London: Routledge and Kegan Paul, 1953)

Larrissy, Edward, ed., *W.B. Yeats: The Major Works* (Oxford: Oxford University Press, 2001)

Lawrence, Dan H., ed., *Selected Correspondence of Bernard Shaw: Theatrics* (Toronto: University of Toronto Press, 1995)

Leake, Laurel Lynn, 'Defining Drag: a Vymifesto', *Velour: The Drag Magazine*, Collected Issues 1–3 (House of Velour, 2018), 54–5

Lerner, Alan Jay, *My Fair Lady: A Musical Play by Alan Jay Lerner* (New York: Coward-McCann, 1956)

Lojek, Helen, 'Brian Friel's Plays and George Steiner's Linguistics: Translating the Irish', *Contemporary Literature*, 35.1 (1994), 83–99

———, *The Spaces of Irish Drama: Stage and Place in Contemporary Plays* (Basingstoke: Palgrave Macmillan, 2011)

LSJ: The Online Liddell-Scott-Jones Greek-English Lexicon, http://stephanus.tlg.uci.edu/lsj/ [accessed 20 December 2015]

Mamet, David, *Writing in Restaurants* (London: Faber and Faber, 1988)

Marcel, Gabriel, *Being and Having*, trans. by Katherine Farrer (Westminster: Dacre Press, 1949)

Marshall, W. F., *Livin' in Drumlister: The Collected Ballads and Verses of W. F. Marshall*, intr. by J. A. Todd (Belfast: Blackstaff, 1983)

Maxwell, Constantia, *Irish History from Contemporary Sources: 1509–1610* (London: George Allen & Unwin, 1923)

Moloney, Karen M., 'Molly Astray: Revisioning Ireland in Brian Friel's *Molly Sweeney*', *Twentieth Century Literature*, 46.3 (2000), 285–310

Morash, Chris and Shaun Richards, *Mapping Irish Theatre: Theories of Space and Place* (Cambridge: Cambridge University Press, 2014)

Murray, Christopher, ed., trans., and bib., *Brian Friel: Essays, Diaries, Interviews: 1964–1999* (London: Faber and Faber, 1999)

———, *The Theatre of Brian Friel: Tradition and Modernity* (London: Bloomsbury, 2014)

Murray, Isobel, ed., *Oscar Wilde: The Major Works* (Oxford: Oxford World Classics, 1989)

National Library of Ireland, 'National Library of Ireland Collection Development Policy, 2009–2011' (Dublin: National Library of Ireland), https://www.nli.ie/en/udlist/reports-and-policy-documents.aspx [accessed 26 April 2022]

———, 'National Library of Ireland Diversity and Inclusion Policy 2018–2021' (Dublin: National Library of Ireland, 2018), https://www.nli.ie/en/Policy.aspx [accessed 10 March 2020]

———, *Treasuring our Heritage: Donation of Materials to the National Library of Ireland*, https://www.nli.ie/GetAttachment.aspx?id=41a1a39f-86bb-498f-9519-efd20c0d3df6 [accessed 26 April 2022] in 'How we acquire', www.nli.ie/how-we-acquire-our-collections.aspx [accessed 26 April 2022]

Nietzsche, Friedrich, *The Birth of Tragedy or Hellenism and Pessimism*, trans. by William A. Huassmann (The Floating Press, 2016)

O'Byrne, Emmett, Aidan Clarke, and Judy Barry, 'Bagenal (O'Neill), Mabel', in the *Dictionary of Irish Biography*, October 2009. https://doi.org/10.3318/dib.006953.v1 [accessed 24 June 2022]

Ó Crualaoich, Gearóid, 'The "Merry Wake"', in J. S. Donnelly and Kerby A. Miller, eds., *Irish Popular Culture, 1650–1850* (Dublin; Portland: Irish Academic Press, 1998), 173–200

O'Faoláin, Seán, *The Great O'Neill: A Biography of Hugh O'Neill, Earl of Tyrone, 1550–1616* (Cork: Mercier, 1970)

Paz, Octavio, *The Labyrinth of Solitude: Life and Thought in Mexico*, trans. by Lysander Kemp (Middlesex: Penguin Books, 1985)

Pelletier, Martine, *Le Théâtre de Brian Friel: histoire et histoires* (Villeneuve d'Ascq: Presses Universitaires du Septentrion, 1997)

Pine, Richard, 'Brian Friel and Contemporary Irish Drama', *Colby Quarterly* 27.4 (1991), 190–201

———, *Brian Friel and Ireland's Drama* (London: Routledge, 1990)

———, *The Diviner: The Art of Brian Friel* (Dublin: University College Dublin Press, 1999)

Plunkett, James, *The Trusting and the Maimed and Other Irish Stories* (New York: Devin-Adair, 1955)

Proust, Marcel, *The Maxims of Marcel Proust*, ed. and trans. by Justin O'Brian (New York: Columbia University Press, 1948)

Regan, Padraig, 'Some Interpretation: Padraig Regan', *The Carcanet Blog*, 12 January 2022, <https://carcanetblog.blogspot.com/2022/01/some-int erpretation-padraig-regan.html> [accessed 27 November 2022]

Reid, Alistair, 'My Father, Dying', in *The New Yorker*, 15 November 1976, p. 50

'Report of the Bloody Sunday Inquiry Volume 1 Chapter 5', https://webarc hive.nationalarchives.gov.uk/20101017064040/http://report.bloody-sun day-inquiry.org/volume01/chapter005/

Roche, Anthony, *Brian Friel: Theatre and Politics* (Basingstoke: Palgrave Macmillan, 2011)

———, ed., *The Cambridge Companion to Brian Friel* (Cambridge: Cambridge University Press, 2006)

Sacks, Oliver, 'A Neurologist's Notebook: To See and Not See', *The New Yorker*, 10 May 1993, 59–73

Scharmen, Fred, *Space Forces: A Critical History of Life in Outer Space* (London: Verso, 2021)

Schneider, Rebecca, *Performing Remains: Art and War in Times of Theatrical Reenactment* (Abingdon: Routledge, 2011)

Shaffer, Peter, *Four Plays: The Private Ear / The Public Eye / White Liars / Black Comedy* (London: Penguin, 1981)

Steiner, George, *After Babel: Aspects of Language and Translation* (Oxford: Oxford University Press, 1975)

———, *In Bluebeard's Castle: Some Notes Towards the Redefinition of Culture* (London: Faber and Faber, 1971)

――, *Real Presences: Is There Anything in What We Say?* (London: Faber & Faber, 1989)

――, 'Silence and the Poet', in *Language and Silence: Essays and Notes, 1958–1966* (London: Faber & Faber, 2010)

Stone, Amy L. and Jaime Cantrell, eds., *Out of the Closet, Into the Archives* (Albany: SUNY Press, 2015)

Sutherland, Stuart, 'The output from the mouth', *TLS*, 1 January 1982, p. 16

Sylvester, David, *Interviews with Francis Bacon* (London: Thames and Hudson, 1975)

Taylor, Diana, *The Archive and the Repertoire: Performing Cultural Memory in the Americas* (Durham and London: Duke University Press, 2003)

Taylor, Lawrence J., 'The Languages of Belief: Nineteenth-Century Religious Discourse in Southwest Donegal', in Marilyn Silverman and P. H. Gulliver, eds., *Approaching the Past: Historical Anthropology through Irish Case Studies* (New York: Columbia University Press, 1992), 143–175

Tertz, Abram (Andrey Sinyavsky), *A Voice from the Chorus*, trans. by Kyril Fitzlyon and Max Hayward (London: Collins and Harvill Press, 1976)

Thomas, Dylan, *Under Milk Wood: A Play for Voices* (London: J. M. Dent & Sons Ltd, 1972)

Tutter, Adele, 'Text as Muse, Muse as Text: Janáček, Kamila, and the Role of Fantasy in Musical Creativity', *American Imago* 72.4 (Winter 2015), 407–50

Tyrrell, John, ed., *Intimate Letters: Leoš Janáček to Kamila Stösslova* (London: Faber and Faber, 2005)

Valvo, Alberto, *Sight Restoration after Long-Term Blindness: The Problems and Behavior Patterns of Visual Rehabilitation*, ed. by Leslie L. Clark and Zofia Z. Jastrzembska (New York: American Foundation for the Blind, 1971)

von Senden, Marius, *Space and Sight: the perception of space and shape in the congenitally blind before and after operation*, trans. by Peter Heath, appendices by A. H. Riesen, G. J. Warnock, and J. Z. Young (London: Methuen, 1932)

Wall, Maureen, *Glenswilly: a talk on her native Glen, given by Maureen Wall in Foxhall on the 17th July 1969, for the first Glenswilly Festival*. See National Folklore Collection, University College Dublin.

Walsh, Victoria, '". . . to give the sensation without the boredom of conveyance": Francis Bacon and the Aesthetic of Ambiguity', *Visual Culture in Britain* 10.3 (2009), 235–252

White, Hayden, 'Between science and symbol', *TLS*, 21 January 1986, pp. 109–110

Wilder, Thornton and Richard H. Goldstone, 'Thornton Wilder, The Art of Fiction No. 16', *The Paris Review* 15 (Winter 1956) https://www.theparisreview.org/interviews/4887/the-art-of-fiction-no-16-thornton-wilder

Winkler, Elizabeth Hale, 'Brian Friel's *The Freedom of the City*: Historical Actuality and Dramatic Imagination', *The Canadian Journal of Irish Studies*, 7.1 (1981), 12–31

Zeki, Semir, *A Vision of the Brain* (Oxford: Blackwell Scientific Publications, 1993)

Zemanová, Mirka, *Janáček: A Composer's Life* (Boston: Northeastern University Press, 2002)

Manuscripts

Dublin, National Library of Ireland (NLI), Brian Friel Papers
———, Brian Friel Papers (Additional)
———, Correspondence of D.E.S. Maxwell
Dublin, Trinity College Dublin, Dr Charles R Browne, photographs, IE TCD MS 10961

Stage

Brian Friel, *Dancing at Lughnasa*, dir. by Annabelle Comyn (Belfast: Lyric Theatre, 26 August–27 September 2015)
———, *Molly Sweeney*, dir. by Abigail Graham (Belfast: Print Room; Lyric Theatre, 8 February–21 March 2014)
———, *Performances*, dir. by Adrian Dunbar (Derry: Millennium Forum; University of Ulster, Magee Campus, Great Hall, 14–16 and 19–23 February 2013)
———, *Translations*, dir. by Adrian Dunbar (Derry: Millennium Forum and on tour, 13 March–27 April 2013)

Other Media

Don't anticipate the ending: creative encounters with the Brian Friel Papers, Museum of Literature Ireland, https://exhibitions.moli.ie/brian-friel
Interview with Jessie Keenan, Museum of Literature Ireland, 26 July 2021
Interview with Robbie Blake, Museum of Literature Ireland, 26 July 2021
Interview with Zosia Kuczyńska, Museum of Literature Ireland, 26 July 2021
Robbie Blake, 'Running the Ending (graphic score)'. See 'Running the ending', *Don't anticipate the ending: creative encounters with the Brian Friel Papers*, Museum of Literature Ireland, https://exhibitions.moli.ie/brian-friel/m/running-the-ending

Jessie Keenan, 'So What is Surfacing (trio). See 'So what is surfacing', *Don't anticipate the ending: creative encounters with the Brian Friel Papers*, Museum of Literature Ireland, https://exhibitions.moli.ie/brian-friel/m/so-what-is-surfacing

Škampa Quartet, *Janáček: String Quartets Nos 1 & 2* (Supraphon, 2001)

Index

A
Achebe, Chinua, 200, 201, 235, 258
Andrews, J.H., 63, 70–72, 85–89, 93, 102, 104, 256
archive, the, 1, 3, 4, 6, 7, 9, 10, 14, 17, 54, 69, 76, 95, 98, 99, 102, 124, 146–148, 151, 157, 174, 191–198, 203, 215–222, 224, 225, 229–232, 245–251, 258
Augustine, Saint, 124, 132, 134, 143, 144

B
Bacon, Francis (early modern philosopher), 111, 112, 225
Bacon, Francis (twentieth-century painter), 2, 4, 17, 18, 32–48, 50, 52–57, 67, 132, 138, 145, 192, 225, 246, 255
Bagenal, Mabel, 47, 48, 50
Ballybeg, 91, 93, 95, 96, 99, 100, 123, 201, 257
Barthes, Roland, 120, 141

Blake, Robbie, 4, 191, 195–198, 203–215, 218–221, 225–232, 247, 249
  artistic practice of, 4, 191, 204, 205, 208, 211, 225, 246
  director of Tonnta, 196
  interviews, 198, 204, 205, 209, 210, 212, 230, 234, 236–239, 243
  Running the Ending. *See* 'Don't Anticipate the Ending'
blindness, 165, 167, 168, 172–174, 177, 180, 183
Bloody Sunday, 27, 28, 47, 59, 60, 254
Bonner, Brian, 70, 102, 256
Brenton, Howard, 31, 33, 60, 239, 256
Brian Friel Papers, The, 1–6, 14, 20, 32, 57, 67, 85, 86, 124, 129, 146, 155, 191–194, 196–198, 209, 215, 217, 229, 232, 245, 248, 249

access, 6, 57, 177, 196–198, 216, 218, 220, 230, 232, 245, 247, 248, 250
acquisition, 2, 11, 193, 247
organisation, 11, 204
Brown, Warren, 28, 60, 254
Burntollet Bridge, 27

C

Chaucer, Geoffrey, 125, 258
Chekhov, Anton, 255
chorus, 21, 43, 47, 58, 96, 254
Cioran, E.M., 132, 133, 138, 143
civil rights, 27, 28, 84
Colby, Thomas, 70–72, 74, 77, 85–89, 92, 93, 95, 102, 125, 256
Colgan, Michael, 148, 183, 186, 189
colonialism, 69, 73, 74, 77, 83–85, 88, 89, 91–93, 97, 99, 100, 103, 125, 165, 200, 209
comedy, 115–117
Conroy Murphy, Bláthnaid, 207, 212, 214, 218, 221, 225, 227, 228
conversation, 118–122, 137, 205
Cronin, Marion, 207, 212, 214, 218, 221–223, 226–229
culture, 29, 49, 53, 68–70, 76, 78–84, 88, 90–93, 96–100, 114, 122, 128, 193, 194, 196, 200, 208, 213, 246–248, 258
Cvetkovich, Ann, 3, 15, 192, 195, 196, 233, 234

D

Daldry, Stephen, 116
dance, 10, 69, 76, 121, 122, 128, 135, 175, 194, 197, 202, 203, 205, 208–211, 215, 217, 218, 220–222, 224–227, 231
Dante, 54, 152

Deane, Seamus, 257
Derry, 27, 59, 73, 94, 183, 254
Donoghue, Denis, 5, 14, 107, 119, 120, 122, 125, 126, 128, 129, 131–138, 145, 151, 157, 166, 197, 225, 232, 246
  The Arts Without Mystery, 16, 123, 124, 126–129, 132, 135–138, 142–144, 258
  Ferocious Alphabets, 111, 119–122, 132, 137, 141, 225, 256
'Don't Anticipate the Ending'
  exhibition, 6, 191, 192, 195, 212, 226, 232
  project, 194, 195, 247, 250
    and COVID-19, 208, 210, 212, 215, 218, 220, 222, 224, 229, 232
  origins of, 4, 196, 197, 229
  workshops (in person), 197, 205, 207, 208, 217, 220–226
  workshops (on Zoom), 218, 219
  Running the Ending, 191, 203, 205, 207–210, 212, 214, 215, 247
    development of, 205, 206
    filming of, 209, 212, 213
  So What Is Surfacing (Trio), 191, 215, 226, 228, 247
    development of, 216–219, 222, 224
    filming of, 6, 225, 226
Doon Well, 124, 258
Dowling, Patrick John, 70, 76, 77, 85, 87, 92, 93, 103, 246, 256
Duffy, Eamon, 54, 64, 258
Dunbar, Adrian, 94, 146, 155, 164, 183

INDEX 273

E
Edwards, Hilton, 7, 13, 21, 22, 26, 58, 59, 253
Eliot, T.S., 80, 132, 143
embodiment, 9, 10, 67–69, 72, 76, 82, 92, 93, 95, 96, 98–101, 135, 161–164, 169–171, 181, 183, 194–196, 211, 247, 251
engrams, 166, 177–179

F
farce, 111–118, 121, 122, 140
Farrell, Suzanne, 153
Field Day, 11, 69, 117
Foster, Roy, 70, 85, 88, 105
Frayn, Michael, 117, 256
Frege, Gottlob, 19, 20, 57
French Revolution, 97
Friel, Brian
  and art, 4, 17, 18, 20, 21, 24, 26, 30, 43, 47–49, 53, 56, 126–128, 138, 147, 151, 152, 156, 157, 160–162, 164, 169, 171, 176, 182, 192, 212
  and artistic practice, 1, 3, 4, 6, 7, 14, 17, 18, 20, 26, 31, 33, 34, 36, 39, 42, 46, 47, 49, 50, 52, 53, 56, 111, 138, 145–147, 149, 151–157, 159, 162, 164, 168, 169, 191, 192, 197, 247
  and chance, 3, 4, 17, 18, 31–33, 35–39, 42, 46, 52, 56, 138, 192, 246
  and civil rights, 27
  and the 'core' of the play, 5, 13, 14, 33, 55, 107–115, 118, 120–125, 132–134, 136, 137, 145, 197, 202, 209, 216, 217, 246
  and culture, 29, 53, 70, 77, 78, 200
  and dance, 167, 197, 200, 202, 203, 205, 208, 210, 220
  and encounter, 3–6, 17, 18, 32, 35–37, 47, 48, 51, 53, 56, 57, 99, 122, 146, 191, 192, 216, 218, 246, 250
  and fact, 4, 17–20, 23, 24, 30, 39–41, 43, 46–50, 56, 57, 90, 110, 157
  and faith, 14, 33, 35–37, 55, 56
  and feminism, 146, 154, 155, 158, 159, 176
  and fiction, 18–20, 23, 24, 30, 47, 49, 50, 56, 85, 86, 110, 149, 168
  and form, 5, 13, 14, 22, 23, 28, 30, 33–36, 39, 43, 45, 46, 50, 51, 53, 56, 57, 97, 107–114, 118, 121–125, 128, 129, 131, 133, 134, 136, 137, 174, 177, 197, 202, 217, 230, 246, 257
  and gender, 5, 26, 41, 42, 79, 145, 146, 148–157, 162, 164–166, 168, 170–176, 182, 183, 246
  and historiography, 2, 48, 51
  and history, 2, 22, 48–52, 74, 76, 81, 83, 85, 86, 95, 97, 129, 200, 258
  and language, 28, 29, 32, 39, 40, 45, 48, 69, 70, 74, 76, 78–80, 82, 88, 90, 93, 95, 96, 98, 100, 111, 120, 122, 125, 128, 130, 132–134, 136–138, 157, 160, 178, 202, 220, 221, 225
  and linguistics, 2, 78, 96, 111, 118, 119
  and memory, 18, 31, 42, 69, 74, 94, 95, 97, 99, 110, 122, 135, 177, 179, 200, 203
  and music/musicians, 122, 123, 129, 133, 134, 147, 150, 153,

154, 159–164, 174–176, 197, 203, 225
and mystery, 123–128, 130–133, 135–138, 157, 168
and officialdom, 23, 28–30, 47, 50, 53, 56
and performance, 9, 43, 100, 134, 135, 145, 147, 160–164, 166–170, 176, 181–183, 246
and performers, 145, 147, 159–164, 167, 171, 175, 176, 183, 220
and philosophy, 19, 34, 124, 126, 127, 133, 134
and pilgrimage, 124, 125, 129, 133, 135
and politics, 27, 28, 30, 69, 76, 77, 86–88, 91, 117, 146, 157, 165, 170, 176, 246
and questions, 12, 13, 24, 36, 37, 109, 113–118, 134, 173, 192, 195, 203, 211, 215–217, 220, 229, 232, 246
and race, 76, 77, 81, 83, 84, 93, 100, 246
and reality, 19–21, 23, 24, 29–31, 47, 53, 54, 56, 80, 94, 108, 109, 167, 175, 176, 179, 199, 202, 203, 208
and the role of the artist, 4, 21, 30–33, 35, 39, 42, 43, 52–54, 56, 129, 147, 148, 150–156, 158–160, 163, 164, 168–170, 175, 176, 181
and space, 4, 9, 20, 30, 47, 53, 67, 68, 91, 93, 94, 110, 120, 134, 135, 167, 225, 246, 249
and time, 2, 3, 17, 24, 30, 47, 84, 91–93, 97, 98, 113, 114, 117, 122, 124, 125, 129–131, 133–135, 137, 167, 232, 246, 247. *See also* time

and violence, 26, 33, 40–43, 46, 47, 49, 50, 52, 53, 56, 80, 86, 164, 199
Aristocrats (1979), 8, 122, 154, 155, 171, 211, 255
Bannermen, 40
Communication Cord, The (1982), 5, 12, 107, 111–113, 120–123, 137, 139, 141, 154, 225, 256
creative process of, 2, 3, 5, 7, 11–14, 22, 28, 31, 36, 50, 55, 57, 67, 70, 84, 85, 87–89, 92, 93, 95, 96, 99–101, 108, 111–115, 117, 118, 120–122, 124, 125, 127, 131, 133, 136, 146, 168, 171–174, 176, 177, 182, 183, 191, 192, 197, 198, 200–205, 207, 210–212, 215, 216, 220, 221, 229, 230, 232, 233, 245–247, 250
Crystal and Fox (1968), 4, 18, 22, 23, 25–29, 43, 175, 254
Dancing at Lughnasa (1990), 5, 44, 53, 122, 137, 168, 191, 197–199, 201, 202, 204, 205, 208, 210–212, 218, 221–223, 226, 230, 248, 257, 258
film adaptation, 194, 198, 203
productions of, 208, 209, 215
Enemy Within, The (1962), 154, 185, 219, 241
Faith Healer (1979), 4, 17, 18, 20–24, 26, 31–33, 35, 40, 41, 43–48, 51, 53, 54, 56, 57, 62, 113, 164, 168, 174, 175, 192, 211, 248, 255
Foundry House, 8, 254, 255
Freedom of the City, The (1973), 4, 18, 20, 22, 26–29, 43, 44, 46, 47, 50, 58, 60, 248, 254
Gentle Island, The (1971), 7, 254

Give Me Your Answer, Do! (1997), 4, 18, 40, 53–56, 62, 64, 145, 154, 210, 233, 258
Hedda Gabler (2008), 173
Home Place, The (2005), 6, 146, 253, 259
Living Quarters (1977), 8, 20, 21, 28, 44, 254
Lovers: Winners and Losers (1967), 19, 20, 23, 28, 46, 57, 59, 60, 109, 139, 253, 255, 257
Loves of Cass McGuire, The (1966), 21, 107–109, 138, 253, 255
Making History (1988), 4, 12, 18, 20, 47, 48, 50, 51, 53, 63, 64, 113, 155, 171, 188, 256
Molly Sweeney (1994), 5, 12, 13, 53, 146, 164–183, 187–189, 258
   productions of, 147, 179, 180–182
Mundy Scheme, The (1969), 101, 109
Performances (2003), 5, 122, 138, 145–149, 151–162, 164, 167, 168, 172, 175, 183–186, 259
   productions of, 146, 155, 159, 164
'Self-Portrait' (1972), 18, 49, 57, 58, 65, 240
The Game, 40–43
Translations (1980), 4, 14, 32, 49, 67–72, 77–79, 81, 82, 85, 86, 88, 94, 97, 100, 101, 111, 121, 137, 163, 165, 182, 248, 256
   productions of, 94
Volunteers (1975), 110, 254
Wonderful Tennessee (1993), 5, 107, 113, 123, 125, 127, 129, 134–137, 175, 204, 257, 258
Frye, Northrop, 21, 58, 255

G
Gill, Peter, 255
Giroux, Robert, 26
Glob, P.V., 254
Goffman, Erving, 111, 112, 118–121, 141, 256
Gola, 254
Graham, Alex S., 253
graphic scores, 203–205, 207, 210, 212, 219, 225, 229, 236
Greene, Graham, 253
Gregory, R.L., 177, 181, 188, 258

H
Harris, Roy, 111, 112, 118–120, 141, 256
Heaney, Seamus, 165, 187, 254
Herman, Vimala, 10, 15, 67, 68, 94, 101, 105, 110, 139
Hone, Joseph, 199, 200, 235, 258

I
imperialism, 69, 73, 74, 83, 99
Irish (language), 69, 71, 72, 74–76, 84, 85, 90
Irish Rebellion 1798, 96, 97

J
Jakobson, Roman, 119
Janáček, Leoš, 147–150, 152–159, 161–164, 168, 171, 181–185, 187, 246, 259
Janáčková, Zdenka, 148, 149, 184

K
Keenan, Jessie, 4, 191, 195–198, 205, 215–226, 229–231, 245, 247, 249
   artistic practice of, 191, 215, 217, 221, 223, 224, 229, 231, 246

interviews, 197, 210, 215, 217, 221, 223, 224, 230–232, 234, 238, 240–244
So What Is Surfacing (A Study), 231, 243
So What Is Surfacing (Trio). See 'Don't Anticipate the Ending'
Kickham, Lucia, 207, 212, 214, 218, 221–223, 226–228
Kilroy, Thomas, 256
Kipling, Rudyard, 83, 103

L

Lacan, Jacques, 127, 131
LaCapra, Dominick, 51, 63, 257
Landes, David S., 124, 125, 129, 130, 134, 142, 143, 246, 258
Langer, Susanne K., 127–129, 143, 144
Larcom, Thomas Aiskew, 71, 72, 74, 88–91
Lewis, Oscar, 28, 29, 254
LGBTQ+, 3, 7, 8, 10, 31, 42, 193–195, 213, 215, 229
Liddell, Alice, 152
Lough Derg, 113, 123

M

Mac Liammóir, Micheál, 7, 8
MacLoone, Fr. Bernard, 198, 201, 258
Mamet, David, 111, 256
mapmaking, 68–73, 76, 78, 90, 92
Marcel, Gabriel, 126, 127
McCann, Eamonn, 27
#MeToo, 146, 158
Miller, George A., 111, 189, 256
Moore, Thomas, 175, 259
musedom, 2, 145–160, 162–164, 166–170, 176, 181–183

Museum of Literature Ireland (MoLI), 6, 191, 192, 195, 198, 210, 212, 226, 227, 232–234, 236–244
music, 10, 122, 128, 129, 133, 134, 137, 147, 150, 153, 154, 157, 159, 160, 162, 163, 181, 191, 197, 205, 211, 220, 225, 227, 228, 236
mystery, 127, 151, 152, 167

N

National Library of Ireland (NLI), 1, 2, 11, 15, 17, 57, 101, 138, 176, 184, 193, 197, 233, 234, 238, 248
Philadelphia, Here I Come! (1964), 7, 13, 18–20, 55, 107, 108, 112, 138, 248, 257
New Irish, The, 109, 112
New Yorker, The, 2, 8, 15, 150, 154, 184, 188, 253, 255, 258, 259
Nietzsche, Friedrich, 127, 128, 131, 255

O

O'Donovan, John, 70, 72, 74–76, 85–87, 89, 90, 96, 103–105, 256
O'Faoláin, Seán, 256
Ono, Yoko, 152, 153
Ordnance Survey, 69–74, 76, 77, 85, 88, 89, 91, 93, 96, 125
O'Rourke, Michelle, 207, 212, 214, 218, 221, 225, 227, 228

P

Pascal, Blaise, 54–56
Paz, Octavio, 129, 143, 246, 258
pilgrimage, 123–125, 131–133
Pirandello, Luigi, 28, 109, 253, 255

place-names, 69–75, 90, 95, 99
Priestley, J.B., 116
Prose, Francine, 5, 150–155, 157–159, 162–164, 184, 185, 188, 246, 259
Proust, Marcel, 17, 21, 22, 24–26, 29, 30, 43, 47, 53, 57, 58, 60, 63, 246, 254

R
race, 153
Reader's Encyclopedia of World Drama, The, 21, 58, 113–117, 140, 255, 256
Reid, Alistair, 8, 15, 255
Ricci, Matteo, 125
Richards, I.A., 119
Romanticism, 82, 91, 92, 100, 150, 157
Ryan, Sarah, 207, 212–214, 218, 221–223, 226–228

S
Sacks, Oliver, 172, 173, 175–177, 179, 180, 188, 189, 258
Schneider, Rebecca, 3, 10, 15, 192, 195, 197, 218, 229, 233, 243, 251
Schulzová, Anežka, 156
Shaffer, Peter, 113, 256
Shaw, G.B., 187, 194
 Galatea, 169, 170
 Pygmalion, 169, 170
Sinyavsky, Andrei (Abram Tertz), 2, 31, 32, 60, 255
space, 2, 4, 8–10, 20, 30, 47, 53, 67, 68, 91, 93–96, 100, 110, 120, 122, 134, 135, 137, 164, 167, 173, 179–181, 192, 198, 211, 221, 223, 225, 230–232, 246, 249, 250

speech, 28, 29, 67, 68, 70, 81, 90, 93–96, 99, 110, 121, 122, 130, 135, 155, 161, 181, 222, 225
Steiner, George, 5, 32, 33, 46, 53, 55, 56, 68, 70, 78–87, 91–100, 122, 132, 145, 157, 160–162, 164, 176, 225, 246
 After Babel, 5, 14, 32, 57, 61, 70, 78, 79, 90, 91, 94, 98, 99, 103, 141, 144, 255, 256
 In Bluebeard's Castle, 5, 68, 70, 79–84, 86, 91–93, 96–98, 100, 103, 141, 186, 187, 256
 Language and Silence, 160, 186
 Real Presences, 160, 186
storytelling, 10, 34, 69, 125, 134, 135, 194
Stösslová, Kamila, 147–149, 153–159, 163, 164, 182, 184, 185, 187
Sylvester, David, 38, 61
 Interviews with Francis Bacon, 17, 32–35, 37–43, 45–47, 49, 52, 60, 233, 255

T
Taylor, Diana, 10, 15, 67–69, 76, 96, 99, 101, 194, 195, 197, 218, 234
Thomas, Dylan, 125
 Under Milk Wood, 51, 125, 257, 258
time, 2–4, 6, 7, 10, 17, 20, 24, 25, 28, 30, 36, 47, 48, 52, 68, 72, 77, 80, 82, 90, 92, 93, 97, 110, 113, 114, 124, 125, 127–131, 133–135, 153, 154, 157, 167, 171, 180, 195, 199, 208, 212, 216, 218, 219, 222, 226, 227, 229, 232, 233, 236, 245–247, 249
Times Literary Supplement, The, 2, 9, 12, 31, 32, 55, 60, 70, 105, 111,

117, 148, 149, 184, 187, 246, 256
Tutter, Adele, 171, 181–183, 188, 189
Tyrrell, John, 148, 150, 156–158, 185–187, 259

U
Uganda, 200, 201, 258

V
Valéry, Paul, 34, 43
Valvo, Alberto, 177, 178, 188, 189, 258
Veyne, Paul, 48, 49, 63, 257
von Senden, Marius, 177, 178, 180, 188, 189, 258

W
Wagner, Richard, 21
Waking the Feminists, 146, 182
White, Hayden, 48, 49, 51, 52, 63, 257
Wilde, Oscar, 25, 26, 59, 254
Wittgenstein, Ludwig, 54, 78, 258

Y
Yeats, W.B., 236
Young, J.Z., 177, 188, 189

Z
Zeki, Semir, 177, 189, 258
Zemanová, Mirka, 148–150, 153, 156, 157, 162, 184, 185, 259

Printed in the United States
by Baker & Taylor Publisher Services